Video Production Handbook

Second edition

Gerald Millerson

Focal Press

Focal Press
An imprint of Butterworth-Heinemann
Linacre House, Jordan Hill, Oxford OX2 8DP
225 Wildwood Avenue, Woburn, MA 01801-2041
A division of Reed Educational and Professional Publishing Ltd

Ⓡ A member of the Reed Elsevier plc group

OXFORD   AUCKLAND   BOSTON
JOHANNESBURG   MELBOURNE   DELHI

First published 1987
Reprinted 1988, 1989
Second edition 1992
Reprinted 1995 (twice), 1998, 1999

British Library Cataloguing in Publication Data
A catalogue record for this book is available from the British Library

Library of Congress Cataloguing in Publication Data
A catalogue record for this book is available from the Library of
Congress

ISBN 0 240 51321 5

Composition by Scribe Design, Gillingham, Kent
Printed and bound in Great Britain

Contents

Preface

This book has been specially designed to save you time and effort, to give you essential facts in an interesting, easily digested form. So let's start immediately by answering some basic questions.

What is this book all about?

It is a journey into the basics of budget program-making with the video camera; whether you are working alone, or with a small multi-camera crew.

It covers the techniques and organization involved in transforming the ideas in your head into a persuasive presentation on the screen. It is an introductory workbook, showing you how to use your video and audio equipment effectively.

Whether your aim is to instruct, inform or entertain, you will find here sure-fire methods enabling you to produce interesting results at minimum expense.

There is no substitute for hands-on experience, and the know-how you will develop as you work through this book will provide a firm foundation for your future studies. We shall be concentrating on the *practical* features of video program-making, so that you achieve encouraging, worthwhile results right from the start, even with quite modest facilities. This book will help you to get the best out of your equipment.

Who is the book written for?

It is designed for anyone, anywhere, using a video camera, wanting high-grade results on a modest budget.

It will be particularly helpful for a wide range of communications and audio-visual students using video in community colleges, high schools, university courses, training schools, etc.

You may be:

● taking an introductory course in TV production

- working on a class project
- using video in the classroom as a teaching aid
- making programs for work training, promotions, sales, staff instruction, etc.
- in a local access CATV group
- an enthusiastic hobbyist

The same underlying production principles apply whether you are on the beach, shooting the family vacation, or in a well-equipped studio making commercial instructional programs.

This text does not assume that you have a technical background, or any previous experience – or that you are really interested in the nuts and bolts of the equipment.

We are going to discuss the basics of good picture-making, and good audio, that underlie persuasive program-making. Why spend your time and effort making poor video programs that leave your audience bored, puzzled or sceptical, when you can create an interesting, even memorable production?

What equipment do you need?

Even if you have modest equipment, and little or no assistance, there is no reason why you should not make really successful programs. This book will help you to make the most of your system.

Its text is keyed to *low-budget production*. But 'low budget' does not mean 'second best'. High-grade results come from know-how and imagination.

Isn't all this equipment complicated to use?

Although you need to understand certain techniques to get the best out of your equipment, you will find that good handling quickly becomes a habit.

Television is a highly technical medium. But so is the technology behind your home TV, your calculator, your phone ...! Concentrate on learning how to handle your equipment effectively, leave the expert to worry about the technicalities, and keep it up to top performance.

Why do we need to learn 'techniques'?

Great ideas do not automatically make great programs. It is not enough simply to show what is going on. The *way* you present your subject will influence how your audience responds. You need to choose your picture and sound carefully, to convey your ideas in an interesting persuasive way. Use them carelessly, and your production can become a *bore!*

How can this book be used?

As a conventional *class textbook* it can provide the material of course lectures, leaving students free to concentrate on what the instructor is saying, without the preoccupations of extensive note-taking. Any class-notes or supplementary information can be margin annotated to personalize the text.

Using this book as a *preparatory study text* students can learn relevant principles at their own pace before each tuition period. This is not only relieves the teacher of repetitive formal lecturing on basics, but enables precious class-time to be devoted to group involvement. So there are increased opportunities for check-questions, discussions, demonstrations, practical work and critiques.

As a tutorial workbook, the text is ideal for *self-paced home study*, for its step-by-step coverage helps the reader, through theory and practice, to build up a self-assured appreciation of principles.

And then?

For those who want to explore aspects of television production in greater detail, there are the author's companion books, all published by Focal Press:

The Technique of Television Production
Effective TV Production
Video Camera Techniques
TV Scenic Design Handbook
Lighting for Video
The Technique of Lighting for Television and Film

Remember!

The video camera and recorder give you an enormous advantage. You can check your results as you shoot! Unlike the film-maker, who has to wait for processing before seeing results, you can make sure that you have the best possible version, shoot alternatives perhaps, experiment, for the videotape is reusable. The result is that you can make comparisons in techniques, correct errors, and *learn faster!*

A final word

Some people feel very strongly about the literary convention of using masculine terms in a text, when both sexes do a particular job (e.g. cameraman rather than camera operator). But remember, this is still only a conventional brevity, in a world that is becoming increasingly enlightened. Video production is an opportunity for us *all!*

Preface to the second edition

There have been exciting advances in the equipment available to video-makers working on a modest budget. Cameras and video recorders have become even more sophisticated, with enhanced picture quality, and additional facilities. Desktop computers now provide us with all manner of amenities, ranging from elaborate graphics and video effects, to advanced video editing. Techniques are now practicable in consumer video, that previously could only be achieved with costly professional equipment.

You will find that this new version of *Video Production Handbook* has been updated and extended to reflect this world of opportunities. My sincere thanks to program-makers who have suggested various ways in which the text could be enhanced to suit current video courses.

As before, we are mainly concerned here with *principles and practices*, for these are the timeless essentials of *persuasive video production*. Even more know-how has been crammed into this new edition, to help your programs to have audience appeal.

The great thing about video production today, is the way in which program-makers are increasingly stretching their facilities, to develop polished, imaginative creations. In the end, what really matters, is what you have to say, and how you say it!

Chapter 1

Video production today

The special features and opportunities of the video medium.

1.1 What is video production?

The differences between 'video production' and 'television production' have become increasingly blurred.

Most 'video production' is concerned with *non-broadcast* program-making. Productions are recorded *closed-circuit on videotape, distributed, and viewed by a small audience.*

Television productions, on the other hand, are usually broadcast, i.e. shown to a large public audience by over-air or cable transmission – either 'live' (during performance) or 'taped' (carefully edited video recordings).

In practice though, you'll find broadcast material packaged for home or closed-circuit viewing, and see video productions aired in broadcast programs (e.g. music videos and pop promos).

Television transmissions are obliged to conform to closely controlled technical standards. Equipment is in constant use for many hours daily, so needs to be stable, robust, reliable, and capable of continuous high-grade output. Video productions are made with equipment ranging from the most sophisticated professional broadcast standards, to low-cost consumer items.

There is no intrinsic reason though, why the screened end-products should differ in quality, style or effectiveness as far as the audience is concerned. Video programs today range from ambitious presentations intended for mass distribution, to economically budgeted programs designed for particular audience sectors. This book will help you, whatever the scale of your production.

Breaking the ice

1.2 The need for 'know-how'

Video production appears deceptively simple. After all, the video camera gives us an immediate picture of the scene before us, and the microphone picks up the sound of the action. Most of us start by pointing our camera and microphone at the subject hopefully, but find the results pretty unsatisfying. Why? Is it the equipment or us? It may be a little of both. But the odds are, that it is *us*!

As you may have discovered already, there is no magic recipe for creating attractive interesting programs. All successful production springs from a foundation of *know-how*.

1. Knowing how to handle your equipment properly. The effects of its various controls.

2. Knowing how to use your equipment effectively. The skills underlying good camerawork and sound pick-up.

3. Knowing how to convey your ideas convincingly. Using the medium persuasively.

4. Knowing how to organize systematically. Practical planning, preparing, and operations.

As you work through this book, the know-how you develop will soon become part of your regular approach to program-making. Knowing what your equipment can do, will enable you to select the right tool for the job, and use it in the right way. Remember, in the end, clumsy operation and inappropriate treatment get between you and your audience!

1.3 It's designed for you

Many people are scared of technology. There's even a name for it: *technophobia!* But however unfamiliar the various units may be at first, remember, most equipment has been designed for speedy uncomplicated handling.

After all, it is there for one fundamental purpose – *to enable you to communicate your ideas to an audience!* Video equipment is as much a communication tool as a typewriter or a telephone.

1.4 First impressions

We all feel a little stupid when we have to operate equipment for the first time! We are apprehensive about which controls to use, and exactly what will happen when we operate them. Some people adopt a 'try it and see' approach – but this can be pretty frustrating, even disastrous. It needs self-control to find out step by step, and patiently build up techniques.

And then there is that private embarrassment most of us have when all these new technical terms come pouring in. Our minds block off, our eyes grow glassy, and mental ear-muffs descend! Take heart, this phase soon passes. Don't let technology scare you off! It really is surprising how rapidly it all becomes a daily routine, as you acquire confidence and get the right results every time.

As for your equipment – if it has been well designed, adjusted and serviced, it will reward you with reliable performance (provided you treat it with care).

1.5 Learning basics

You don't need to know *how* equipment works, but you should know *what* it does if you are going to get reliable results.

Even with the most sophisticated video and audio equipment, you need to know the answer to only a handful of basic questions to use it successfully:

What is the equipment *for*?
What can it *do*?
What are its *limitations*?
Where are the *controls* and any *indicators* (lights, meters, etc.)?
How and when do I *adjust* them?
What is the *result* when I do so?
Can I cause any problems (or damage) by *misusing* them?

1.6 Remember the purpose

There is no short cut to experience. As you handle equipment, you grow increasingly familiar with its peculiarities.

But don't let slick handling preoccupy you. Many a raw cameraman has tried to show his 'skills' by zipping around, fast zooming and cute composition – where an experienced one would have avoided these distractions, and held a steady shot, letting the subject work to the camera instead!

Smooth accurate operation is important, but *appropriateness* is even more desirable. In the end, it is *audience-impact* that really counts – the effect your camera treatment has on your viewer.

1.7 Resources

Nowadays, it is true to say that, for certain subjects, a single person with sufficient time, talent, experience, and suitable equipment, can make great video productions unaided at home. Topics ranging from coin collecting to electronics, from agriculture to archeology, can be treated effectively with minimal resources. However, decide to tackle drama or make a documentary, and it's a very different ball-game!

Clearly, the kind of equipment and technical knowledge you need for your production, will really depend on the sort of programs you are going to make. If for instance, you are using video as a living picture album, to capture memories of the family and recall enjoyable vacations, then you might even find that just a video camera and a videotape deck connected to your regular TV set will suffice.

But if you aim to make carefully staged packaged productions, with precise editing, music and effects, you will find that more flexible facilities are necessary. Successful productions usually depend on teamwork; each member of that team contributing their individual expertise and experience.

1.8 Simplicity

Don't get preoccupied with hardware! You do not need elaborate or extensive facilities to produce successful programs. Even the simplest TV equipment may provide you with the essentials you need. It really depends on the type of presentation you are involved in. For some purposes, one camera is ideal. For others, a dozen may be insufficient.

Of course, you may be hampered occasionally if you do not have a special gizmo that enables you, for example, to produce a multi-segment screen, or turn the picture upside-down. But surprisingly often there is another method of achieving similar or equally effective results. *What* you do is more important than *how* you do it. If you can get an effective moving shot along a hospital corridor by shooting from a wheel-chair, rather than a special camera-dolly, your audience will not know – or care!

Sometimes extra 'goodies' on your equipment can tempt you to use them *because they are there*, rather than because you *need* them! You will see examples every day on broadcast TV where wipes, star filters or diffused shots are used in the wrong place, at the wrong time, just for the sake of variety; because they are readily to hand.

What appears at first sight to be sophisticated, stylish presentation, may have far less impact on your audience than a single still shot that lingers to show a person's expression.

Video production approaches

1.9 Video production methods

You can shoot action in several different ways:

> Single camera – 'live'
> Single camera – 'videotaping'
> Multi-camera treatment – 'live'
> Multi-camera treatment – 'videotaping'

You will find that there are particular advantages and drawbacks with each of these techniques.

1.10 Using a single video camera – 'live'

You can use a single video camera to present the action as it happens; i.e. shooting it 'live'. When your audience knows that they are watching reality (so anything can happen!) there is tension and expectancy, a strong impression of spontaneity. They feel as if they are actually participating in the events from a ringside seat.

This is a simple, straightforward method of presenting any subject. But it has major limitations. For example, you can't change the camera's viewpoint rapidly to see the action from another angle, or to show reaction shots, or to make quick visual comparisons. It can be difficult to keep up with fast-moving action. Because you are showing everything in real time, it is difficult to avoid including the less interesting periods as well as the highlights.

You can overcome some of these problems, as you will see later, but whenever you shoot action 'live' or 'live-on-tape' (i.e. a straight-through recording without subsequent editing) the single camera has certain productional limitations.

1.11 Single camera – 'videotaping'

Like film-making, a great deal of video production is carried out with a single camera. The camera's picture and the associated sound are recorded, either on a videotape recorder (VCR) attached to the camera, or on a separate recorder unit nearby.

Later you replay ('review') these videotapes, and select the shots you want from all the material that has been shot – making a careful note of all the required 'takes', and the sort of transitions you want between them – i.e. cuts, mixes (dissolves), wipes, etc. This preparation (*off-line editing*) saves a deal of time when you later edit the program.

'*Editing*' involves playing the selected shots, and re-recording them on a master tape. But more of that later in Chapter 8.

1.12 Multi-camera techniques

Broadcast television and large-scale video productions regularly use *multi-camera* production methods. Two or more cameras shoot the action from various angles, and their shots are selectively intercut, using a *production switcher*. This is an extremely flexible arrangement, even when action is continuous; whether you are shooting live or videotaping the production.

However, multi-camera treatment does have disadvantages. You need a closely coordinated production team, and a separate control center with quite an elaborate technical set-up – intercom, preview monitors, production switcher, etc.

There is always the possibility when intercutting shots of continuous action 'on-the-hoof', that you might miss an unexpected opportunity, switch to the wrong camera at a crucial moment, or a shot might go wrong. If you are taping the show, and action can be repeated, you can re-shoot ('re-take') the faulty section, and edit the corrected version in later.

Figure 1.1 The versaility of video

Carrel study

• Home study
• Video promos
• Entertainment
• Further education

• Instruction
• Workshop training
• Product information
• Trouble-shooting

• Training
• Self-assessment

• Group training
• Overflow meetings
• Conferences
• Public relations
• Staff coordination

• Exhibitions
• Displays
• Promotions
• Trade fairs

EXHIBITION

• Nature programs
• News
• Hobbies

• Classroom demonstrations
• Critiques
• Field instruction
• Sales
• Community study

The versatility of video

The video medium

- The TV camera provides you with an instant image in full color.
- Video cameras may be automated, and can be remotely controlled.
- Video pictures can span from the microscopic to the infinities of outer space.
- Video pictures from several sources can be combined (inset, split screen).
- The image can be modified and manipulated. (Color, tonal values, shape and form, sharpness, etc.)

Video presentation

- The video picture can be shown on screens ranging from pocket-size to giant display. From a single screen to a 'videowall' (multi-screen) display.
- The video signal can be distributed instantly by cable (wire, fiber-optic), wireless transmitter or infra-red link, satellite.
- Video pictures can be intercut, superimposed, or blended in various ways.
- All forms of photographic material can be televised (photo-stills, slides, film of any type.)
- Video artwork can be created electronically (computer graphic).
- Titles, text, patterns can be generated electronically (computers, character generators).
- A video image can be printed onto paper in full color (photographic, printers).

Video recording

- The video signal can be stored in several forms (photographic, magnetic tape or disc – using analogue or digital recording.)
- Video recordings can be played back immediately, and replayed many times. It can be stored indefinitely.
- Videotape can be wiped in selected parts, or completely. New recordings can be made on the erased tape.
- Videotape recordings can be reproduced at faster or slower speeds than normal. A single moment of action can be frozen ('still frame', 'freeze frame'). A day's events can be played back in a few seconds.
- Taped programs can be edited to omit faulty or irrelevant shots, enhance the presentation, adjust program duration, etc.
- Video programs can be transferred to standard motion picture film for projection.

Recorded sound

- The action sound normally recorded in synchronism with the picture on videotape recording, can be augmented or replaced (e.g. music, commentary).

Limitations

- There are many incompatible video-recording systems.
- Video tape is easily damaged or destroyed.
- Tape faults or damage result in picture defects of various kinds.
- To select individual shots from the tape, it is necessary to play or spool (fast wind) through it. Tape has to be rewound after play through.
- When tape is copied during editing or devising special effects, picture quality deteriorates.
- Tape wear develops during freeze-frame replay.

1.13 Multi-camera variations

When the action cannot be repeated, or events are unpredictable, some directors make use of an *ISO* (isolated) camera. This simply means that while all the cameras are connected to the switcher as before, one of them is also continuously recorded on a separate VCR. This ISO camera takes wide shots of the action (cover shots), or concentrates on watching out for the arrival of the guest for instance, without any fear of missing the important moment. Shots on the ISO tape can be played back during a live show, or edited in where necessary later.

In another multi-camera approach, each camera has its own associated video-recorder (*dedicated VTRs*). Instead of intercutting between cameras with a switcher, shots from their separate video-tapes are edited together later during a post-production session. Any voice-over narration, sound effects, video effects, music, etc., are then added.

Figure 1.2 Basic video systems
The flexibility of video equipment allows you to arrange it in a number of ways

1.14 What facilities do you need?

An ever-increasing range of video and audio equipment is now available at quite moderate costs. Further items can be hired or rented from production houses (facility houses) as you require them.

Looking through any manufacturer's or supplier's catalogue, or a video magazine, you will find that the list of available equipment seems endless! But how necessary is it all?

Well, it depends on several things:

- *The kind of productions you are going to make.* Equipment that is essential for some situations (e.g. an underwater camera) would have little value for other productions. Even a microphone may be superfluous, if you are going to 'shoot mute', and add all the sound to silent shots during editing!
- *Whether the equipment is complex or simple.* You may able to *improvise*, making your own facilities, e.g. light reflector boards.
- *Whether there are alternatives.* Sometimes you can tackle a situation *indirectly*, and avoid the need for extra equipment (e.g. shoot via a wall mirror to get a longer shot of a room).
- *Whether the situation is critical.* Where editing is broad and non-critical (e.g. when interconnecting general shots of a scene), even simple intercutting may be all that you need. But if you have a series of intercut close shots of people speaking, even a lip-synchronizing error of a frame or two may be distracting.
- *Time saving.* Improvisation is fine when it works. However, the makeshift device may not do the job so well. It can involve time, and trial-and-error experiments. It might even fail at a critical moment! There are times when it pays to have the right equipment to ensure success.

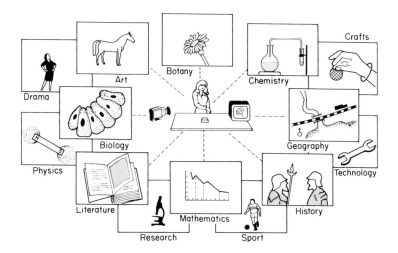

Figure 1.3 The classroom camera
Video in the classroom provides a valuable tool that can extend normal teaching opportunities.

1.15 Subjects influence production methods

As you will see, a number of issues influence how you can tackle any subject – from the purpose of your program, to the budget and talent at your disposal.

Even such basics as:

whether you have freedom to move your camera,
whether the subject itself is moving around,
which features you particularly want to emphasize,

can directly affect your decisions.

Just think for a moment, about some typical situations you might encounter:

- A *static subject* such as a building (e.g. telling the history of a church).
- A *long procession* (e.g. a Mardi Gras parade).
- A *sports meeting* with events taking place around the field.
- An *interview* in someone's home.
- An *unpredictable* event (e.g. programs on wildlife).
- A production in which there is scripted dialogue and moves for actors/performers (e.g. a soap opera).

Each presents its own particular opportunities, limitations and problems.

Technicalities

1.16 Equipment performance

Thanks to careful design, even the most complex equipment continues to perform faultlessly for long periods with little attention. But it is good practice to make very regular checks, and carry out routine maintenance.

It is simple enough to check that parts are clean (lenses, tape heads), that controls are working correctly and ready for use. Even the simple action of running a head-cleaner tape through a recorder at intervals, will reduce the likelihood of problems during taping sessions.

Whether you carry out equipment checks yourself, make basic readjustments, or have the services of an experienced engineer to keep its performance up to specification, will depend of course, on your particular circumstances; on how much you understand about that particular piece of equipment, and the test gear you have. It is quite practicable for instance to adjust a series of preset controls on a vectorscope to place markers within their appropriate boxes, without having the slightest idea what is happening technically within the circuitry.

But remember, don't tweak controls unless you know what is going to happen, and you can correct any mistakes!

1.17 Technical basics

Although you don't need to know how your equipment actually works to use it effectively, it certainly does help if you have a general idea about the purpose of the various units in the video and audio system. So in Chapter 13 we shall look at a general outline of the way video works, and typical units you may meet in the video chain.

Chapter 2

Meet your camera

Get to know your camera's controls so well that you use them instinctively.

2.1 A range of designs

Video cameras today come in a variety of shapes and sizes, to suit all pockets and applications. They range from units as small as a peanut, to broadcast cameras that need a couple of people to lift them. Performance ranges from satisfactory to state of the art.

You can use a video camera as stand-alone unit, or combine it with others in a multi-camera production.

You can record the video camera's picture on a separate videorecorder – either a VCR (video cassette recorder) or a VTR (reel-to-reel system). This can be carried in a backpack, a shoulder bag, or on a small wheeled cart.

An increasing number of video cameras take the form of *camcorders*, with a VCR either built-in to the camera unit, or attached at its rear.

Another approach is to fix a radio transmitter to the camera, and to pick up both picture and sound at a mobile support vehicle/base station (a station wagon or truck), where the program is recorded and/or passed on to a studio center.

Figure 2.1 Video camera designs
Video cameras range from small hand-held and shoulder-mounted units to systems incorporating their own videotape recorders.

2.2 Cameracraft

It is very easy to operate any video camera. Designers have gone to a lot of trouble to make controls simple to use. Popular hobbyist cameras have been so automated, that you need do little more than point them at the subject, and press a button to get results. If you are shooting for fun, and just snapshooting around, that's fine. Why make camerawork any more complicated?

It really depends on whether you are aiming to use your camera as a *creative tool*. The weakness of automatic controls, is that your camera can only be designed to make *technical* judgments. And these are usually something of a compromise. It can't make *artistic* choices of any kind. Auto-circuitry can help you to avoid poor-quality pictures, but you can't rely on it to produce attractive, meaningful pictures. Picture appeal will always depend on how *you* use your camera, and the choices *you* make.

As you will see, good picture-making is much more than just 'getting the shot'. It begins with the way you handle your camera, and use its controls. It is not just a matter of getting the shot sharp, but of selecting which parts of the scene are to be sharp, and which are soft focus. It involves carefully selecting your viewpoint, and arranging the framing and composition for maximum impact; deciding what is to be included in the shot, and what is to be left out. It is the art of adjusting picture tones by careful exposure.

Automatic camera circuitry can help, particularly when shooting under difficult conditions, and save you from having to worry about technicalities at all. But it cannot create meaningful pictures for you.

Camera features

2.3 Main features

Let's take a look at the main features of your camera:

1. The *lens system*, which projects a small image of the scene onto the camera's pick-up device.
2. The light-sensitive pick-up device, which converts the lens image into a corresponding video signal. An increasing number of video cameras use a solid-state *CCD* (*charge-coupled device*); or an *MOS* (*metal oxide semiconductor*) *chip* in less expensive cameras. Earlier, *camera tubes* were universal.
3. Its *viewfinder*, which displays what the lens sees, and enables the cameraman to assess the picture.
4. The way your camera is *supported*.
5. The camera's *power supplies*.
6. The *microphone* which is often attached for general sound pick-up on portable cameras.
7. The *supplementary controls* which affect picture quality.

The handbook issued with your equipment will give you details and specifications of your particular camera. There is a list of typical features in Table 2.1.

2.4 The lens system

If you look at the front of your camera's lens, you will see two important numbers engraved there:

Figure 2.2 Parts of the camera
Camera designs vary, but the following are typical facilities found in the video camera:
1 Microphone – electret, unidirectional
2 Lens hood
3 Lens aperture (iris) – f/1.6 max.
4 Focus control
5 Manual zoom control
6 Aperture control
7 White balance adjust; black adjust
8 Video gain (0 dB, 6 dB, 12 dB), color bars, camera standby/operate switch
9 Color compensation filter – 3200 K, 5600 K, 5600 K + 12.5% ND, closed
10 Viewfinder, adjustable – 1.5 in (37 mm) with LED indicators
11 Power selection, intercom, audio monitoring jack
12 Camera back: VTR connector, video output, camera cable, monitor video output, gen-lock connection for multi-camera set-ups
13 Eyepiece
14 Snap-on battery pack
15 Side of camera: mike input connector, external d.c. socket
16 Viewfinder controls
17 Power zoom switch
18 Auto-iris on/off

The lens' focal length – or in the case of zoom lenses, its range of focal lengths. This gives you a clue to the variations in shot sizes the lens will provide.

The lens largest aperture or *f/stop* (e.g. *f/2*) – the smaller this *f/stop* number, the larger the lens' maximum aperture, so the better its performance under low-light conditions.

2.5 Focal length and lens angle

The term *focal length* is simply an optical measurement – the distance between the optical center of the lens and the image sensor, when you

Continued on page 15.

Table 2.1 Camera features

As well as the main lens control, the camera has various extra controls to ensure that shots taken under different conditions will match. Otherwise picture brightness, color, and tonal values could vary noticeably from shot to shot. Other features offer you extra facilities.

AGC (Automatic gain control)	Circuitry which automatically adjusts video amplification to keep it within preset limits. Reduced during bright shots, and increased under dimmer conditions, it arbitrarily alters overall picture brightness and contrast.
Auto-black	After capping up the lens to exclude all light, this switch automatically sets the camera's circuitry to produce a standard black reference level.
Auto-fade	Although you can manually adjust the lens aperture, to fade the picture out to a black screen, or up to full strength from black, it is not always easy to do this smoothly while holding the camera steady. So a facility is fitted to some cameras for doing this automatically at the touch of a button. This may fade the audio at the same time.
Auto-focus	A facility that automatically adjusts the lens focus for maximum sharpness on the nearest subject in a selected zone of the frame. Whether this is the one *you* want sharpest, is another matter. When you are shooting through foreground objects, or focusing selectively, or anything is likely to move between the camera and your subject, you should switch the camera to manual focusing.
Auto-iris	This device automatically adjusts the lens aperture (*f*-stop) to suit the prevailing light levels (light intensities). By doing so, it prevents the picture being very over-or under-exposed ('washed-out' or 'murky').
	However, there are times when the auto-iris 'misunderstands', and changes the lens aperture when it should remain constant, e.g. during zooming, or when a lighter area comes into the shot. Then it is necessary to switch the lens aperture control to *manual* or *aperture lock*, and operate it by hand.
Auto-white	This control automatically adjusts camera circuits' 'color-balance' to suit the color quality of the prevailing light, and ensure that white surfaces are accurately reproduced as neutral. Otherwise all colors will be slightly warmer (red–orange) or colder (bluish) than normal.
	You simply press the *auto-white* button while shooting a white surface, or place a white plastic cap over the lens, or point the camera at the scene (averaging out its colors).
	If the color quality of the light is outside the circuit-adjustment limits, a warning indicator may show that a color correction filter (below) is needed on the lens to suit the illumination.
	Where white balance adjustment is entirely automatic, a *white balance lock* can prevent it from making wrong adjustments (e.g. when shooting large color areas).
	Some cameras use a *manual white balance adjustment*, which is turned while watching a meter or viewfinder indicator.
Black stretch or gamma adjustment	Some cameras include an operator-controlled circuit adjustment to make shadow detail clearer and improve tonal gradation in darker picture tones. This is the opposite of 'contrast compression', which emphasizes the contrast in picture tones.
	With a higher gamma setting (e.g. 1.0) picture tones are more contrasty, coarser and dramatic. A lower gamma setting (e.g. 0.4) provides more subtle, flatter tonal quality.

Table 2.1 *continued*

Cable correction	When a camera is cabled to a central control unit, corrective circuits can be switched in to compensate for video losses (fall-off in definition) that increase with cable length.
Camera cable	This may be a short 'umbilical' multi-wire cable connecting the camera to a portable VCR (videorecorder), or a more substantial cable routed to a camera control unit (CCU or CPU). This cable provides power, syncs, intercom, etc., to the camera, and takes video and audio from the camera to the main video/audio equipment.
Color correction filters	Because the brain compensates, we tend to assume that most everyday light sources such as sunlight, tungsten light, quartz lamps, candlelight, etc., are all producing 'white' light. But in reality, these various luminants often have quite different color qualities. They may be bluish or reddish-yellow, depending on the light source and the conditions.
	Unless the camera's color system is matched to the prevailing light, its pictures will appear unnaturally warm (orange), or cool (bluish).
	How far auto-white adjustment is able to re-balance the camera's color response, to compensate for variations in the color quality of the prevailing light, depends on equipment design. For greater compensation you may need color correction filters. There are often fitted inside the video camera, just behind the lens (perhaps on a 'filter wheel'). Alternatively, you can fit a suitable filter over the front of the lens.
	Typical correction filters include *daylight, artificial/tungsten light* and *fluorescent light* (perhaps marked 6000 K, 4700 K and 3200 K). The filter wheel may also include or combine neutral-density (ND) filters to improve exposure.
Macro	Many zoom lenses have a *macro* position. This allows the lens to focus on very close objects; much closer than the lens' normal MFD (*minimum focused distance*). You cannot zoom with the lens in *macro* mode.
Remote camera control	Small infrared hand control unit, providing remote control of camera/VCR unit.
Remote VCR control	A trigger to remotely stop/start a videorecorder from the camera.
Reverse/normal switch	Reverses picture tones and colors for negative effects.
Self-timer	A device that automatically delays the start of videotaping, to allow you to get into the shot.
Shutter speed	To avoid movement blur and improve detail in fast action, a much briefer exposure rate than the normal 1/60 s (PAL 1/50) is needed. A variable high-speed electronic shutter (settings from e.g. 1/125 to 1/400 s) reduces blur considerably, but needs higher light levels, and is liable to produce unnatural break-up or flicker on some subjects.
Slow motion control	Where an interval timer ('intervalometer') is fitted, the camera records a brief shot at regular adjustable intervals (e.g. 10, 20, 60 s). When replayed at normal speed, the time lapse effect will show a flower grow, a day's weather, in just a few minutes.
Standby switch	A device used to save battery power, by switching off unused units when rehearsing or during standby. Some cameras have *auto switch-off* which cuts the system's power, when the camera has not been used for several minutes.
Sync – Int/Ext	When working alone, a video camera generates its own *internal* synchronizing pulses to stabilize the scanning circuits. These pulses are also combined with the picture video and sent to the camera's video output. In simpler camera designs, these sync pulses are imprecise, and rely on the TV receiver's circuits to compensate for any resulting jitter.

Table 2.1 *continued*

In multi-camera production, the camera is switched to *external sync*. It then uses the accurate synchronizing signals sent along the camera cable from a separate communal *sync generator*.

Title generator	A small keyboard used to provide titles and data (choice of colors) and overlay them onto the background scene. Several frames may be composed and stored ready for use. Although the print style limits its use, it is a convenient way of introducing titles/subtitles, and shot identification such as time, date, location, shot number (a built-in 'slate').
Video/RF output	As well as its normal *video output*, some video cameras have an *RF (radio frequency) output* that can be fed directly into a TV receiver or VCR's antenna (aerial) socket (e.g. Channel 3).
Zoom lens iris	Some lens systems can be switched to allow manual, auto-iris, or remote manual control at a CCU, by a video operator/shader.

In addition, there will usually be various controls for selecting and setting – tape speed, clock, character generator (titles), etc.

are focused at a great distance (infinity). It is measured in millimeters (mm) or inches.

Cameramen often identify a particular lens, or assess its coverage by referring to its focal length. If you know the focal length of the lens, *and* the size of the image sensor (CCD active area) you can work out the *lens angle*; i.e. how much of the scene the lens will take in.

However, in practice, you will find it a lot easier to think in terms of *lens angles* than to juggle with formulae. So, instead, we usually speak of 'narrow-angle' (or 'telephoto') and 'wide-angle' lenses instead. This lens angle immediately tells us how much of the scene will appear in shot from any camera position.

When the lens has a *long focal length* ('long focus'), it behaves as a '*narrow angle*' or '*telephoto*' lens. The subject appears closer, but you can only see only a small part of the scene. Space appears compressed.

A lens with a *short focal length* ('short focus') takes in '*wide angle*'. It will show more of the scene, but subjects look further away, and space appears exaggerated.

2.6 The zoom lens

Most video cameras today are fitted with the familiar *zoom* lens. This system has several advantages.

The zoom lens is designed to have a *variable focal length*; so its angle of view is *adjustable*. This is a great help. It provides you with controllable coverage. You can easily alter the size of the subject on the screen, and select how much of the scene appears in the shot. The actual variation depends on the zoom lens design (e.g. 8 : 1; 18 : 1).

This is a lot more convenient than having to move around to vary the size of the shot, as with the *prime lens* fitted to many photographic cameras, which has a fixed focal length.

But the zoom lens does have disadvantages! Zoom lens design involves many technical compromises, particularly for small systems, and the problem of

Figure 2.3 Camera lenses
Part 1 *Prime lens.* The prime lens (fixed focus lens, primary lens) has adjustable focus, and iris (aperture, stop), but its lens angle (focal length), is fixed.

Figure 2.3 Camera lenses
Part 2 *Zoom lens.* A. This has adjustable focus, iris and focal length (lens angle). Altering the focal length varies the lens coverage. Changing it while on shot produces 'zooming': zooming in as the focal length increases, and zooming out as it decreases.

The focal length may be adjusted (B) manually (knob on lens barrel), or (C) with a motor system (power zoom), operated with a rocker-switch, from wide angle to telephoto (narrow angle).

Nearby switches also control the iris (lens aperture): auto, manual, and remote control.

providing high performance, lightweight, robust zoom lenses at reasonable cost has been a challenge for manufacturers. So the optical quality of budget systems is generally below that of an equivalent prime lens.

As you'll see, it's easy to *misuse* a zoom lens, so that your shots show distortion and varying perspective. 'Zooming' too, can be a very distracting effect. You need to use the zoom lens with care!

2.7 Changing the lens system

The camera's zoom lens is usually attached to the camera head with a screw threaded *lens mount*. On some video cameras, it is possible to remove the zoom lens and fit a different lens system instead.

You may for instance, want the highest picture quality for a particular purpose (e.g. high grade macro shots), and decide to use a 16 mm or 35 mm film camera *prime lens*. Or you might want to affix a special purpose periscope or microscope attachment.

To do this, you need a suitable lens mount. It might be a 1 in. or ⅔ in. 'C-mount' as used with 16 mm film cameras, or a ½ in. 'D-mount'. Adaptors also allow T-type, P-type or quick-release bayonet-types of lens fittings to be used with 35 mm camera lenses.

2.8 Zoom lens control

Your zoom lens has three sets of controls.

- *Focus adjustment.* You adjust focus by turning a broad ring at the front of the lens barrel. This moves the lens system in and out. A scale shows the distance at which sharpness is maximum – although as you will see, things nearer and father away may still look reasonably sharp. As well as *manual focusing*, many video cameras also include an automatic focusing device (*auto focus*).

- *Iris or lens aperture adjustment (f-stop).* Along the lens barrel nearer the camera head, you will see another ring. This turns against a scale marked in *f-stops* or *transmission numbers*. If you look into the lens as you turn the aperture ring, you will see the opening of its small variable iris or diaphragm change. The size of this aperture controls the brightness of the image falling onto the image sensor (CCD or camera tube). Again, you can adjust the iris manually, or with automatic circuits (*auto iris*).

- *Zoom control.* As we saw earlier, the zoom lens has a variable focal length, which allows its coverage to be adjusted to any angle within its range; from *wide angle* to *telephoto*.

Figure 2.4 Pan-bar controls
When the camera is fitted to a mounting, the lens focus and zoom actions can be adjusted from extension controls on the pan bars, e.g. a twist-grip for zoom and a hand-crank for focus.

Zoom control

Focus control

To adjust the focal length, you turn a third ring on the lens barrel (it has a small knob to make operation easier). A scale shows the selected setting. You can either choose a particular lens angle and shoot at that setting, or vary the angle while on shot to produce the familiar 'zooming' effect.

In a *pump zoom* lens (often used for photographic cameras), a large ring on the lens barrel rotates to *focus*, and slides along the barrel to *zoom*; not usually the smoothest of movements!

You can switch most video zoom lenses from *manual* to *power zoom* operation.

A rocker switch actuates a small motor, which drives the zoom in and out between maximum coverage (wide angle) and minimum angle (telephoto). The speed of the zoom may be variable, depending on the switch pressure.

When a video camera is mounted on a movable dolly, it is not really convenient to reach round to the front of the camera to adjust the lens. Instead, flexible cables or an electrical servo system are fitted. These allow focus and zoom to be adjusted from behind the camera, by controls attached to the *pan-bars* (*panning handles*).

2.9 Altering the iris

For all practical purposes, it does not matter whether your lens system is calibrated in *f-stops* (based on the size of the aperture), or in *transmission numbers* (based on the amount of light it passes at various openings).

When the iris aperture is fully opened (probably around *f*/1.4) it lets in the most light. Its minimum opening when 'stopped right down' (under very bright lighting), may be *f*/22. Remember, the smaller the opening, the bigger the number. Some irises can be closed down until the picture fades out altogether.

When you alter the lens iris, two things happen simultaneously:

1. It alters the brightness of the lens image reaching the image sensor (CCD; camera tube), so affects the *exposure*.
2. It affects the relative sharpness of subjects in the shot, as the *depth of field* changes.

Figure 2.5 Lens aperture
The lens aperture is adjustable from a maximum (e.g. *f*/2) to a minimum (e.g. *f*/16).
Large aperture: small *f*-number, shallow depth of field, but less light is needed.
Small aperture: large *f*-number, increased depth of field, but more light is needed.

In practice you will usually find that you choose the iris *f*-stop to suit the prevailing lighting conditions; adjusting the *f*-stop until it gives the best tonal gradation in the main subject (correct exposure). Moving around on location, you may need to readjust the lens aperture for the best exposure as the light changes.

In a studio, where you have direct control of light levels, you can either adjust lighting to suit a convenient *f*-stop, or light to a comfortable level,

Figure 2.6
Part 1 *Depth of field*. Within the depth of field, things appear sharp, although focus is maximum at the *focused distance* (FD). Outside these distance limits (Df and Dn), things look defocused.

Part 2 *Aperture and depth of field*. As you stop the lens down (to a smaller aperture), the depth of field increases. (FD: focused distance)

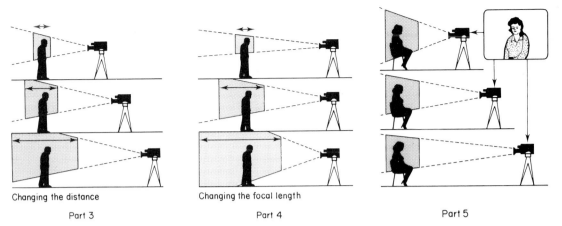

Changing the distance   Changing the focal length

Part 3   Part 4   Part 5

Figure 2.6 *continued*
Part 3 *Distance and depth of field* As you get farther from the focused subject, the depth of field increases.
Part 4 *Altering the focal length*. As you *decrease* the focal length (i.e. widen the lens angle or zoom out), the depth of field in the shot *increases*.
Part 5 *Depth remains the same*. If you alter the camera distance, then adjust the lens angle to get exactly the same size shot, the depth of field will be the same as before. Only the apparent perspective will have changed.

and adjust the lens for correct exposure. In a multi-camera production, where cameras are controlled at CCUs, a video control operator may vary the lens aperture slightly, to match different shots.

Sometimes you may particularly want to use a small lens aperture, so that most of the shot is sharply focused ('deep focus'). Or, alternatively, you may want a restricted depth of field so that you can focus selectively (using a large aperture). Then you will need to adjust light levels or use neutral density lens filters to suit the appropriate stop.

2.10 Lens accessories

There are two often-neglected accessories that fit onto the lens: the *lens cap* and the *lens hood* (*lens shade*).

When you are not actually using your camera, get into the habit of clipping the *lens cap* over the end of your lens. The lens surface has a special bluish coating ('blooming'), which improves picture contrast and tonal gradation (by reducing the internal reflections that cause 'lens flares' or overall graying). This thin film is easily damaged by careless cleaning, or scratching (e.g. blown sand, grit). Your lens cap not only prevents anything from scratching or rubbing against the lens surface, but helps to keep out grit or moisture.

One of the problems with *camera tubes*, is that bright lights or strong reflections (speculars) can burn the light sensitive target. So one needs to avoid these potential hazards wherever possible. Now although CCD image sensors are not as easily damaged, it is still good practice to steer clear of problems, and avoid leaving your camera pointing at a lamp or into the sun, and to cap up the lens during stand-down periods.

The *lens hood* (*sun shade; ray shade*) is a cylindrical/conical shield that fits round the end of the lens. It prevents stray light reaching the lens, and so reduces the likelihood of lens flares. It is particularly useful when you are shooting towards a light source that is just off-screen.

2.11 The image sensor

The type of pick-up device your camera has, will affect the quality of the picture – its resolution (definition), picture defects, limitations.

Most video cameras today are fitted with CCD image sensors. The solid-state CCD has many advantages over camera tubes.

- It is small (6.8 mm × 8.8 mm or 6.4 mm × 4.8 mm), compact, rugged, consumes low power, and has a long life.
- CCDs have high sensitivity, and produce little 'lag' under low-light conditions.
- The CCD resolves moving detail well, and handles a wide brightness range (dynamic range) effectively.
- It produces pictures at switch-on (no warm-up time), does not suffer from burn-in ('stuck-on' after-images of bright lights and reflections), and there is no 'comet-tailing' behind moving lights.
- There is no geometric distortion.
- Strong magnetic/radio fields (e.g. nearby radar) do not affect the system.

The CCD is not without its drawbacks though.

- It is liable to have background blemishes, and the resolution (particularly vertical detail) may be limited.
- There can be a noticeable smear on movement. (Vertical smear on highlights.) It is flicker sensitive.
- Picture noise may form a fixed background at low light levels.
- There can be strobing effects on fine line structures.
- The depth of field on small format CCDs (12 mm/½ in.) can prove excessive, so that selective focusing is difficult.

2.12 Sensitivity

All camera systems must have a certain amount of light to produce good clear pictures. How much, will depend on camera design and adjustment, and on how light or dark the surroundings are.

Lighting intensities (light levels) are measured in footcandles or lux (1 fc is roughly 10 lux), and modern camera systems typically need around 75–150 fc (805–1600 lux) at $f/4$.

But what if the surroundings are not sufficiently bright to get good pictures? You have two options. Either you can adjust the camera, or you can improve the lighting – e.g. move the subject nearer the light; adjust or add light.

The simplest solution is to open up the lens aperture to let more of the available light through to the CCD; up to the maximum lens-stop available (e.g. $f/1.4$.) But then the depth of field becomes shallow, and that can make focusing difficult for closer shots.

Another solution where there is insufficient light, is to switch in increased *video gain* (*video amplification*) in the camera system. Although the image sensor itself still lacks light, this electronic boost will strengthen the picture signal. Most cameras include two or three boost positions. A 6 dB increase will double the gain, while a 12 dB increase will quadruple it. With a 6 dB boost you may get very acceptable pictures with quite low light levels, e.g. around 15 fc (150 lux) at $f/1.6$; while with a high 12 dB boost, only about 8 fc (80 lux) would be needed. However, it is best to keep boost to a minimum wherever possible, for it increases picture noise (grain) and picture sharpness deteriorates.

So you see, a camera's sensitivity will depend on both the f/stop and the amount of boost switched in. A camera with a typical specification requiring 186 fc (2000 lux) at f/8 (3200 K, 89.9% reflectance), will only need 1.2 fc (13 lux) when opened up to f/1.8 and 18 dB gain. With the iris fully opened (f/1.4) even 0.7 fc (7.5 lux) will produce satisfactory pictures!

2.13 The viewfinder

The simplest arrangement is an *optical viewfinder* – either an attached or through-the-lens system. This has the advantage that you can rehearse shots at any time, even when the camera itself is switched off, for it uses no battery power. However, it does have major disadvantages. You are not seeing the actual *television picture* your camera is producing, so you cannot monitor picture quality in any way, or assess exposure. In simpler optical viewfinders, it may not show the exact area taken in by the lens in closer shots (parallax errors).

Most video cameras are fitted with an *electronic* viewfinder, containing a small black and white picture tube (typically 1.5 in. (38 mm)). With its flexible eyepiece held against one eye, you can not only frame-up and compose the magnified TV picture, but get a good idea of exposure, and the relative tonal values in the shot.

You can usually secure the viewfinder on whichever side of the camera is more convenient. It may also tilt up and down (or swivel) – with the eyepiece hinged out of the way – so that you can still see its screen when using the camera above or below eye-level.

Like larger picture monitors, viewfinders have their brightness, contrast and focus (sharpness) adjustments. Some also have a *crispening* control that emphasizes detail in the viewfinder picture to make focusing easier. (remember, viewfinder adjustments do not affect the camera's picture in any way.)

Some video camera systems can be modified to suit your particular shooting conditions (*configuration changes*).

When used on location, where lightweight, portable cameras are essential, they can be fitted with compact zoom lenses and viewfinders. In the studio, where the cameras are mounted on dollies, larger high quality lens systems can be attached, and bigger viewfinders fitted.

The 5–7 in. (12.5–18 mm) diameter picture tube of an open-screen type viewfinder is easier to watch for sustained periods, and focusing can be more precise. A hooded visor keeps stray light from falling onto its picture.

Although it would be more useful to have a viewfinder with a color picture, the lower resolution of color screens does make focusing more difficult. On location, small color monitors or clip-on *LCD screens* (*liquid crystal displays*) can provide color viewfinders when color is important to shots, but in the studio cameramen may prefer to use a nearby full-size picture monitor instead.

When using a camcorder, the electronic viewfinder has particular advantages. It not only shows you the video picture while you are shooting the action, but can switch so that you can watch a replay of the videotape you have just recorded. You can check for any faults in camerawork, performance, continuity, etc., and re-shoot the sequence if necessary.

Its screen can be used to display test data of various kinds, when checking camera performance.

Some systems allow you to display *another camera's picture* superimposed upon your own. This can be a very useful facility when two cameras are combining to create a special effect: for example, where one is shooting a map, and another is taking a shot of a city name. Thanks to the combined viewfinder image, the second camera can position the name accurately at the right spot on the first camera's map. If the second camera zooms in, the name grows dramatically, spreading right across the screen.

The only other ways of carrying out this trick, would be for the cameramen to watch the superimposition on a nearby picture monitor, or work from intercom instructions.

However, the electronic viewfinder does have its drawbacks.

● On a battery-powered camera, it does consume current all the time the camera is working. That is easy to overlook, especially if you have lengthy rehearsals, and review your recordings in the viewfinder.

● Because the picture is black and white, you may overlook the effect of *color* in the shot; inadvertently including a distracting brightly colored area perhaps.

● Because the viewfinder image is small, unwanted details can go unnoticed that will be very obvious when seen on a large TV screen.

2.14 Indicators

Even if you are operating your video camera in a completely automatic mode (*full auto*), you'll need information from time to time about such basics as how much tape you have left, and the state of the batteries.

Video cameras carry a range of indicators giving a variety of information and warnings – small meters, liquid crystal panels, indicator lights, switch markings. Most of the indicators are on the body of the camera, but because your attention is concentrated on the viewfinder much of the time while shooting, several are arranged within the viewfinder or on its screen.

These indicators take the form of warning lights, words or patterns on the viewfinder picture. You will find a selection of typical indicators in Table 2.2. No camera has them all!

2.15 Audio circuits

Most portable video cameras are fitted with a microphone (usually an electret type) intended for general program sound pick-up. It may be built-in or removable, perhaps for use in a portable handgrip.

A foam sponge or cloth *wind shield/wind gag* cover over the mike reduces low-pitched wind rumble.

To position the microphone more effectively, it is sometimes attached to a telescopic 'boom', which can be extended to reach out in front of the camera.

The sound pick-up is usually mono, although stereo microphones are increasingly used.

Sometimes, when shooting documentaries, the camera operator/director uses the mike to record information and sound notes as a guide track alongside the video. This can be a useful aid when writing the program commentary later.

An *audio monitor* earpiece jack, enables you to monitor your sound pick-up during recording. You should continuously assess sound quality, balance, background, etc. Quite often you will find that *background*

Table 2.2 Typical camera indicators

A variety of indicators of various kinds are fitted to video cameras, including the following.

Autofocusing zone selected	Shows whether autofocus is controlled by a small central area of the shot, or the nearest subject in the scene.
Back light exposure correction	System that opens the lens an arbitrary stop or so above the auto-iris setting, to improve exposure against bright backgrounds.
Battery alarm	Warning light showing that the battery is OK, or that it is getting exhausted.
Boost setting	Amount of video amplification (gain) being used.
Call light	Indicator light showing that CCU operator wants to contact camera on inter-com/private-wire system.
Date and time indicator	Displays details on screen, for overlay into picture.
End of tape warning	Shows that only e.g. 1 min of tape remains available.
Full auto-indicator	Shows that camera is in fully automatic mode (i.e. auto-iris, auto-focus, etc.)
Low light level warning	Insufficient light falling onto CCD, causing underexposure. (Open iris and/or increase boost.) An overexposure indicator light may also be fitted.
Manual aperture setting	Shows lens iris is manually operated.
Manual focus correct	Lens focus is manually operated, and correctly adjusted.
Playback	Indicates that VCR is replaying the tape.
Shutter speed	Indicates which shutter speed has been chosen, to capture fast movement.
Standard or long play selected	Shows whether normal tape speed or half-speed (for tape economy) has been selected on VCR.
Tally light	A cue light showing that the camera is recording; or when used with a switcher unit, that this camera has been selected 'on-air'.
Time indicator	Shows running time (elapsed time/tape time used) and/or the time remaining on cassette.
Titles	Small character generator provides titles, which can be superimposed on picture.
Video/audio recording	Indicates that VCR is recording (picture and sound).
Video level	Some cameras can superimpose a display on the viewfinder, showing the video signal's strength and exposure.
White balance	Shows if color temperature adjustment is satisfactory.

noises which seem quite slight to the ear, prove very obtrusive on the soundtrack.

You can also use the earpiece to listen to a replay of the recorded video-tape soundtrack.

Figure 2.7 Camera microphone
When the camera microphone is fitted to a telescopic boom, it can be extended towards the action, and get over nearby obstacles.

Narrow-angle microphones attached to the camera are more stable, and require no attention.

An *external mike* socket on the camera, allows you to plug in a separate microphone; for better sound quality, and more accurate mike positioning. (It may also include a power supply for the extra mike.)

An *audio input* socket may be included, to allow a second sound source (e.g. music or effects) to be recorded on a separate track during video-taping.

When a camera is used in a multi-camera production, and cabled back to a central control point (CCU, CPU), *intercom* (*talkback*) *circuits* allow the cameraman to speak with the director and video operator, through a headset mike. Some cameras have a duplicate socket, for a second operator (e.g. a sound man or an interviewer) to plug into the intercom circuit.

2.16 Power

Your video camera will normally require a 12 volts d.c. power supply. This can come from a number of sources including: an on-camera battery pack, a battery-belt worn by the cameraman, the battery used to power the VCR, or a heavy-duty battery (car battery) on a small cart or trolley. When you are working near regular utility supplies (mains supplies), you can use a special adaptor to convert the 100–240 volts a.c to 12 volts d.c.

When using batteries, there are a number of precautions that you should take if you are to avoid being left without power at a critical moment. The most obvious is to either switch your equipment off when it is not actually being used, or switch to a standby (warm-up) mode so that it is only using minimum power. (See Appendix A, Battery Care.)

Remember, the camera system (including its viewfinder), the videotape recorder, any picture monitor you may be using, an audio recorder, lights fitted to the camera, these are all drawing current. And when setting up shots, organizing action, shooting, doing retakes, reviewing

Figure 2.8 Camera power
The video camera can utilize several types of power supply:
1. Internal battery (2 Ah)
2. Battery belt (4–6 Ah)
3. Shoulder pack
4. Trolley battery (e.g. 7 Ah)
5. Car battery (using cigar-lighter socket)
6. Snap-on ('on-board') battery
7. A.c. power adapter
8. Power from a portable VCR.

the recording, writing up notes, it is very easy to find that you are squandering valuable battery power. Fully charged standby batteries are a must!

2.17 Camera arrangements

Video cameras are designed to suit a wide range of applications.

As you have seen, there are fundamentally two approaches to video production:

- Single camera shooting, in which a camera works quite independently.
- Multi-camera shooting, where a group of cameras work together.

This leads to a number of different configurations:

1. *Single camera*

- The camera may be completely self-contained; as in a typical *camcorder*. The camera carries its own battery power supplies and VCR system – either built into the camera, or attached to the camera body ('pick-a-pack'; 'on-board').
- The camera may carry its own power supply, but its video (and sound) passes through a lightweight umbilical cable, to a *separate portable VCR*.

● In a variation, the camera is cabled to a portable VCR as before, but is *powered from the VCR unit.*

2. *Multi-camera*

● Each video camera may carry its own power supply and circuitry, sending its video signals to a pick-up point or base unit some distance away. (A system used on location for remotes.)
● Various forms of interconnection are used in these systems, including cable, radio mini-link, laser link, infrared link. Each has its particular advantages and limitations.
● The camera may be cabled to a central control point at a base station in the vicinity. This cable carries video and audio from the camera, together with the intercom, and provides the camera with power, synchronizing signals, scanning-voltages, etc., generated by units at the base station. (A system universally used in studios.)

Controlling the camera

2.18 Supporting your camera

There are four basic ways of supporting your camera:

● Hold it in your hands.
● Rest it on your shoulder.
● Use some kind of body support.
● Mount it on some kind of camera dolly.

Hand held video cameras are extremely light. Depending on design, you steady them against your head while looking through the viewfinder eyepiece, and/or support them with a molded grip (pistol grip) beneath the unit. The grip usually has a trigger-switch, so that you can start/stop/pause the VCR during recording.

You can attach the camera to a *mounting* (monopod, tripod) with a screw-socket in its base.

Many video cameras have a moulded saddle-type base (or shoulder pad) that rests on one shoulder, positioning the viewfinder in front of the opposite eye. A quick-release base-adaptor plate is used to attach the camera to a mounting.

2.19 Handling your camera

Pictures that are shaky, bounce around or lean over to one side, are a pain to watch. So it is worth that extra care to make sure that your shots are steady and carefully controlled. There may be times when your audience's attention is so rivetted to exciting action on the screen that they are quite unconcerned if the picture does weave from side to side, or hop about. But don't rely on it! Particularly when there is little movement in the shot, an unsteady picture can be very distracting and irritating to watch.

As a general rule, you need to hold your camera perfectly still, unless you are deliberately *panning* it (i.e. turning it to one side), or *tilting* it (pointing it up or down) for a good reason.

So what stops us from holding the camera steady? There are a number of difficulties. Even 'lightweight' cameras are still quite heavy (particularly if fitted with a lamp, battery, large zoom lens, etc.), and seem to grow heavier with time. Muscles tire. Body movements (breathing, heart

Figure 2.9 The hand-held camera
Above: Holding the camera.

Right: Keeping the camera steady.
1. Legs braced apart, and elbows tucked in.
2. Seated, with elbows on knees.
3. Kneeling, with elbow resting on leg.
4. Elbows resting on the ground.
5. Resting the back against a wall.
6. Resting the elbows on a low wall, fence, railings, car, etc.
7. Leaning your side against a wall.
8. Supporting one foot on a step or box.
9. Resting your body against a post.
10. Pulling up on a string (chain) fastened under the camera, with its lower end trapped under one foot.
11. Use a monopod (single-leg telescopic tube).

beat) can cause camera movement. Wind can buffet the camera. You may be shooting from an unsteady position such as a moving car or a rocking boat. And on top of all that, if you are using a narrow lens-angle, any sort of camera-shake will be considerably exaggerated anyway!

To overcome or reduce this problem, and provide a stable base for the camera, several methods of camera support have been developed.

2.20 Hand-held cameras

The lightest, smallest cameras are easily hand-held. The secret is to stand in a comfortable well-balanced position, with your legs apart and slightly bent, and your elbows tucked in to your sides. You support the camera firmly but not too tightly, with the hand-grip beneath the camera in your right hand. Within easy reach are the VCR start/stop (pause) switch, and the power-zoom rocker switch. The left hand adjusts the focus control (or the manual zoom lever) on the lens barrel. With the eyepiece pressed against one eye (keep them both open, so that you can see what is going on around you), this position holds the camera steady enough for short periods.

You can improve picture steadiness further by resting your elbows or your body against something really secure. This may be a wall, a fence or perhaps a nearby car.

The simplest aid, when you are hand-holding a camera, is a string or chain suspended from the camera-base. You hold its free end under your foot, pulling the camera gently upwards, to make it just that bit more stable.

There are situations where you can use a special camera mount attached to a C-clamp, or an alligator spring-clip (gaffer-grip), to attach the camera to a firm nearby support such as scaffolding, fencing or furniture.

2.21 Shoulder-supported cameras

This familiar method of holding the camera is mainly used when the camera has to be very mobile, and able to change position quickly, or when shots are very brief. So we see it mostly when news-gathering, and at sports events, where the camera has to move around at the run, to follow action.

With the body of the camera on your right shoulder, and your right hand through a support loop at the side of the lens, your fingers are free to operate the power-zoom rocker switch, while your thumb can press the VCR pause switch. Your left hand adjusts the manual zoom lever, the focusing ring, f-stop (lens aperture), and the macro lever when necessary.

The comfort and success of this method depends largely on your stamina, and how long you are using the camera. Standing with upraised arms supporting a shoulder-mounted camera can be very tiring. So there are several body-braces and shoulder harnesses that help to keep the camera steady if you are shooting for long periods. A typical arrangement has a metal prop fixed beneath the camera, and resting on a chest pad or a belt support.

2.22 The monopod

This is a cheap, easily carried, lightweight mounting. It consists of a collapsible metal tube of adjustable length, that screws to the camera base. Braced against your knee, foot or leg, the monopod can provide quite a firm support for the camera, yet allow it to be moved around

Figure 2.10 The shoulder-mounted camera.
Part 1 A U-shaped saddle holds the camera firmly on the shoulders.

Part 2 *Hand positions*. With the right hand through the support loop (fingers operating power-zoom, and iris selection), and the left hand adjusting focus (perhaps iris), the camera can be supported firmly, even in difficult conditions.

Part 3 *Body brace* A body brace from the camera to the belt (or the chest) helps to support the camera firmly.

rapidly to a new viewpoint. Its main disadvantage is that you can accidentally lean the camera sideways, and get sloping horizons. And of course, the monopod is not self-supporting.

2.23 The panning head

If you were to bolt your camera straight onto any form of mounting, it would be held rigid, and unable to move around to follow the action.

So instead, you need to fit a *panning head* (*pan head*). Not only does this enable you to swivel the camera from side to side (*pan*), and tilt it up and down, but you can adjust the freedom of movement (friction, drag), and lock the head in either or both directions.

Although you can control the camera on the panning head by holding its body, it is better to use a small panning handle (pan-bar) attached to the head to guide it.

Figure 2.11 Monopod
This lightweight extensible tube, can be set to any convenient length, and used in various ways.

Whenever you pan or tilt the camera, you need to feel a certain amount of resistance in order to be able to control it properly. If there is too little, you are likely to overshoot or twitch the camera at the end of a pan or tilt, and you will have difficulty in following action accurately. On the other hand, if too much effort is needed, panning will be bumpy and erratic. So the friction (drag) for both pan and tilt is generally adjustable.

Panning heads for video cameras may use either friction or a fluid (silicon) to dampen movements. The cheaper, simpler friction head has disadvantages, for as you gradually exert pressure to start a pan, it may suddenly move with a jerk. And at the end of a slow pan, it can stick unexpectedly. With a fluid head though, all movements are very steady and controlled.

A panning head is usually fitted with *locking controls* that you can use to prevent it from panning and/or tilting. You should always apply these to lock-off the camera whenever you are leaving it unattended; otherwise there is the danger that the camera may tilt suddenly, and not only jolt its delicate mechanism but even overbalance the tripod altogether!

Locking controls are very useful too, when you want to avoid any trace of camera shake, e.g. when shooting a title card, or when heavy winds are likely to buffet the camera, or when you are holding a shot on a very narrow-angle lens.

2.24 Using a tripod

A tripod is a very compact, convenient method of holding your camera steady, provided you use it properly. It has three legs of independently adjustable length, that are spread apart to provide a stable base for the camera.

Unscrewing the tripod from the camera usually takes a little time. So most people leave the tripod attached and just close its legs together when they move to a new position. If you have a quick-release mounting plate fitted to your camera, the tripod can be removed rapidly.

Tripods are certainly not foolproof! In fact, you need to take certain precautions to avoid disaster, so here are some useful tips:

Don't leave your camera on its tripod unattended, particularly if people or animals are likely to knock against or trip over it! Take special care whenever the ground is slippery, sloping or soft.

To prevent the feet of a tripod from slipping, they normally have either rubber-pads for smooth ground, or spikes (screw-out or retractable) for rough surfaces. (Be sure though, not to use spikes when they are likely to damage the floor surface!)

If the ground is very uneven (e.g. on rocks or a staircase), you can fix the tripod legs at different lengths so that the camera itself remains level when you pan around. Otherwise horizontals will tilt as you pan! Many tripods are fitted with spirit-levels to help here.

A very lightweight tripod is a false economy. It is intended for small photographic cameras, and will be far too flexible and insecure for a video camera.

Figure 2.12 Tripod
A simple three-legged stand, with independently extensible legs. Height cannot be adjusted during a shot. It can be set up on rough uneven ground. A spider (spreader) will prevent the feet from slipping, or sinking in soft ground.

Because any tripod fitted with the camera tends to be top heavy, you should always make sure that its legs are *fully* spread, and resting on a firm surface. When a tripod is set to full height (e.g. 6ft. (2 m)), it is particularly unstable. A low tripod (e.g. 2ft. (55 cm)) is effective for low-angle shots, but it may not be easy to see into the viewfinder.

Most times, you will want to work with the camera viewfinder at around your natural eye-height. You adjust the camera's height, by selecting how far the tripod legs are extended before locking them. But do not try to vary height by altering the distance apart of the legs. Some tripods have a central camera-support column that can be raised or lowered by a hand crank, although not while actually shooting.

There are several techniques for improving a tripod's stability. Simplest is a central weight (e.g. a sandbag or bag of stones) hung by rope beneath the tripod's center. The legs can be tied to spikes in the ground. Or you can use a folding three-blade device known as a 'spreader' or 'spider', which provides a portable base. On very soft ground, sand or mud, the tripod is best used on a flat triangular wooden base.

2.25 The rolling tripod

One practical disadvantage of the tripod is that you cannot move it around while shooting. However, fix the tripod to a castered (wheeled) base or 'skid', and you have a rolling tripod. This useful economical general-purpose *dolly* can be pushed around easily on a flat level floor. Uneven surfaces, though, will shake the picture. If the floor slopes at all, it can be very difficult to control the rolling tripod while dollying.

Rolling tripods may be fitted with *brakes* (to prevent wheel movement), *direction locks* (to hold the wheels in a chosen direction), and *cable guards* (to prevent the wheels overrunning cables).

Although it sounds obvious, before you move a rolling tripod, remember to check that the brakes are off, that the wheels are free, and there is no cable or obstruction in your path. You will find that it helps if you give a slight push to align the casters in the appropriate direction, before you dolly. Otherwise the picture may bump a little as the tripod starts to move.

2.26 Other mobile mountings

A number of other types of camera mounting are used in video production.

The *Steadicam-Jr* is a special stabilizer, that takes the shake and shudder out of even wide camera movements. While carrying a camera weighing up to 4 lb (1.8 kg), it allows you to take smooth traveling shots while panning, tilting, walking, running, climbing, etc. A 3 in. LCD color screen (treated to reduce reflections) allows you to monitor the shots, and a small camera light (videolight) (3200 K) helps out in those awkward corners.

And then there are the various types of lightweight *pedestal* mountings, *jibs*, and *small cranes* which are used with heavier cameras, or when shooting for sustained periods.

The main theme you will find running through this book, is *it's the result that matters, not how you get it!* You need to be able to support your camera firmly. Your audience does not know or care whether you are using a tripod, or are resting it against a handy lamppost.

You could take a moving shot, from a car, the back of a motor cycle, a hospital trolley, or even roller skates or skis. It is the result that counts – although some methods are a lot safer and more convenient than others!

2.27 Handling care

It's very easy to hazard your equipment, especially when shooting on location. Although some units are pretty rugged and almost foolproof,

Figure 2.13 Rolling tripod
A tripod on a castered base (skid/skate/rolling spider). The height is preset with a hand-crank (or pneumatic). Caster foot-brakes and cable-guards may be fitted. Easily wheeled on a flat smooth surface, steering may be erratic.

Figure 2.14 The Steadicam-Jr
A compact balanced support, that holds the camera rock steady, even when you are moving around. It incorporates a video light and an LCD color monitor.

others are easily damaged or fouled up. A moment's oversight can leave you with unreliable performance, or even put your equipment out of action altogether: a camera momentarily rested on the ground, a spilt drink, the jolts and vibration of a traveling vehicle. It takes just a moment to protect your camera with a waterproof cover ('rain hood') against wind-blown dust and grit, sea-spray, or rain. Extreme cold, heat or moisture can create problems too. A car's trunk (boot) can become an oven in the hot sun. High humidity can wreak havoc with videorecorders.

Moving from a cold exterior to warm surroundings, is liable to result in condensation (dew) in VCRs, and can cause tape or machine damage. Wrapping up the equipment (even in a plastic bag) may help. Similarly, when moving from an air-conditioned interior into a hot sunny exterior.

There's always the temptation to wonder what is inside, or wonder what would happen if. . . Resist it! Always bear in mind the old adage: "If it ain't broke, don't fix it!" It's a good general principle not to open up equipment unless you do really know what you are doing. It can easily cause additional faults. There is nothing more annoying or time wasting, than wrestling with equipment to make it work, and wondering: "Am I doing something wrong, or has it 'gone on the blink'?".

Chapter 3

Using your camera

Why put up with the second best, when your camera can create interesting, persuasive images?

3.1 Why bother?

Have you seen how casually some people use their video camera? They adopt a 'point and squirt' approach, assuming that automatic circuits will take care of the problem. After all, they might argue, the camera is not gobbling up costly film. It is easy to discard anything you don't want.

It is only when they come to check over the results later, that they too often seem disappointing. many shots are plain boring. The audience's attention will wander. Picture quality varies. Subjects are not all that clear. Editing looks clumsy.

This is a pity, considering that by mastering a handful of working principles, you can produce effective pictures with a professional polish!

3.2 What gets on the screen?

You will often hear the camera described as 'an extension eye' or 'the eye of the audience'. But these are very misleading over-simplifications. You can use your camera to *deliberately* create those impressions, but the camera doesn't automatically convey a true picture of any situation to your audience. If someone is at the spot, their eyes flick around, refocusing, taking in what is happening. They know where they are, and can decide for themselves what they look at. Everyone makes their own selection from the scene.

Your audience can only see what you have chosen to show them. Just that part of the scene selected by the lens is visible on the 4 × 3 rectangular screen in front of them.

They can only guess at what lies outside the lens' 'angle of view'. Other things quite near the camera would fill the screen if the lens turned just a little; but they remain unseen, 'out of shot', for the camera is highly selective.

The director's skill lies in choosing just the right section of the scene *for his purpose*, and satisfying his audience that this is exactly what *they* want to see at that moment.

Figure 3.1 The camera isolates

The camera only shows what is going on in its 4 × 3 shaped segment of the scene. The audience does not know what is outside the field of view.

3.3 How close should we be?

Close-up shots are fine for revealing detail – sometimes too much! They also restrict how much of the scene and the action your audience can see, and so encourage them to concentrate on particular features of the subject.

But you have to take care not to thrust detail at your audience too blatantly as if to say: 'Now see this! Pay attention! Look at these details!' Good production techniques are based on *persuasion*. And there are many subtle ways of influencing exactly where your audience looks, without thrusting big close-ups at them all the time. You can do this by the way in which you arrange the composition of the picture, move people around or position the lighting.

A *wide shot* (long shot) shows your audience where the action is located. It helps them to follow movement. It lets them see how one thing relates to another. It gives them a good idea of space.

An overall view of this sort does have its disadvantages, too. Your audience cannot see subject details at all clearly. They can see the speed with which the player runs after the ball, but not his expression when he drops it!

Long shots give broad impressions. But they also give your audience the opportunity to gaze around, and start thinking about whatever happens to catch their attention, rather than concentrate on the particular point you are making in your program at that moment!

Any well blended program treatment, needs a series of closer and more distant shots, each carefully chosen for its purpose: to help your audience locate themselves, see what is going on, interpret action, see details, and so on.

Figure 3.2 Shots of people

Shots are classified by the amount of a person appearing in the picture. There are various alternative terms:

DETAIL SHOT
　Extreme close-up (ECU). Isolating detail.
FACE SHOT
　Very close-up (VCU). From mid-forehead, to above the chin.
BIG CLOSE-UP
　(BCU); Tight close-up; Full head. **Full head** height nearly fills the screen.
CLOSE-UP
　(CU). Framing from just above the head, down to upper chest, just below necktie knot.
CHEST SHOT
　Bust shot; Medium close-up (MCU). Cuts the body at lower chest (breast pocket, armpit).
WAIST SHOT
　(WS); Mid-shot; medium shot (MS); Close-medium shot (CMS). Cuts the body just below the waist.
KNEE SHOT
　(¾ Shot). ¾ length shot, cutting just below the knees.
FULL LENGTH SHOT
　(FLS); Medium long shot (MLS). Entire body plus a short distance above/below.
LONG SHOT
　(LS). Person occupies ¾ to ⅓ screen height.
EXTRA LONG SHOT
　(ELS) (XLS); Vista shot. Extreme long shot.

3.4 How much can we see?

How much of the scene your camera shows will depend on:

● The camera's viewpoint.
● How far the camera is from the subject.
● The angle its lens covers.

As we saw earlier, the lens' coverage (*lens angle, angle of view*) varies with its focal length. The *zoom lens* can be adjusted to any focal length within its range. If it is a 6 : 1 (six to one) system, than its widest angle will be six times the narrowest. (Its shortest focal length is 1/6 of its longest.) Typical systems include 6 : 1, 8 : 1, to 18 : 1; but ranges of up to 44 : 1 or greater are available!

Some larger zoom lenses are fitted with an *extender lens* (*range extender*). This can be flipped in when you want to push the zoom range beyond its normal upper limit, perhaps effectively doubling it – although with a noticeable light loss (e.g. 1½ stops) and degraded definition.

Another way of altering the maximum or minimum angle of your lens system, is to clip on a *supplementary lens* (*diopter lens*). A 1½ times *teleconvertor* lens will effectively make a 1 : 6 zoom lens' narrowest angle that of a 1 : 9 lens. A *wide-angle conversion lens* will increase its widest coverage.

An *adaptor ring* can effectively double the original lens' focal length. It screws between the original lens and the camera body. Results can be quite good, but definition falls off when you zoom in to detail, using the narrowest lens angles.

In fact, each of these methods of altering the lens performance has its limitations, but they do provide ways of extending your present system.

Finally, as you know, you can always replace your lens with a photographic prime lens that has a more appropriate fixed focal length.

3.5 Using a different lens angle

A so-called 'normal' lens angle provides a picture with very natural-looking impressions of space, distance and proportions. Typically, it covers an angle of around 20–28°.

If you change the angle covered by the lens (alter its focal length), some interesting things happen.

A *narrow angle* or *long focus* lens (long focal length) will give a telescopic view of the scene. This shows a relatively narrower segment, which is magnified, and appears closer.

A narrow lens angle has great advantages when you cannot move the camera closer (or do not want to). But there are snags too. it often has the effect of flattening subjects, squashing space, and compressing depth. It can make things look unnaturally close. Movements too are affected. Even fast-moving subjects seem strangely slowed by a narrow-angle lens, as they move up to, or away from the camera.

You will find that it is difficult to hold a camera steady when using narrower lens angles, for even the slightest vibration is magnified, and shakes the picture. (Rest the camera on something firm, or use a tripod or some other type of mounting.)

A *wide-angle* lens on the other hand, shows us a much greater area of the scene. But now everything in the picture looks unusually distant. The lens seems to emphasize space and depth. Movements towards and away

Figure 3.3 Lens angles

Changing the lens focal length alters its coverage in proportion. Using a focal length three times the present one, the lens angle will be one-third of the original, so the subject appears three times as large in the picture. It is the equivalent of having reduced the camera distance to one-third, and only one-third of the original scene is now visible.

from the camera (or forward/backward camera moves) seem faster than they really are.

The wider the lens angle (i.e. the shorter the focal length), the easier it is to hold the camera steady, and to move around smoothly while shooting. But don't let that tempt you to use a wide-angle lens all the time. Otherwise, your subjects will look too distant. If you move in close to them, subjects will look very distorted shot on a wide-angle lens.

3.6 So why move around?

If you make things appear closer and further away simply by altering the lens angle, why change your distance from the subject? Why not just alter the zoom setting? It's far less trouble.

Although at first glance, changing the lens angle *seems* to give similar results to varying the camera distance, if you look at the picture carefully you will see that something else is going on at the same time. The impression of distance you get in the picture, is varying with the lens angle you use! If you are shooting in a large room for example, it will look much smaller than it really is when shot on a narrow lens, and much larger than normal if you switch to a wide lens.

This may not matter. It might be just the effect you want – to make a room look bigger than it really is perhaps. There will be times when you simply have to accept any spatial distortions in the picture, for there is no other way of getting the shot. If you want a close-up of a distant statue high up on a building, you will probably need to use a narrow-angle lens; and if that squashes space and reduces the form of the building, that is hard luck!

However, as a good working principle, it is best to use a *normal* lens angle for general purposes, and move nearer or father from the subject whenever you want to adjust its size in the picture (dolly in/out; track in/out).

If you cannot move around to change the size of your shot, i.e. there just isn't time, or there are obstructions, you may have to change to a different lens angle to get the shot. And if you want the camera to *seem* to be getting nearer or farther away, you will have to zoom in or out on shot.

Vary the lens angle as you *need*; to overcome a problem, or to get an effect. Don't just alter it casually. If you are shooting a parade from a balcony, and are getting useful group shots with a normal lens angle, don't hesitate to use a wide-angle lens to take in the lengthy procession, or a narrow-angle lens to show details. If you didn't alter the lens angle, you could only take one type of shot from that position. And you certainly cannot rely on running up and down to new viewpoints to give you the variety of shots you need.

Figure 3.4 Adjusting proportions

If you widen the lens angle, them move the camera closer to bring the main subject to its original size, other subjects in the scene will appear further away; relative proportions in the picture will alter.

Narrow the lens angle, and the reverse happens.

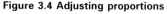

The warnings here are:

● Try not to alter your lens angle casually. A 'normal' lens angle provides natural-looking perspective for most shots.

● If you alter the lens angle, you must expect perspective, distance, depth, proportions to appear to change.

● Remember that smooth camera handling becomes more difficult at narrower lens angles (longer focal length).

● As we shall see, focusing is harder, when using a narrow lens angle (shallow depth of field).

● Don't be tempted to use a wide-angle setting just because it makes focusing easier (greater depth of field). It falsely exaggerates depth, and distorts perspective badly – especially in close shots.

A final word here: how obvious these various changes are, between one lens angle and another, very much depends on where you are shooting. In or amongst buildings, the effects can hit the eye. But on the beach or in open country, even a critical viewer may overlook the difference altogether.

3.7 Zooming

As you alter the zoom lens' focal length, its shot broadens (*zooms out*) or narrows (*zooms in*).

Zooming can be a valuable productional option. It allows you to adjust the shot width unobtrusively, without having to move the camera. Zooming can be a much smoother change, than dollying the camera in and out. You can zoom to produce an exciting swoop in to a subject, or a rapid withdrawal. When you zoom on a fast-moving subject, any perspective changes are not obvious. But zooming is a very artificial effect, and often misused. Our sense of space and dimension is upset. Lens handling alters as the angle changes. Focusing becomes increasingly difficult as you zoom in. Rapid in-out zooms can be nauseous!

Manual adjustment, allows you to control the zoom lens subtly at any speed. But if you are following focus and/or adjusting exposure at the

Figure 3.5 Zooming

Zooming simply magnifies and reduces the picture. It does not produce the changes between planes that arise as you move through a scene (dollying; tracking).

Increasing the focal length narrows the lens angle, filling the screen with a smaller and smaller section of the shot (zooming in).

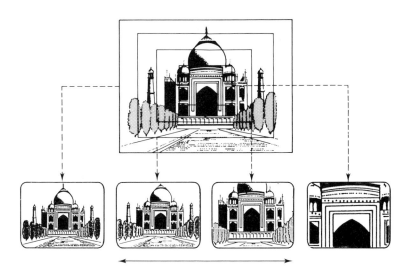

same time, adjustment on shot may cause camera shake. The motorized *power zoom* fitted to most systems, ensures a smooth but often less accurate zoom. Depending on design, its rocker-switch control may provide single-speed, two-speed (fast/slow), or variable-speed changes. (The last depends on switch pressure, a full zoom taking from e.g. 5 to 20 s.) The power zoom's main disadvantages are that it consumes battery power, and like the auto-focus system, is liable to be overheard by the camera mike.

3.8 Focusing

Focusing quickly becomes a reflex action. You adjust for the sharpest image, turning the control just a little to keep subjects sharp ('follow focus') if they begin to soften. But as we shall see, focusing is not always as straightforward as that.

To begin with, a lens cannot focus on subjects closer than its 'minimum focused distance' (MFD). And with a long-focus (narrow-angle) lens, that could be as little as a foot and a half (0.5 m) away. You cannot focus on subjects nearer than that. At very narrow angles, the MFD may be several yards/meters from the camera!

Figure 3.6 Following focus

The camera cannot focus on anything closer than the *minimum focused distance* (MFD).

For a 'long focus' lens (long focal length; narrow angle), the MFD may be some distance from the camera. With a 'short-focus' lens (short focal length; wide angle), focusing may be possible right up close to the camera.

As the subject gets closer to the camera, the depth of field becomes shallower, so focusing is more critical. How noticeable a fall-off in sharpness is depends on the amount of detail and fine tonal contrast in the subject.

At the other end of the scale you have the *macro lens* systems, which are designed to provide a sharp image almost up to the actual lens surface. But it is difficult to avoid a camera shadow when lighting such close subjects. When you are using the macro setting, the lens' zoom action is inoperative.

3.9 Auto-focus

Most video cameras are fitted with an *automatic focusing* facility. This is a really useful device for those occasions when you are extremely preoccupied with following action, are not sure where the subject is going to move to next, are shooting in a hazardous situation, and might get the focusing wrong in the heat of the moment. But why not switch auto-focus in all the time, so that it frees you of that chore altogether?

Well, if you rely entirely on automatic features in the camera to control your pictures, you must expect results to vary. The auto system simply sharpens focus to maximum in a selected zone of the shot, irrespective of what is appearing there. So you need to use it with care.

Camera systems have different degrees of sophistication. Some have a two- or three-step focus zone (small angle, to full frame width). Some include an *auto-focus check*, so that you can check the auto effect while still in the manual mode. There are even 'fuzzy logic' circuits which readjust as a subject moves around within the shot, or the shot is altered.

There are three types of auto-focus systems: *infrared* (*IR*), *ultrasonic* (*piezo*), and *electronic* (*image*).

- In the infrared system, the camera sends out a brief burst of IR light which is reflected from the nearest object, and detected by an IR sensor. Circuits interpret the return beam's angle (triangulation), and adjust the lens focus.
- The ultrasonic (piezo) system emits a short bleep of inaudible sound, and measures the time taken to return. Circuits calculate distance and adjust the lens.
- The electronic (image) system is quite different, for it examines the video signal, and adjusts the lens focus for maximum sharpness. (Video strength and contrast fall when the picture is defocused.)

Each of these methods can work well most of the time, but there are situations where they can produce very surprising results!

Different auto-focus systems can be fooled by the subject or by conditions, and give inaccurate results:

Infra-red. Small subjects, surface color (especially black), shiny angled surfaces.
Ultrasonic. Subjects behind glass, water, etc. Broken-up foreground (trellis, foliage, branches). Metallic noises. Rain, snow, fog.
Electronic. Dim lighting, low contrast or flatly lit subjects.

Keep a lookout for problem occasions:

- When the subject is not in the center of the picture. If you place two people either side of the frame, auto-focus may sharpen on an unimportant distant object in the center of the screen, and leave the subjects soft-focused!
- You may want to focus on someone near the camera and a distant person at the same time, but auto-focus may sharpen on one or the other – or neither!
- If you shoot a subject through a foreground framework (e.g. trellis or branches), the system will focus on this foreground rather than the more distant subject.
- If you are following a moving subject (e.g. a person within a crowd), the auto system may re-adjust and focus on other subjects.
- If you zoom to change the size of the shot, the auto-focus system may refocus as you recompose the picture.
- If you are shooting a distant view, and anyone (or anything) moves into the shot, closer to camera, the system may refocus on them instead, and defocus on the real subject. If, for example, you are panning around a scene and look past a foreground tree, the system may readjust to focus on the tree.
- There could be times when the background behind subjects become confusing or intrusive, due to ambiguous focusing.

If you meet such situations, the best solution is to switch to *manual* focusing, to avoid problems. Nevertheless, if you use it wisely, auto-focus is a very useful facility.

3.10 Depth of field

Strictly speaking, when you focus a lens, only objects at that distance on the focusing scale will appear really sharp in the picture. Anything nearer or farther away becomes increasingly defocused.

In a distant view, everything seems pretty clearly defined. But refocus the lens onto something a few feet away, and you will find that only a limited amount of the shot appears really sharp. Now focus on something very close to the camera, and sharpness becomes restricted to a very shallow zone indeed.

How obvious this effect is varies with the amount of detail there is in the scene.

The focused zone, which is called the *depth of field*, varies with:

● the *distance* at which the lens is focused,
● the *focal length* of the lens (or the position of the zoom),
● and the lens *f*/stop (*aperture*).

Alter any of these, and the depth of field changes.

Depth is *greatest* when:

● the lens is focused at a distance,
● you are using a short-focus (wide angle) lens,
● the lens aperture is stopped down (e.g. *f*/16).

Depth is *shallow* when:

● you are focusing on close subjects,
● using a long-focus (narrow angle) lens,
● the lens aperture is opened up (e.g. *f*/2).

Don't be misled into thinking that you can use a wide-angle lens to improve depth of field in a shot. When you change to the wide-angle, the subject will look smaller, and by the time you have got closer to compensate, the focused depth will become the same as before! And now you will have distortions and exaggerated depth too!

3.11 Maximum sharpness?

Should one always try to get everything in the picture as sharp as possible? Not always. There will certainly be situations where you *do* want to see everything in the shot clearly. You may be showing widespread action, as in a ball game. Or the camera could be looking around an interesting building. Or you may want to compose your picture in depth, and have your shot include both a person near the camera and another some distance away, all sharply focused.

Then you could use a wide-angle lens, stopped down as far as the light levels will permit.

There will be other times though, when you want your audience to concentrate on a particular subject, and disregard the surroundings. And you can achieve this, by deliberately *restricting* the depth of field, using a larger lens aperture and/or a narrower lens angle. Now, thanks to the limited depth, your subject will appear sharp against a defocused background, where anything likely to confuse or distract merges into an indistinct blur.

3.12 Difficult to focus?

Sometimes you will find that there is insufficient depth of field to focus clearly on the *whole* subject. That is a particular problem in close shots. Stopping the lens down would help of course, but there may not be enough light for you to do so, without under-exposing the picture. Yet you are unable to increase the light level. What do you do then?

Well, there are several regular compromise solutions here.

The best method, may be to sharpen focus on the *most important part* of the subject, and leave the rest defocused.

Figure 3.7 Limited depth of field

Part 1 If the depth of field is too limited for your purposes, you can:

Part 2 *Stop down* – increasing focused depth, but higher light intensity is needed.

Part 3 *Focus on one subject* – letting others soften.

Part 4 *Split focus* – spreading the available depth between both subjects (now none is really sharp).

Part 5 *Move subjects closer* – so that they are roughly the same distance from the camera.

Part 6 *Use a wider lens angle* – so that depth increases, but subjects now appear smaller (Figure 2.6).

Part 7 *Pull the camera back* – so that depth increases, but the shot is now smaller.

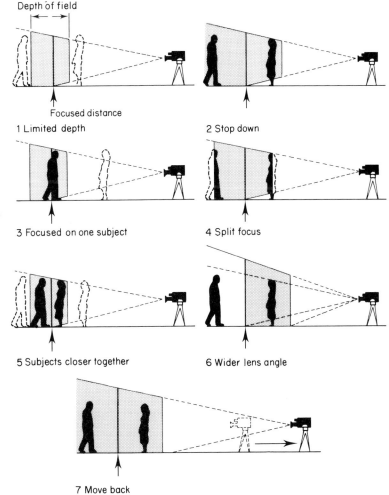

1 Limited depth

2 Stop down

3 Focused on one subject

4 Split focus

5 Subjects closer together

6 Wider lens angle

7 Move back

Figure 3.8 Pulling focus

As he turns, you refocus on the visitor.

Alternatively, you might *split focus*, and choose a compromise focusing distance so that all subjects are clearly enough focused in the circumstances.

Sometimes you can *pull focus* (*throw focus*) if this is appropriate. Supposing, for example, that you are shooting two people at different distances from the camera, and cannot get them both in sharp focus. You might start by focusing hard on one, than at a suitable moment, alter focus while still on shot, to sharpen on the other person. The method works, but the effect of changing focus in this way can be very dramatic. So it's a technique you need to reserve for the right occasion!

Finally, you could improve matters by moving the subjects, or altering the camera position, so that they are both about the same distance from the camera and within the available depth of field.

3.13 Pre-focusing the zoom lens

The zoom lens is a fine tool for the creative cameraman, but it holds some nasty pitfalls for the unwary. At the very moment you are concentrating on following some tricky action, you are most likely to meet up with its sneakiest traps!

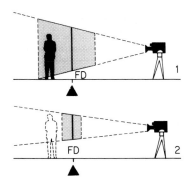

Figure 3.9 Pre-focusing the zoom

If you have not focused the lens accurately in a long shot, the picture will become defocused as you zoom in.

Part 1 Although focus appears satisfactory here, this is due to the available depth of field (wide lens angle).

Part 2 But on zooming in, the depth becomes restricted (narrow lens angle), and is insufficient to keep the subject sharp.

You soon discover that it is a lot more difficult to *hold shots steady* when you are working at the narrow-angle (long focus, telephoto) end of its range, than when you are zoomed right out (widest angle, shortest-focal length). That is really what you would expect of course (section 3.5), but to find that camera handling varies from moment to moment can be unnerving at first, especially when you zoom into a close detailed shot and then find that you cannot keep it steady!

As we have seen, the available *depth of field* also changes throughout the zoom lens' range, and that can pose practical focusing problems.

When you are zoomed out, there is normally considerable depth of field available, and focusing is easy. Usually, so much looks sharp in the picture that you can't judge exactly where the 'best' focus is. But zoom in to a close shot, and depth becomes relatively shallow.

In fact, there is always the danger that instead of being focused exactly on the subject as you thought, you were really focused some distance nearer or farther away! Consequently, when you zoom in from a good sharp long shot to a close-up, you may find it completely defocused, and then have to fumble to correct focus, while on shot!

The only solution to this dilemma is to remember to *pre-focus the zoom*, before you take the shot. All this involves is taking a trial close-shot of the subject immediately beforehand so that you can focus crisply, then zoom back to the wide shot (without changing your distance), ready to start shooting the action.

That sounds fine, but if you have been shooting a bank of flowers, then suddenly decide to take a big close-up of a butterfly that has just landed on a nearby blossom, you are unlikely to be pre-focused. In this situation, you can only hope, and correct the focus on the close-up surreptitiously. If the shot is badly defocused, then focus it correctly, and cut out the fuzzy picture during editing.

Exposure

3.14 Tonal range

Your camera can only handle a limited tonal range. If surfaces in the picture are too bright relative to your *f*/stop setting, they will block off (burn out; crush) to a blank white. Areas in the picture that fall below the system's lower limit will reproduce as black.

The trick is to choose the *f*/stop so that *the tones in the subject you are most interested in* are clearly visible. This process is called 'adjusting the exposure'.

You can use a *light meter* to estimate exposure; to judge whether the light levels are appropriate for the lens aperture you want to use. (A video camera's sensitivity may be roughly equivalent to ASA 100.) You can also check whether lighting is reasonably consistent throughout the acting area. Measuring and adjusting the amount of light falling on the subject is regular film practice.

However, a light meter gives only a *general* indication. As you will discover, exposure is a *subjective* choice. The video camera shows you immediately, whether the exposure is appropriate. You adjust the lens aperture to get the most pleasing effect in selected parts of the shot; usually people's faces.

Let's take a practical example. Perhaps you are shooting someone standing out in the open air. You adjust exposure by altering the lens aperture, until they look good in your viewfinder; or better still, on a high grade picture monitor. Their face tones in particular, should appear quite natural – neither too light nor too dark.

Now look carefully at the picture, and you are quite likely to find that their white shirt reproduces as washed-out and without detail, or the trousers look black, with no signs of modeling in the material at all. Perhaps you can simply accept the results. But if this is a fashion shot, showing off the quality and attractiveness of the clothing, it would scarcely be acceptable.

You can seldom expect to show good tonal gradation in *everything* in the scene. There will usually be something in the shot that crushes out to white or black.

How successfully you can expose a shot will depend not only on the range of tones appearing in it, but on the effect you are aiming at. You might deliberately 'underexpose' a picture to make it look more shadowy and mysterious. You might 'overexpose' a picture of the seashore, to create a high-key effect.

In the studio, one can control tones by careful selection, by lighting or by adjustments. But elsewhere, particularly on location, you have to make the most of what is available, and at times the lens aperture you select may have to be something of a compromise.

If parts of the location scene reproduce as large blank white or black area in the picture, there may not be much you can do about it. The obvious remedy is to reframe the shot, or change the camera position, to keep them out of picture altogether. If you have lighting equipment available, you may be able to lighten darker tones or shadowy areas. Occasionally you can mask off a troublesome surface (e.g. have someone standing in the foreground obscuring a large blank white wall). If it is only a small object that catches the eye (e.g. sun reflected in a table mirror), you may be able to re-angle it, or remove it altogether.

3.15 Underexposure and overexposure

When a picture is *underexposed*, all of its tones will appear that much darker. Results are usually dull and lifeless. Detail and modeling may be clear in light tones (even clearer than usual), but mid to dark areas look muddy and merge to black.

There is always a certain amount of 'noise' in any video picture, but when it is underexposed, a grainy sparkling 'snow' over the darker tones becomes very obvious and degrades its quality. The effect worsens in the videotape recording and any subsequent re-recordings (dubbings).

It is worth remembering too, that when the camera receives insufficient light from the scene, other picture defects also develop such as *lag* (image smearing on movement), and picture noise.

To remedy underexposure, you open up the lens aperture to provide the camera's CCD with a brighter lens image. (But at the same time of course, this will reduce the depth of field to some extent, and could make focusing harder, particularly when using a narrow-angle lens.)

Increasing the video amplification on a camera cannot really compensate when the camera sensor is not getting enough light for maximum performance. It just boosts the video signal. But it will certainly strengthen the reproduced picture, perhaps even making it look bright and well contrasted.

When a picture is *overexposed*, all of its tones will appear unusually light. Even fairly light tones in the scene will block off, while darker areas of the scene will often be easier to discern than normal. Stopping down a little improves reproduction in light tones, but reduces the visibility of shadows.

3.16 Automatic exposure

If judging exposure is a matter of artistic choice, how is it that so many video cameras are fitted with an automatic iris? Well, leaving aside those people who would otherwise be careless about exposure, the auto-iris is a very useful facility when you are in a tight spot. It continually adjusts the lens aperture to maintain an average video signal.

Under typical location conditions, whether in the open or within buildings, light levels can change considerably as the camera alters its viewpoint. Try walking around with a light-meter, and you will see its needle bouncing up and down as you reposition. So your camera may well need to be stopped down to $f/16$ in a sunlit courtyard, yet have to open up to $f/2$ as you move inside a house.

Strictly speaking, therefore, if you are following along with action that moves from the exterior to the interior, you would need to keep an eye on your viewfinder, and adjust the exposure to match these different light levels.

But surely, you will say, you are already having to follow *focus* as you move, and keep the shot properly framed. How can you accurately adjust exposure at the same time? A very valid point! That is why even experienced cameramen under these conditions will leave exposure to the auto-iris, and concentrate on focusing and composing the picture.

Ideally, you set the lens aperture to suit your main subject. If the same subject appears in a succession of shots in the same scene, you want the exposure to be *constant*, not yo-yo about as incidental background tones vary. Yet changes of this kind are really unavoidable when using an auto-iris.

It is easy to fool an auto-iris. If you bring a lighter tone into the shot (e.g. open a newspaper or take off a jacket and reveal a white shirt), it will close down a little, and darken all the other tones in the picture, including the face you are really looking at. Take the light area out of shot, or pan away from it, and the auto-iris will open up. Picture tones will lighten. Take a long shot, and face tones may look dark, but zoom in to a close shot, and because other picture tones are now excluded the face reproduces much lighter.

Under certain conditions, the auto-iris can cause bad underexposure. Normally, if you are shooting inside a room, the system will open up and produce successful pictures. But suppose the person you are filming moves over to the window. The auto-iris will see the intense daylight, and stop the lens down. As a result, the person now appears as a silhouette, while the sky is well exposed.

Some cameras have a *backlight* control that you switch in under such conditions. This opens up the iris an arbitrary stop or so above the auto-iris setting, to improve the subject's exposure. This may overexpose lightest areas, but the person will now be more clearly visible.

Although the auto-iris system is by no means infallible, these variations are often preferable to badly overexposed or underexposed pictures. And in practice, they may be too slight to worry about, or even pass unnoticed. For all that, they are still there. It depends how critically you are watching the final result.

Handling your camera

3.17 Why all these rules?

There are a lot of "do's" and "dont's" in this section. You could simply follow them, but it would be better to try shooting situations in which you *deliberately* break each of these principles. Then re-shoot the same scenes the right way. If you sit down and critically compare the results, they should speak for themselves!

3.18 Panning and tilting

If you cannot get a sufficiently wide shot of your subject to show it completely, or you feel that the distant view does not have enough detail, there are two general solutions.

You can take a series of separate shots which are then intercut to build up an overall image in the minds of your audience. However, you must avoid this sequence simply developing into disjointed random 'potshots'.

Alternatively, you can pan your camera carefully and systematically over the scene, to relate various parts. Take care, though, to avoid a series of brief erratic pans, or long 'empty' pans that wander over unimportant things. See that each pan has a clear purpose and finishes by settling on an interesting feature of the scene. Above all, do avoid panning from side to side over the scene, as if you were using a water-hose. Although this can be a great temptation, it is not something you are likely to do more than once, when you have played back the results!

Like all camerawork, panning and tilting need to be smooth and controlled. You should not overshoot, but bring each movement to a

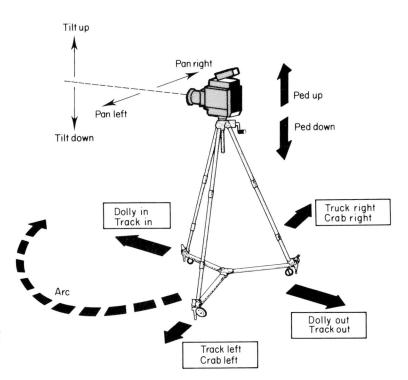

Figure 3.10 Camera movements

Although some camera movements have alternative terms (dolly, truck, arc – track, crab), others are universal. People often speak of 'panning' up/down as well as panning sideways.

smooth finish. If your pan has a jerky start or finish, or is hesitant, or its speed is uneven, or it wavers up and down, the result can look pretty crude in the finished production.

Don't be tempted to pan around too quickly, for your picture will only become an indecipherable blur. Most of us fall into that trap at first, when shooting a landscape. We pan around briskly, trying to show everything, only to find that the result on the screen is extremely disappointing, as details become broken up ('strobing') during the movement.

Try panning across a scene, so that an object takes around five seconds to travel from one edge of the screen to the other. That is about the fastest rate to avoid movement break-up.

Very occasionally, you can deliberately use a rapid *whip pan* (zip pan) for startling dramatic effect, but it is really one of those ideas that you try, then seldom use again!

If your camera is hand-held or shoulder-mounted and you want to follow action over a wide arc, do not try to rotate your body by turning on your heels. Instead, position yourself facing mid-way, ready to make a smooth balanced movement, and twist your body to follow the action. The result will be much more controlled. Keeping your knees slightly bent can help.

When you are using a tripod, remember to check that it is level before panning, or you will find the framing moving upwards or downwards as you pan.

3.19 Following moving subjects

There is a lot more to taking shots of a moving subject, than simply keeping up with it! The way you cope with movement is a hallmark of good camerawork.

When you hold your camera quite still, anything moving around in the shot can very soon reach the edge of the frame and pass out of sight, particularly if it is moving quickly in a 'tight' shot filling most of the screen.

There are several ways of treating this situation:

● You can let the moving subject *pass out of the frame altogether* ('exit'). And you will certainly do this if you want the audience's attention to pass on to a new subject.

● You can *widen the shot;* zooming out or moving back to include the movement. That is often the best solution, if you have someone pacing to and fro, or waving their arms about.

● You can *pan and/or tilt* to keep the subject in shot, for example, to follow somebody as they move around a room. But don't use too close a shot here. Not only will the subject itself look very cramped in the frame, but you'll find it quite difficult to follow the action smoothly.

● You can move the camera position (e.g. arc round) so that the subject remains in shot.

● You can move along with the subject ('traveling shot') keeping it in frame as you go.

● Instead of following the movement, you can let it leave frame, and then pick up the action from a new viewpoint.

If you are shooting with a *single* camera, the last option listed above means that you have to stop recording, get over to the next position, set up the new shot, and re-start recording again. In the meantime, you're missing some of the action. Unless, of course, you can have it repeated, and take up the action from just before you moved to your second viewpoint.

If you are using *two or more* cameras, you need not miss any of the action; just cut to the second camera at the right moment.

Which of these methods you choose, will depend on which you consider is most appropriate, both artistically and practically.

3.20 Framing movement

At first sight, it seems logical to keep a moving subject exactly in the middle of the picture. However, you will find that the picture looks unbalanced and rather boring. Instead, when you are panning with a moving subject, try to position it lagging just a little behind center-frame all the time ('offset'). The picture looks more dynamic. The faster the movement, the greater the offset.

Above all, don't let the subject 'hop around the frame' through uneven panning. (This can happen if there is *insufficient drag* on the panning head.)

Worst crime of all, don't have the subject 'popping in and out' of the shot, as you lose it and find it, while trying to keep up with it! (This will most likely to happen if you try to follow a fast moving subject in a close shot on a narrow-angle lens, or if you have *too much drag* on the panning head.)

3.21 Walking

If you are going to use a shoulder-mounted camera a lot, it is a good idea to make practice recordings, as you move around on shot – towards the subject, away from it, in an arc, sideways. It is not easy as it seems, to keep level steady well-composed shots in sharp focus.

When your subject moves away, the obvious thing to do is to walk with them. But beware! Unless you have checked over the route beforehand, ensure that there are no carpets, steps, cables, people or posts. You may meet unseen hazards as you concentrate on the viewfinder picture. That is why experienced cameramen develop a habit of flicking a glance around, to check out their surroundings, and nearby action, and try to keep both eyes open when using an eyepiece viewfinder.

There is always a certain amount of bounce in the camera's shot as you walk, especially if you are moving at all quickly. This unevenness may be unimportant, even dramatic if you are following someone over uneven ground, through a crowd, or pushing through a forest. But it can be quite distracting if you are walking around within a building.

If you have a cable between the camera and a second operator (e.g. carrying batteries, sound equipment, video recorder, or a light) fast moves can be difficult. But at least you have a person nearby who can warn you of hazards in your path – particularly when you are moving backwards!

3.22 Shooting from vehicles

Whenever you are shooting from any vehicle, there are a number of points worth bearing in mind.

Where possible, it is best to hand-hold the camera, and shoot through an open window. Resist any temptation to rest the lens or the camera on the glass or the vehicle's body, for vibration can damage the equipment and blur the picture. Smeary, rain-speckled, dusty or tinted windows can degrade picture quality to a considerable extent, especially if sunlight is falling on them. Your pictures will show flattened contrast, defocused blurs and changing color values, that become particularly obvious when intercut with other shots.

Your position in a vehicle will influence the audience-impact of your pictures. Facing forwards, subjects appear to move towards the camera, getting closer and closer and increasingly clearer. So this is a powerful viewpoint that provides continual interest. A rear view, however, shows everything moving away from the camera, and audience interest tends to fall. No sooner does something come into shot than it quickly becomes too small to see properly. Side windows are a good way of shooting distant subjects, but anything close rapidly zips across the screen out of focus.

Shooting someone inside a moving car can need a certain amount of agility! A wide-angle (short-focus) lens is essential, to enable you to get sufficiently wide shots of the driver. Typical camera positions include: seated beside the driver, crouched in the passenger's foot space, or leaning over from a rear seat. Cameras can also be mounted outside the car, using bolt-on brackets or suction-held pads (limpet mounts).

Picture-making basics

3.23 Practical conditions

There are no absolute 'rules' for effective picture-making. In fact, if you arrange your pictures too systematically the results can look very mannered and artificial. But there *are* certainly a number of situations to avoid!

During a busy shooting schedule, there simply isn't time to linger, experimenting over the composition of each shot. You have to make quick decisions. But if you understand compositional basics you will know what to look out for, and realise how to adjust the shot for the most appropriate effect. Once you recognize the sort of thing that make pictures unsuccessful, and many are a matter of commonsense, you will avoid them instinctively.

Unlike a painter, who can arrange objects on the canvas to suit his ideas, a video cameraman usually has to make the most of what is there already. But that does not mean that you cannot control what the viewer sees! You can do a great deal to change a picture's appeal: by selecting your viewpoint carefully, by the lens angle you choose, or by the way you frame the shot. Sometimes you will be able to reposition items to improve the picture further.

3.24 Selecting the shots

Whether you shoot the subject with one camera, or intercut between two or more, you must create a smooth-flowing sequence of pictures that makes sense to your audience. This will not happen automatically.

The worst thing you can do is to take a series of random 'good shots' of the subject without any thought about how they are going to be interrelated on the screen. You could finish up with a collection of unrelated bits and pieces. For reliable results, you should aim to work out beforehand what you want to show, and how you are going to show it. Try to plan ahead.

3.25 Persuasive shots

Picture-making is not about creating *beautiful* pictures. it is about providing *appropriate* pictures. There will even be moments when you quite deliberately introduce an *ugly* shot, to shock your audience with harsh reality. The color camera too easily glamorizes. A scene of squalid decay can become 'a vision of interesting textures and hues' in the evening sunlight.

A well-chosen sequence of shots does much more than just *illustrate* the subject for your audience. The pictures you choose and arrange are expressing your point of view; how you have interpreted a situation; what you want to say about it. That is what program-making is all about. It is almost as if you were there beside them guiding their choice and interpretation of events.

When you show them pictures of a bustling marketplace, you may be making the unspoken invitation; 'Look around at anything that happens to interest you'. More often though, you want to draw their attention to certain aspects of a scene, so you invite them through the shots you select, to concentrate on an interesting feature: 'See how this object differs from that one. Notice the intricate details there'. Or on another occasion you might be saying: 'See how she is reacting to what he said. See what she is doing . . . watch how she is doing it'.

3.26 What is it all about?

As each shot appears on the screen, your audience is seeing and hearing it *for the first time*. In an instant, they have to interpret what you have selected to put there. It is not surprising that they can occasionally become confused!

Unless you are careful, they may 'look at the wrong thing', as their attention alights on something else in the picture that is more prominent, more colorful or more interesting!

The duration of a shot is important, too. If you hang on to any shot for too long, your audience will certainly begin to drowse.

If your shots are too brief, they may 'flick past the eyes without entering the brain'!

Your aim is to help your audience to understand; to guide their thoughts, whether you are describing a technical process or telling a joke. You do not want to confuse or distract them by irrelevancies. You need to present a logical sequence of ideas that can be followed easily. Your audience cannot ask what you meant, or turn back to re-read what you said. They have to get the point first time round.

If you do not take the trouble to choose shots carefully, people have to look around each picture, trying to decide what it is all about, correctly or incorrectly. If they do not have any idea what they are supposed to be looking at (or don't find it interesting), they will look at whatever draws their attention. Random pictures produce random thoughts.

Very occasionally, you may actually *want* to puzzle or intrigue your audience, in order to create a dramatic or comic build-up of tension. The camera enters a quiet room. They are left wondering . . . they see a threatening shadow of someone standing there . . . but a moment later realise that it is only coming from garments on a coat-rack. They have been fooled.

But, in most situations, if your audience is left puzzled, wondering where it is, or what it is supposed to be, or why you have switched away from something they found interesting to this new unexplained scene, then something is very wrong!

Some directors do this all too often, when they try to introduce some variety, or do 'something different'. The shot cuts to a building reflected in a puddle, or some wayside flowers, or watches a dog sleeping beside the road . . . that seems to have nothing to do with the story! Even shooting the subject through a decorative foreground screen can be puzzling at times.

If a shot is appropriate and helps the story onwards, it can be as unusual as you like. But if your audience is distracted by it, or begins to think how interesting the *shot* is, rather than the subject, then it has failed.

3.27 Clutter

If you do not guide your audience's attention to particular features of the scene, they are just as likely to finish up looking at the wrong thing or becoming bored.

When a picture is absolutely full of things (a crowd of people, shelves of articles, or a wall of paintings), it is hard for the viewer to concentrate on any one of them properly, or even see them clearly. You may simply be trying to say: 'Aren't there a lot of different versions?', or 'See how big the collection is!'. But you could finish up with an audience who feel that they are missing out, for they can't see any of the items clearly.

It is often far better to *isolate* the item you want to show:

- Get closer (tighter framing).
- Change the camera's viewpoint.
- Use a shallow depth of field, so that only the main subject is in focus.
- Move it apart from the rest.
- Use contrasting tones.
- Use strong compositional lines.
- Position the subject higher in the frame.
- Use lighting to isolate it (light pool, shadows).

3.28 I can't see it properly!

There will be times when you use diffusion, or sneaky lighting, to make a subject look strange, mysterious or just different. But most times you want your audience to be able to see the subject *clearly*, especially in a demonstration of any kind.

Look out for those moments when they *cannot see* what you are trying to show them, because the shot is too distant, or something is shadowing the subject, or even someone's thumb is over the label we are supposed to be reading.

Close-up shots are great when we want to show detail. But sometimes a close shot can prevent your audience from seeing *sufficient* of the subject. It may show a few cogs, when we really need to see much more of a piece of machinery, to see how it works.

Another hazard is overexposure. It can bleach out detail in light-toned subjects – particularly when back-light bounces off a paper being shown to camera, and we cannot see what is written on it.

All this is very obvious, but problems of this sort happen regularly, and very frustrating they can be too!

Composing pictures

3.29 Theory and practice

There is an old joke about a centipede who walked around happily, until he was asked how he knew which leg to move first. Trying to work it out, he fell in a ditch, unable to budge. Many of us feel that way when we try to apply the *rules of composition*. They sound so complicated and so restrictive, they seem to turn the pleasures of picture-making into a mathematical process.

Let's forget about learning 'rules', and consider instead what we do and do not *like to see* in pictures. By following this path, we shall meet all the most important compositional principles we need to know.

3.30 The brief shot

As we look at a *still* picture, whether it is on the printed page, a projected slide, or hung in an art gallery, there is an opportunity to linger. We can scrutinize it for as long as we want.

On TV and film screen, shots do not encourage browsing. Each is there only for a brief time, from a fraction of a second to perhaps half a minute at most. Then it is replaced by another. Each shot has to make its point rapidly. Each creates its impact.

3.31 'Dull' is in the mind

What makes a shot dull? A lot depends on your *attitude* to what you are seeing. Any shot is dull when you personally find little worth looking at

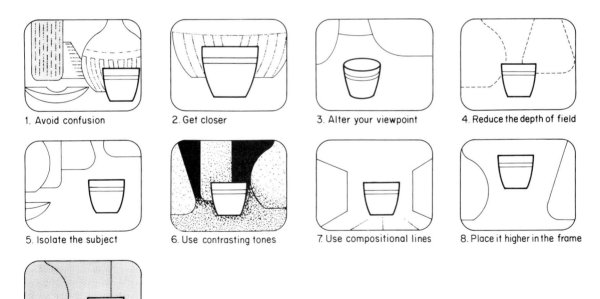

1. Avoid confusion   2. Get closer   3. Alter your viewpoint   4. Reduce the depth of field

5. Isolate the subject   6. Use contrasting tones   7. Use compositional lines   8. Place it higher in the frame

9. Isolate it with lighting

Figure 3.11 Concentrating attention

in it; when you could not care less who the people are, or where they are, or what they are doing. That's why other people's vacation slides may lack some of the appeal for you that they have for those who took them.

A shot may seem to show just a boring stretch of ocean. But if the commentary tells us: 'At this dangerous spot, after years of painstaking searching, divers found the Spanish treasure ship ...' we look at the picture with new eyes, although in reality there isn't anything special to see! You will meet this sort of thing regularly. Without the influence of the commentary, such shots could be an instant yawn. But because our interest is aroused, and they are only there for a short time, they attract and hold our attention.

So the appeal of any picture depends partly on what it *shows*, partly on what it is *about*, and partly on how *interested* you have persuaded your audience to be in it.

A shot of open desert may quickly pall, but when the audience sees a tiny moving shape in the distance, its curiosity is aroused. What happens if you continue to hold that shot? Usually, people lose interest. But in different circumstances, using exactly the same shot, they may be on the edge of their seats, waiting perhaps to discover which of the travelers has managed to survive.

If there is *too much* to see in the picture, the eye flits around hopefully, but probably finishes up concentrating on nothing. If there is *too little* in the shot, attention soon falls.

When there are no visual accents to grab the attention, the eye wanders. But if you can arrange things so that your main subject stands out from its surrounding, then your audience will concentrate on it, and is less likely to heed other things in the picture.

3.32 Clever shots

It is tempting to devise shots that are *different*; shots that make the eye stop and wonder. Wildly distorted perspective from a close wide-angle lens, very low angle shots, or pictures using weird reflections are fine when you need them for a dramatic or comic effect. But unusual viewpoints don't just make a picture look different; they draw attention to themselves. They distract you from the real subject.

3.33 Fitting the frame

The TV screen has a horizontal rectangular shape, and many subjects fit comfortably into this format. So we can get quite a close shot of them, filling all of the screen, without losing parts outside the frame area.

Others are too tall for the screen. So you can only show them completely in a long shot, or shoot them in sections, either by panning over them, or by intercutting a series of close shots. Sometimes when the subject does not fit the screen, you have to select an oblique viewpoint to get it all into the picture.

Once you get fairly close to any subject, you are bound to lose parts of it outside the frame of the picture. Most TV receivers are adjusted to get the maximum picture size possible, so they cut off the edges of the shot. If you do not want your audience to miss anything important, such as titling, you need to compose the shot to keep these details within the 'safe area' of the screen.

Picture borders. The picture edges are usually lost on the screen (due to over-scanning the picture tube). To ensure that no important action or titling is lost, keep it within the borders shown.

Framing people. Don't let the frame cut people at natural joints; intermediate points are much more attractive. Avoid having people seem to lean or sit on the edge of the picture.

Tight framing. If you frame shots too close to contain the subject's actions, it will keep moving in and out of the picture. The result is very cramped and distracting.

Figure 3.12 Fitting the frame

Figure 3.13 Headroom

Keep a check on the distance between the top of heads and the top of the frame. If this headroom is too little ('tight'), the frame will appear to crush down on people, and parts of heads may be cut off by the receiver overscan. Too much headroom ('loose') unbalances the shot, and may attract the audience's attention.

Too little headroom   Too much headroom   Just right

If you shoot a person so that the frame chops off their heads, hands or feet, the result looks odd. But alter the shot slightly so that the frame cuts partway along their limbs, and the effect seems natural enough.

There is nothing unusual about seeing a person leaning against a post, but adjust the shot so that they seem to be resting on the frame of the picture, and it appears comic.

It is interesting to see how the frame of the screen affects how comfortable we feel with the picture. If you take a shot in which the subject just fills the screen, it will look cramped and hemmed in by the frame. Go a little closer, so that parts of the subject are cut off, and all is well. Take a shot in which the subject only fills a small part of the screen, and we may get the impression that there is 'too much air around them'.

There are circumstances, of course, when you will deliberately aim at a crowded-screen effect, or isolate the subject, for dramatic reasons, but not for regular shots.

3.34 The rule of thirds

If you divide the screen into even proportions (halves, quarters), either vertically or horizontally, the result is generally pretty boring. You should avoid for example, an horizon located exactly half-way up the frame.

You will often find the 'rule of thirds' quoted as a useful aid to composing the picture. Here you draw a grid on the monitor, dividing the screen vertically and horizontally into three equal parts. Then you compose shots so that main subjects come on these lines or where they cross. This routine is purely mechanical; for subjects' positions really depend on their size, shape, tone, the background, their relative importance, and so on. In time, you will instinctively compose shots with these features at the back of your mind. In the meantime, this 'rule' can be a helpful starting point.

Figure 3.14 Proportions

An equally divided frame allows only formal balance – usually dull and monotonous. Thirds can lead to quickly recognized mechanical proportions. Dividing the screen in a 2:3 or a 3:5 ratio achieves a far more pleasing balance.

3.35 Well-balanced shots

A good sense of balance is important to us in daily life, and we apply it instinctively to everything we do, even picture-making. It is easier to demonstrate than to talk about, and in a couple of minutes with a camera, you can see how it affects the way you arrange your pictures.

All you need is a reasonably small subject such as a vase or a pile of books on an empty table, with nothing else of interest nearby. Take a shot in which it takes up about one-third of the frame height, and comes in the center of the picture. Figure 3.15 shows the idea, but results on your own screen will be a lot more convincing. What do you notice about this arrangement? Well, it probably looks a perfectly ordinary, stable, rather dull composition.

Tilt your camera down a little. The vase is now in the top of the shot, and you become aware of the space below it in the frame. The picture has become somewhat top-heavy.

Tilt up, until the vase is right at the bottom of the shot. Now the empty space above at the top of the picture has become prominent, and the frame is rather bottom-heavy.

You are seeing how the height at which you locate the subject in the frame, alters the feeling of the picture's vertical balance.

This idea is particularly important when shooting people. If you do not have enough space between the top of a person's head and the top of the picture (too little 'headroom'), the frame will seem to crush down on them. Have too much space, and one's attention goes up to the space, to see what is there.

So when taking shots of people, always look out for the headroom. It will be considerable in a long shot, and reduce correspondingly as your shot gets closer. As a very rough guide, you can think of keeping the eyes about a third of the screen height from the top of the picture, but as you will discover, headroom is influenced by whatever else is visible in the top of the picture.

3.36 Good balance

Looking at a well-balanced picture, we see that it has a settled, stable look. An unbalanced shot, on the other hand, has an insecure, uncertain feel to it.

That might be just what you want. An unstable, incomplete look increases tension and creates a dramatic impact. An easy way to achieve this is to make the picture top-heavy or lop-sided. But usually you will want to arrange shots so that they look balanced and complete.

Back to our experiment. Center up the subject as you did originally, then pan left a little so that it is over to the right of the frame. If there is nothing else in the frame the picture will look lop-sided, heavy on the right. Pan right until the subject is on frame left, and now the weight in the picture has moved across the screen. If you use a dark-toned subject the effect is more pronounced than with light tones.

You can do this experiment with light- and dark-toned pieces of card on a flat surface. The effect will be similar. If you zoom in (or get closer) so that a subject occupies more of the screen, it not only becomes more prominent, but its 'weight' in the picture increases. The farther you place it from the center of the frame, the greater is its effect.

Figure 3.15 Picture balance

Part 1 The frame position of even a simple subject can affect whether the picture looks balanced, top-heavy, bottom-heavy or lop-sided.

1 2 3 4

Part 2 A group that would look lop-sided and unbalance the picture (1) can be counterbalanced by another mass in another part of the screen (2) If centered (3), the picture is balanced, even without other subjects, but continual centering gets monotonous. Different sized masses can balance each other, but take care not to split the audience's attention.

When you have several subjects in the shot, the overall impact will alter, depending on their relative sizes and tones. Obviously, a large subject a long way away may appear smaller than a tiny object close to the camera. It is the effect that counts. You can actually balance a large subject on one side of the frame with several smaller ones on the other side. It is all a matter of their relative sizes, tones and distance from the center of the frame.

There you have the secret of interesting, well-balanced pictures; not shots which are continually, monotonously centered every time, but shots which are balanced across the frame, depending on the tones and proportions of the subjects we see there.

3.37 Juggling proportions

You can vary the relative proportions and positions of things in a picture very simply, by:

- *Adjusting the camera's distance.* As you know, the closer things are to the camera, the larger they appear in frame. Even altering your camera distance, a little changes the apparent size of foreground subjects considerably. Distant things, though, remain about the same size in picture, even for big changes in viewpoint.
- *By changing the camera height.* The lower the camera, the more prominent things in the foreground usually become. From even a slightly higher position, the camera pushes them down to the bottom of the frame, and may shoot past them altogether.
- *By changing the camera lens angle.* Using a wide-angle lens makes things rapidly diminish in size with distance. So you can make something seem much farther away, or smaller, by using a wide lens angle and adjusting your distance from the foreground subjects to get the proportions you want.

When you use a narrow lens angle, the reverse happens. The relative sizes of things do not seem to change much with distance. Even things that are far off still appear pretty close.

So by selecting a suitable lens angle and changing your viewpoint, you have quite a lot of control over proportions in the shot.

Grouping (unity)

If there are a number of separate items in a picture, they will always look better when they are grouped in some way, rather than scattered around the frame. This creates a unity in the picture, and pulls it all together.

You can often create the effect of grouping in the picture, even where subjects are really some distance apart, by carefully selecting the direction from which you shoot them.

3.39 Camera viewpoint

Where you place your camera, relative to a subject, will have a strong influence on what it looks like to your audience, and how they feel about it.

The smaller a subject appears in the frame, the less important it seems to become and the less detail is visible. Its surroundings become more prominent, and can take attention from the subject itself.

Although closer shots emphasize the subject, you need to take care that they do not become so enlarged on the screen that the effect is overpowering! Really close shots often lose scale, and make the audience forget the true size and proportions of the blown-up area.

Looking down at any subject tends to make it look less impressive than looking up at it. Although steeply angled viewpoints are usually too dramatic for most purposes, even a slight variation from an eye-level position can affect the impact of a subject.

3.40 Distortions

Controlled distortion is a technique of cunning cameracraft. A wide-angle lens can distort a halloween mask, for example, to create a frightening effect. That same lens can make quite a small group of trees look like a forest.

But take care that you do not distort the shape of things badly, by accident. You might for instance, be shooting an oil painting high up on the wall of an historic house. Either to avoid light reflections, or to get an unobstructive view, you may decide to take close shots of it from a side position, on a narrow-angle lens. You get a shot, but look at the results! A squashed version that does little justice to the original!

Shooting in a small room, you may have to use a wide-angle lens, to prevent everything looking too close. But beware! It is quite likely that now the room looks larger than life, and if people appear in the shot, you could too easily make them appear plump, fat-faced or large-nosed with receding hair, due to wide-angle distortions.

Anticipating editing

3.41 Continuity

Every time you set up your camera to take the next action shot, give a thought to *editing*. Otherwise you are liable to finish up with a series of shots that do not join together smoothly. This is particularly liable to happen when you re-angle the camera, and repeat the action.

Table 3.1 Common faults while shooting

- Wrong color temperature. (Picture bluish or yellowish.)
- Soft focus.
- Focused on wrong subject.
- Camera shake, unsteady camera (tiredness, windblown).
- Sloping horizons.
- Headroom wrong. (Too little or excessive.)
- Cut off top of head or feet.
- Subject leaning on the frame.
- Subject size. (Too distant or close to see properly.)
- Successive shots too similar.
- Cutting to new camera angle, but similar shot size.
- Inappropriate camera height for the situation.
- Disproportionate number of long shots or close shots.
- All subjects composed center-frame.
- Too much sky in the shot.
- Shots do not interrelate. (Too many isolated subjects.)
- Subject obscured. (Foreground intrusion.)
- Distractions. (Other objects, background, people waving.)
- Background distracting.
- Background objects sprouting from heads.
- Shots too brief (or too lengthy).
- Start of action missed.
- Zooming excessive or distracting.
- Panning not smooth, too fast, or overshoots.
- Speaker's eyeline slightly offset. (Gives a shifty look.)
- Person handling objects badly. (Obscuring, moving around.)
- Poor lighting. (e.g. Black eyes, hot top, half-lit face.)

The most frequent problems are:
- Part of the action is *missing*.
- The action shot from another angle does not *match* that from a previous shot of the subject.
- The *direction* of the action has changed between successive shots.
- The *shot sizes* are too similar, or too extreme.
- Action leaves the frame, and re-enters it on the same side.
- Successive shots show continuity differences; e.g. with and without glasses, different attitudes/expressions, dressed differently.

3.42 Improving flexibility

When you are shooting, you can help editing flexibility in various ways:

Avoid over-brief shots
- Always tape the *run-in* and *run-out* to an action, to allow editing leeway. Not just the actual moment of the action.
- Where possible, start and finish a long panning shot with a 'held' (static) shot.
- When shooting 'continuous action', it can be helpful to begin each shot with the end speech and action of the previous shot.

Extra editing material
- Always shoot some *cutaways* showing the surroundings, general scene, bystanders' reactions, etc.
- Consider whether specific reaction shots/nod shots would be appropriate.
- It is sometimes helpful to shoot the same scene at a leisurely pace, and at a faster pace (e.g. slow pan, faster pan) to allow editing choice.

Faulty takes
- Do not record over (wipe) an unsuccessful shot. Parts of it may be usable.
- If an action sequence goes wrong, it is sometimes better to retake it entirely. At others, change the camera angle (or shot size), and retake the action from just before the fault onwards (a 'pick-up' shot).

Overall shots
- Always begin shooting with a wide 'atmospheric' shot of the scene (*establishing shot*); even if it is not used eventually.
- Consider taking an overall *cover shot* of the action, then repeating action while taking closer shots.

3.43 Crossing the line

Unless you take care when arranging camera viewpoints, you can easily upset the audience's sense of direction, and their impressions of spatial relationships. Having seen someone on the left of the screen, it is distracting to discover them on the cut, at the right of the next shot.

To avoid this happening, draw an *imaginary line* between two people, or along the direction of action (*action line*). Then be careful that cameras shoot from only one side of this line – never crossing it. You can dolly across the line, or shoot along it, or change its direction by regrouping people, but intercutting between cameras either side of this imaginary line produces a *reverse cut* or *jump cut*.

Figure 3.16 The imaginary line

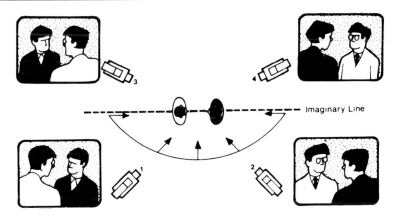

Part 1 *Intercut facing shots*. Shots can be intercut (cross-cut) between cameras located on the same side of the imaginary line; i.e. between 1 and 2, or 3 and 4. But inter-switching between cameras on opposite sides of this line, causes jump cuts (1 and 3, 1 and 4, 2 and 3, 2 and 4).

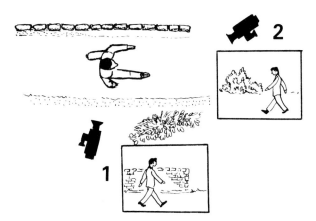

Part 2 *Crossing the line*. Reverse cuts arise very easily, when the camera crosses the line of a subject's route (the *imaginary line* or *action line*). Here the camera has moved to a new unobscured viewpoint on the other side of the path, so the direction of the walk appears to change during editing!

Part 3 *Maintaining direction*. A subject should appear to be moving in the same direction on the cut. To avoid confusion (e.g. intercutting 1 and 3), insert a neutral head-on shot, or a cutaway to another subject.

Chapter 4

Practical lighting

Good lighting can transform even a routine, uninteresting shot into an attractive, appealing picture.

4.1 Lighting for everyone

Don't be scared of lighting! A lot of people are apprehensive about doing the wrong thing and looking foolish. Others think of lighting as an unnecessary luxury for a small production unit. They assume it requires a lot of equipment, and kilowatts of power. It can, if you have to light a large-studio drama, or the inside of a stadium. But everyday video productions are not usually so extensive, and even quite modest facilities will still give you opportunities for some really worthwhile lighting treatment.

As we shall see, there are many situations where just one lamp, or a well-placed reflector, is all that is needed to make a picture spring to life. Even where production is on a larger scale, foresight and imagination can often make a little light go a long way. It is chiefly a matter of knowing what you are aiming at, what to look out for, and what you can do about problems you meet.

Why not simply go around shooting in whatever light is available? You could. On your good days, you will finish up with clear attractive interesting pictures, where realistic color makes the picture sing. But there will certainly be those other days when pictures are lifeless, drab, or crudely over-contrasty; when you can't see the subject clearly, or its texture is lost, or attention goes to the wrong subject; when everything looks uninteresting and dull; when video noise spatters the picture, and color smears in the gloom.

So much depends on where and when you are shooting. Are you inside a building (interior) or out in the open (exterior). Is it day or night? Are the surroundings well illuminated, or in shadowy gloom? Are you shooting quite localized areas, or taking spacious long-shots? And finally, a lot will depend on the sort of atmosphere you are aiming to convey to your audience: a realistic everyday scene or a moody dramatic situation.

Obviously, you are not going to introduce any extra lighting into a scene unless it is really going to enhance your pictures. Often, you will not have the time or the opportunity to make changes anyway. So we shall assume that, at most, you will only be toting around a handful of lightweight lamps. There will be many situations, particularly in the open air, where you do not even need these, provided you know how to arrange your subject in the existing lighting.

4.2 The camera does not compensate

One of the most important things to bear in mind, when you are lighting, is the essential difference between the way your eyes and brain register the scene and the limited, literal way your camera reproduces it.

Your eyes and brain compensate (sometimes *over*-compensate) in many subtle ways, as the lighting of your surroundings varies. You seem to be able to see details in shadows; variations in color values pass unnoticed. You are still able to see a remarkable amount even when the lighting conditions are very poor.

Your camera cannot interpret. It responds to what is there, within its limitations. If a surface reflects too much light for the video system, whether it is a specular reflection from a shiny surface, or a very light tone, it blocks off to a blank white in the picture. Darker-toned furniture, clothing, foliage or shadows often crush-out to black on camera. If you are on the spot, looking at the scene, you have none of these problems. So you have to be alert to how the camera is really reproducing what you are seeing.

As we saw earlier (section 3.14), loss of detail and modeling in certain parts of the picture may not be important, unless you particularly want to see features of a white wedding dress or a black velvet costume. Where the lost tones do matter, you may sometimes need to 'doctor' the scene to make it appear normal on the screen, e.g. by lighting a dark background to bring it within the range of the camera system, or deliberately keeping it out of shot, if you can't!

4.3 The key factors

Did you realize that you already know a lot about the principles of lighting? Although these everyday effects are so similar that you probably don't give a second thought to them, you already have quite a store of knowledge about the way light reflects from different surfaces, how shadows fall, how the appearance of things can vary under different kinds of light, and so on. You will be applying these various observations, as you light your production.

'Lighting' involves a lot more than simply having enough illumination around to let the camera see what is going on. Light influences what your subject looks like, how people feel about what they see, what attracts their attention. So we need to think about not only where to put our lamps, but the sort of light we are getting from them, and how all this affects the quality of our pictures.

For most everyday purposes, we simply refer to illumination as 'light', and leave it at that. But to use it successfully, we should take a look at some of its interesting characteristics.

1. The light's *intensity* (brightness), for this affects exposure.
2. The light's *quality*; whether it is concentrated 'hard' shadow-forming light, or diffuse 'soft' shadowless illumination.
3. Lighting *contrast*; the relative brightness of the lightest and darkest areas in the shot.
4. The *direction* of the light relative to the camera's viewpoint, and the effect this has on the appearance of the subjects.
5. The light's *color temperature*; the luminant's overall color quality.

When using *colored light* for effect, you are concerned with:

its *hue* (the predominant color, e.g. blue, green, yellow),
its *saturation* (chroma, purity, intensity), i.e. its richness or paleness,
its *luminance* (brightness, value), i.e. how light or dark it appears.

If you understand how to control (or compensate for) these various features, you will be able to create consistent high-quality pictures, even when shooting with available light. If you ignore them, results may be fine; but then again, they may be unpredictable.

4.4 The light's intensity

As you know, the camera requires a certain amount of light reflected from the scene, to produce high-grade pictures. If there is too little, the shot is under-exposed (all tones reproduce too dark). If there is too much, it will be over-exposed (all tones reproduce too light). You can measure the intensity of the lighting with a light-meter, or rely on the camera's exposure-indicator, or on the appearance of the picture in your viewfinder.

The camera will not receive sufficient light if:

● the illumination falling on the subject is too dim (low light levels),
● your lens aperture (stop) is too small,
● you are using a filter that is too dense, relative to the tones in the scene, or its overall brightness.

Clearly, you will need less light to achieve good pictures in a white-walled room than a dark-panelled one. Remember, extra video gain can only partly compensate for underexposure, for although it boosts the picture strength, the sensor (CCD) itself is still getting too little light from the scene (causing picture noise, smearing, trailing effects).

4.5 If there is not enough light

If you are shooting inside buildings, or outdoors at night, you are quite likely to find that there is not really enough light around to get high-grade pictures. There are several regular solutions:

● Move the subject to where there is more light.
● Open up the lens aperture – but this reduces the zone of sharpness ('depth of field').
● Increase the camera's sensitivity ('boost' 'video gain') – but this will increase picture noise.
● Increase the local lighting, i.e. switch on more room lights.
● Add some of your own lighting to the scene.

4.6 If there is too much light

If lighting is too intense (high light levels), you may compensate:

● by moving the subject to where there is less light,
● by stopping the lens down (smaller aperture),
● by using a neutral density filter,
● by switching off some of the existing lighting,
● perhaps pulling shades or blinds.

Otherwise, if you are using lamps to light the scene, you may:

● switch off some bulbs (in a multi-bulb light source),
● switch off some of your light sources,
● use lower-power sources,
● use a dimmer (although dimming a lamp lowers its color temperature),

By partly closing the flaps you can limit the spread of the light.

Clipping a piece of diffuser to a barndoor flap.
Reduces the intensity of part of the light beam.

Similar to Pt 2 above but holding a sheet of cooking foil, cutting off the light completely.

Figure 4.1 Controlling the light

- place diffuser material over a lamp,
- take the lamp farther away,
- flood (spread) the lamp's beam,
- use 'bounce light' instead of some of the direct lighting.

4.7 Hard light quality

Because the sun is so distant, it behaves as a localized *point source* of light. Its rays are therefore very directional and travel to us in straight lines. They cast distinct sharp shadows, which emphasize the texture and contours of any subject, especially when the light falls at an oblique angle. Because it is directional, you can easily block off this *hard light*, to prevent it falling on any surface.

Many man-made light sources, such as a match, a candle or a bare light bulb, also behave in this way. Because they are of very limited size, they act as point sources and produce hard light, irrespective of how powerful or weak they are.

Rather than let the light spread around in all directions (as with a bare bulb hanging from the ceiling), many lighting fittings include a specially shaped 'parabolic' reflector, that directs light rays forwards in a narrow beam. They may also be fitted with a 'fresnel' ('stepped') lens to concentrate the beam further. This light-gathering improves the lamp's efficiency, and helps you to restrict the light to selected parts of the scene.

By adjusting the position of the reflector and/or the lens relative to the bulb, you can vary the spread of its beam, and to a certain extent, its intensity. Flaps or light-shields may be attached to the fitting, to cut off parts of the light beam. (These are known as barndoors, flags or snoots.)

The good things about hard light are:

- It is directional, so can easily be restricted to illuminate just those areas you want to light.
- It casts clear-cut shadows and shows up texture.
- Hard light can produce vigorous, bold, well-defined effects.
- The intensity of a hard light source, does not fall off appreciably with distance. So you can illuminate things effectively, with a lamp some distance away.

The *bad things* about hard light are:

- You often want to avoid distracting or ugly shadows (e.g. on the background behind someone).
- Results may look harsh, contrasty and unattractive.
- You may not want to emphasize texture (e.g. revealing the irregularities in someone's skin).
- Hard light sources have restricted coverage, so that you may need several lamps to cover a wide area.
- When you use more than one hard light source, the multi-shadows can be very distracting.

4.8 Soft light quality

Diffused light scatters in all directions. It occurs naturally, when the sun is obscured by cloud, and whenever sunlight is reflected from rough light-toned surfaces.

When subjects are illuminated by this *soft light*, there are no distinct shadows, only slight variations in surface brightness. So texture and surface contours are not very pronounced in the picture. You may not be able to see them at all.

There are several different types of fittings designed to provide soft light.

Some rely on diffusion material such as spun-glass sheet, frosted plastic or tracing paper (sometimes wire mesh) to scatter the light. (You can put a diffuser over a hard light source to reduce its intensity and soften its quality to some extent.) In others, the light from hidden lamps hits a reflector and scatters.

Another form of soft light uses a group or bank of open lamps. Their overlapping beams combine to give shadowless illumination.

At a pinch, you can create a compact 'soft light' source by placing two or three layers of diffuser (e.g. spun glass) over a hard-light source such as a lensless spot.

The good things about soft light are:

- It can produce subtle delicate shading.
- Soft light does not create unwanted shadows.
- Soft light avoids emphasizing modeling and texture.
- Soft light can illuminate the shadows cast by hard light sources, so that we can see details there, without itself casting further shadows.
- Soft light sources can cover a wide area of the scene.

The bad things about soft light are:

- It can flatten out all signs of surface shape and texture in the picture.
- Soft light spreads around, flooding all surfaces with light. It can be very difficult to restrict, and keep off selected areas.
- Soft light quickly falls off in intensity, as you increase the lamp's distance from the subject. So something fairly near the source may be over-lit, while another subject a little way away, is insufficiently lit.

4.9 Lighting contrast

The 'contrast' in a scene is simply the difference between the brightness of its lightest and darkest tones. If the range is too great for the camera to handle (around 20 : 1 to 30 : 1 max.), as it well might be when strong sunlight casts deep shadows, the extreme tones are lost in the picture. Many TV receivers can only reproduce a range of up to 15 : 1 anyway.

The tonal contrasts that your camera sees will depend partly on the tones of the subjects themselves, partly on variations in the light's intensity, and partly on the shadows it casts.

Excessive lighting contrast produces a coarse 'soot and whitewash' effect, with burned-out highlights and detailless lower tones. Whether the result looks highly dramatic, or crude and difficult to interpret, depends on the situation.

When lighting is contrasty (e.g. lots of hard light from one direction, and no fill light), picture quality can alter considerably as you vary the camera's position. Shooting with the light behind the camera, subjects may look very bright, flat and unmodeled. If you shoot towards the light, only the edges of subjects will be illuminated, while the rest of them remains unlit.

The other extreme is the effect you get when the scene is lit with soft shadowless lighting. Now everything is very subtly modeled – perhaps so subtly, that the picture looks uninterestingly flat, as if things had been cut out and stuck onto their background. Even if you move the camera around over a wide angle, the tonal quality of the picture remains reasonably constant under soft lighting.

Figure 4.2 Light direction
As the position of the light changes, relative to the camera viewpoint, its effect alters on the subject. The direction you choose depends on which feature you want to emphasize or suppress.

Top: moving light upwards, and behind.

Bottom: moving light round and behind the subject.

In practice, you usually want to avoid the harshness that comes from a high lighting contrast, and the flatness that you get with a low lighting contrast. The best solution is to use a careful balance of hard lights (which creates a three-dimensional illusion), and some soft light, to illuminate any shadows (i.e. 'fill' them) without casting extra ones.

4.10 Light direction

The direction of light can have a considerable influence on what any subject looks like. The best way to demonstrate this for yourself is to sit in front of a mirror in a dark room, holding a flashlight. Then you will see not only how the effect changes as light from different directions, but you will begin to understand the ways in which light-direction affects portraiture.

First hold your flashlight beside your head, pointing it straight into the mirror. This is the equivalent of a light just beside the camera. Notice how this direct frontal light seems to flatten out the texture and shape of the front of your face. If there is a smooth or shiny surface behind you, the light bounces straight back into your eye (i.e. into the camera lens), and appears as a hotspot on the background. Even a rough surface, such as stone or concrete, may look smooth under direct frontal lighting. It reminds you too, how unpleasantly dazzling it can be for people if you light them this way.

Move your flashlight to above your head, shining straight downwards. See how the light emphasizes every wrinkle! The top of your head and your nose are now bright ('hot') and your eyes are hidden in dark sockets. You have instantly aged many years, and look dreadful! (So always try to avoid top, overhead, downward lighting, particularly when shooting people.)

Figure 4.3 Three-point lighting
Basic set-up. Three lamps are used:
The *key light* which models the
subject, and is some 5–30° to one
side of the camera (vertical angle of
10–40°). The *fill light* (filler) which
illuminates shadows but ideally casts
none of its own (diffused), positioned
say 5–30° on the other side of the
camera. The *back light* placed
behind the subject, to outline it with
light; up to 20° either side of the
dead back position, facing the
camera; vertical angle of 25–60°.

Area lighting. This principle can be
used for lighting areas too.

Hold the flashlight down low, shining upwards, and the effect is spooky,
because we are not used to seeing people lit in this way – except in horror
movies. Now the eyes and the neck are strongly lit. Again, surface details
are emphasized with upward shadows.

Take the light round to one side, and you will see how only half of your
head is lit, and the surface texture and contours of your face are unattractively exaggerated.

If someone takes the flashlight and holds it behind you, shining onto the
back of your head, you will see that only the edges of your head will be
lit (i.e. hair, ears and shoulders if the lamp is high). This sort of *backlight*
is very successful when lighting solid subjects, for it helps to make them
stand out from their background, and creates a three-dimensional
illusion. If the subject is of transparent or translucent material, the
backlight will reveal this.

4.11 Three-point lighting

For most situation, you will find that the best results come from using
three basic light directions.

The main light, or *key light*, is positioned slightly above and to one side
of the camera. This is normally a hard-light source (a spotlight), and it
reveals the shape and surface features of your subject.

A soft light (broad source) on the opposite side of the camera illuminates the shadows and reduces the lighting contrast. The more the key
light is offset, the more important this soft *fill light* (filler; fill-in)
becomes. If the key is nearly frontal, you may not need fill light at all.

Finally, a *backlight* angled down onto the subject from behind gives it
solidity.

Wherever possible, you can add extra lamps to light the background
behind the subject. But where space or facilities are limited, you may
have to rely on spill illumination from your key and fill lights to cover
background areas instead.

4.12 Measuring light levels

The most convenient method of measuring light, is to stand in the
subject's position, and point your light-meter towards a light source, to
measure the incident light. It is usually better to check and balance the
final lighting setup, than to switch on and measure individual lamps.

The best way to learn about appropriate light levels for your equipment,
is by experiment. Set the lens aperture to e.g. *f*/4. Sit someone in front
of the camera, and adjust the intensity of the key light (change power,
distance, diffuser, dimmer) until their face and clothing appear attractively exposed, when viewed on a picture monitor (not the camera
viewfinder). Light tones should not be crushed out, nor darker areas
clogged.

Now read the key light's intensity, and you have a typical guide figure
for future reference. Add sufficient fill light (offset at e.g. 5–30°) to
relieve the shadows, without overlighting them – as *judged by your
monitor picture*. Measure the fill light intensity (re-check the key-plus-fill
brightness). Having noted these figures, repeat the operation for the back
light. You now have useful working data for the future.

The amount of light produced by a particular lighting fixture, depends
on its design, the quality of its light (how hard or soft), its power, how

it is adjusted, the lamp's age and condition, its distance from the subject, etc. Forget formulae! Measure how much light *your equipment* gives at a typical distance under *your* working conditions, and use this as a basis for the number of units you need for a job.

4.13 Typical light levels

If you want to work with a lens aperture of *f*/4 (to get sufficient depth of field), you may need a typical light level from the key light of e.g. 100 fc (1076 lux). This is the main light source, that determines the exposure. Don't *under*light if you can help it. Some people use minimum light, and boost the video to improve the signal, but this degrades picture quality. Worse still, you are unlikely to be able to judge tonal balance accurately at lower light levels. Your eye will overlook distracting shadows, that become all too prominent on camera!

The intensity of the *back light* should usually be similar to the key light (e.g. 100 fc/1076 lux); but it will vary with the subject. Strong back light when appropriate may look 'glamorous'; but hot edges around subjects can also be artificial and distracting too. Weak back light is ineffectual.

The amount of *fill light* (*filler*) you need from soft-light sources, will depend on how contrasty you want the final effect to be. A rough rule-of-thumb is *around one-half to one-third as bright as the key light (e.g. 50–33 fc/530–360 lux). It should seldom be similar (high key situations), and never stronger than the key.* Remember, the purpose of the fill light is to augment, to illuminate shadows, without casting fresh shadows.

4.14 Color temperature compensation

The color quality of light can vary considerably, from the orange–yellow of candlelight or small tungsten lamps to the bluish illumination of daylight; from the warm hues of sunset to the greenish quality of many fluorescent light sources.

For good color fidelity, your camera system's color response, and the color quality of the prevailing light, need to match reasonably well. If they do not, you will find that the pictures have a pronounced bluish or orange–yellow color cast.

You can *match the camera to the lighting* by switching in a compensatory color-correction filter on the camera, and/or readjusting the camera's white balance.

Sometimes you will meet a *mixture* of lighting, e.g. high color temperature daylight coming through the windows, and low color temperature tungsten light inside a room. Then you have the choice of:

- shutting out the daylight by pulling the shades and relying on your quartz/tungsten light alone (camera set to 'tungsten balance'),
- putting light-blue filters (or 'dichroic filters') over the quartz/tungsten light to raise its color temperature (camera set to 'daylight' balance),
- attaching large sheets of orange–yellow color filter material over the windows to match the quartz/tungsten light (camera set to 'tungsten balance'),
- simply shooting the scene with its mixture of daylight and unfiltered lighting, and accepting the results.

With the camera balanced to 'daylight', the daylight will look right and the tungsten over-warm.

With the camera balanced to 'tungsten', the daylight will look very blue, and the tungsten light will look natural. The color-quality of light (its *color temperature*) is measured in kelvins (degrees kelvin (K)). If you want accurate consistent color reproduction (e.g. when shooting for medical records), or need to match several video cameras, you can use a special color-balance meter to check the light, and then introduce appropriate compensation. But for most purposes, it is sufficient to switch the camera to its nearest color-correction position (e.g. 'daylight', 'artificial', 'fluorescent', or 5600 K, 3200 K) and white-balance to these conditions.

4.15 Using colored light

Because your video is in color, it seems reasonable to assume that you would use quite a lot of colored light. But, in practice, you will only find yourself needing colored light when creating decorative effects (e.g. for a display, a dance or musical routine, firelight or moonlight), or to change the appearance of backgrounds (to introduce some color on a plain neutral wall or drapes).

When you do need colored lighting, you clip a sheet of special color media over a light fitting. Make sure that the sheet is not going to restrict ventilation to the lamp (which will overheat and fail). And do not put it so close to the lamp that the color sheet is destroyed by the intense heat.

Various materials are available, but never use colored glass. Colored gelatine is quite cheap, but it burns up, quickly becomes very brittle and torn, and pales out in use. Special plastic sheeting (of acetate, polyester, mylar or acrylic) is expensive, but will last and can be re-used.

If you are shooting under tungsten lighting and want to create an overall warm look to your picture, all you have to do is to set your camera to 'daylight' color correction. Conversely, you can use a 'tungsten' setting when shooting in daylight, to give pictures a very cold blue wintry appearance.

4.16 Shooting in daylight

Although daylight provides us with a free, convenient light source, it isn't a particularly reliable one. Its intensity varies, and so does its overall quality. Clouds pass over the sun, and sharply defined shadows vanish. Instead we may be left with a much weaker, diffused light. Throughout the day, the color quality and the direction of the light alter, and the sun that was frontal in the morning can gradually change to side light by the afternoon. All this may make it difficult to cut together shots that have been taken at different times of the day, where the variations in lighting show in the edited version of the action.

What you always have to bear in mind, is that the effect of light depends on the *position of your camera*.

Strong sunlight, that is more than enough from one viewpoint, may only rim the subject from another angle, leaving it in deep shadow.

You really have four choices. You can:

● Move round your subject until the sun is roughly behind the camera (but then it may not be the background you want!).
● Turn the subject into the light.
● Wait for the sun to move round to a better angle.
● Add (or reflect) lighting to compensate.

Sometimes you will just have to accept things as find them. Suppose, for example, you want to take shots of an impressive building. Sunlight falling at just the right angle would throw wall texture and its various features into sharp relief. Once in a while, the light will be just right, and produce exactly the results you are looking for. There are even tables to tell you where the sun will be at any time of the day. But don't rely on it!

Under dull overcast skies, everything can look uninterestingly flat. Perhaps you could try again later, when the sun is shining. It could be that the particular features you want to show never do get suitable sunlight anyway! If a wall is facing north, it never does get full sunlight. So you may have to shoot the subject as it is, and just hope that results will look all right on the screen.

4.17 Using reflectors

The cheapest way to improve a subject's lighting when shooting in sunlight is to use a *reflector*. This is simply a surface such as a board, screen, cloth or even a wall, that reflects existing light onto the subject from another angle. The quality of the reflected light depends on the surface you use.

A mirror surface (e.g. metal foil or metallized plastic) will reflect a distinct beam of light from a hard light source, creating sharp well-defined shadows. This light travels well, even when the subject is some distance away. (A mirror surface will even reflect soft light to some extent, if placed fairly near the subject.)

Unfortunately, the angle of a mirror-finish reflector can be critical. When the light shines directly at its surface, you will get the maximum effect. But as the surface is angled to the light, the reflected beam, which only covers a restricted angle anyway, narrows and becomes less effective. In a long shot, its limited coverage is seen as a localized patch of light.

If your reflector has a matt-white surface, it will produce a soft diffused light, which spreads over a wide angle. But this soft reflected light is much weaker, and will only travel a relatively short distance, depending on the intensity and distance of the original light source.

Reflectors are easily made from a board covered with aluminium cooking foil (smooth or crumpled and flattened) or matt-white painted, according to the type of light reflection you want. (A board faced with two different surfaces can be very useful.) The bigger the reflector, the more light will be reflected over a broad area, and big cloth or roller-blind reflectors (even portable ciné-screens) can be used. But reflectors of this size are cumbersome to transport and support, and likely to vibrate in any wind.

Reflectors come into their own in strong sunlight. Over a limited area, you can use the reflected light to fill in deep shadows or to provide a frontal key light when the sun is behind the subject. Two or more reflectors can be used together. The main problems are in directing the light to exactly where you want it, and in supporting the reflectors perfectly still, at the right height.

However, as the only alternative is to use powerful lamps, or lights close in to the subject, it is an approach that is certainly worth trying when the sun's direction is appropriate, and tonal contrast is high.

Indoors, you can use reflectors to redirect light from windows into shadowy corners, or reflect sunlight as a filler. And when you are using backlight, a low reflector near the camera can provide useful filler, perhaps to lift the shadows under people's chins and eyebrows.

Finally, while on the subject, when you are shooting in bright sunlight, look out for *accidental colored reflections* from nearby surfaces. Even a smart green shirt may show its wearer with a green complexion!

Figure 4.4 Reflectors
How effective a reflector is depends on its surface (polished, metallic surfaces are best) and on its angle to the sun or other light sources. If you use a reflector beside the camera, and reflect a source directly ahead of the camera, the intensity and coverage of the reflected light is maximum. As you angle the reflector to the source, its output and its coverage fall.

4.18 Bounce light

It is a common trick in *photography* to point a flash-gun at the ceiling or a wall when photographing interiors, to give the scene an overall wash of diffused 'bounce light'. (But don't use a colored surface, or the reflected light will have a similar hue!)

Although you can sometimes use the same idea when shooting video, and point your lamps at the nearby surfaces to get a soft 'base-light', remember that only a fraction of the lamp's output is reflected. So it is really a pretty wasteful, random method. If you use more powerful lamps in order to get stronger bounce light, ventilation can become a problem in a small room. On balance, it may be better to use a strongly diffused broad source instead.

4.19 Do we need to light it?

It is an interesting fact that, if you look around any everyday scene, your eye will often pass without a second glance, over incidental features that seem to stand out in a photograph. You overlook the reflections in a shop window, and concentrate on the items on sale within. You accept a bright blob of light on a tiled surface without a thought. You talk to people, and note their expressions and how they are dressed perhaps, and that is an end to it.

Now look at a video of the same scene, and you are likely to react quite differently. The reflections in the window seem to stop you seeing into the shop. The blob of light on the tiles has become an annoying distraction. You tend to look at the people in the picture in a much more detached, critical way, than in everyday life. You may well be struck by their shadowed eye sockets, how haggard they look under the steep lighting, the hot tops to their heads; you may become aware of ugly neck shadows, bright noses or ears, strongly lit shoulders, the long nose shadow that looks like a mustache.... Various trivial aspects of the everyday scene now have quite a different impact on the screen.

This is why professionals go to so much trouble to re-adjust and light many scenes, where there is obviously sufficient illumination to produce acceptable pictures. It is not enough, for example, to be able to get shots of an audience at a concert; one wants the pictures to be *attractive* too. The available light is often in the wrong direction, or is too flat or too contrasty, or it only illuminates part of the scene clearly. The extra lighting seeks to correct these shortcomings.

4.20 Lighting options

Whatever sort of program you are making, you really have four choices as far as lighting is concerned:

1. You can shoot with the existing lighting, either from your chosen viewpoint, or after moving to another position where the subject looks better.
2. You can increase the intensity of the lighting already there, e.g. take shades off light fittings or replace the bulbs with others of higher power.
3. You can augment the present lighting with extra lamps of your own. These may be anything from a reflector or a single hand-held lamp to a number of lighting units.
4. You can rely entirely on the lighting equipment you have taken along, because either there is no other illumination there, or you have decided that it is unsuitable and switched it off.

Then you have the choice of either lighting the whole action area, or restricting your lighting to suit limited action in one small section at a time.

4.21 Economy lighting

Whenever you shoot in the light that just happens to be there at the time, whether it is daylight or artificial, there is always an element of uncertainty about the quality of the pictures you are going to get.

By lighting the scene, or supplementing the existing lighting, you have some control over the situation, and a far better chance of achieving consistently high quality pictures.

'Economy lighting' is a way of thinking, a matter of turning whatever lighting is available to your advantage.

You begin by asking yourself: 'Can I shoot the scene from the camera position I have chosen, with the present lighting?' Check on whether you can expose the picture properly. Is there good detail and tonal gradation in the subject you are particularly interested in? If part of the subject is in shadow, does that matter? Would some fill light from a reflector, or a hand-lamp beside the camera, help to show details in the shadows? Are there any distractions in the shot, such as a bright sky or a large defocused blob of color?

Perhaps the overall effect would look better if you were to turn the subject slightly towards the light. Then you might not need any fill light for the shadows at all.

Would it be better to wait for the sun to come out, or return another day when the light is right?

If you are shooting an interior and there is daylight around, can you make use of it in some way in your shot, e.g. to save you providing a key light, or lighting a background wall?

And here's a trick, when there is virtually no light, or it's impossible to get good pictures with your video camera. Use a *photographic camera* (either with flash or a time exposure), to take a slide of the scene. Then project this slide in a dark room, and shoot the screen with your video camera!

4.22 Makeshift equipment

If one is on a tight budget, there is a natural temptation to improvise. There are occasions when you can for a short time put a higher-powered bulb into a hinged desk-lamp or a ceiling light-track, clip on a sheet of cooking foil to shade off the wall, and a piece of tracing paper to soften the light. But these makeshift arrangements take a while to set up, easily come adrift, and are very temporary. And they are not particularly safe. Time soon passes, and the fitting overheats.

Lightweight lighting fittings

Supports

4.23 Gaffer grip/gaffer clamp/alligator ('gator') clamp/clip-light

This large spring-loaded or screwed clamp has a support (⅝ in. (16 mm) spigot or socket) to hold a small lamp such as a PAR holder (the bulb incorporates a parabolic aluminized reflector) or a lensless spot.

Take care when lighting

When lighting your productions, it is easy to become preoccupied with the effects you are creating and to overlook some of the very practical hazards that await the unwary. There are a number of things that you should look out for, just in case.

Equipment condition

Check out your lighting equipment to make sure that it is all in good condition. Lamps should be fitted firmly in sockets (never handle lamps with the bare hands). Check that nothing is coming loose, cables are not frayed or cut and that the plug and its connections are OK.

Grounding/earthing

All electrical equipment should be properly grounded (earthed), otherwise you are liable to get a severe electric shock under certain conditions.

Electrical overload

Take care that all your lamps are individually fused, and that you do not connect too many lamps to one outlet and/or overload the power supply. There may already be other equipment using the power circuit you want to plug into, and yours might exceed its capacity. So enquire before connecting to other people's supplies. Find out where fuses or cutouts are located, and who is responsible for them.

Hot lamps

Lamps can get extremely hot, especially quartz lights. So take care when working near lamps that are lit, or only recently switched off. Not only can you burn yourself, but the lamp's filament is fragile when hot and can be destroyed by even a slight knock.

If a hot lamp is within a couple of feet of a surface (0.5 m), there is every chance of scorching or setting fire to it. Wood, drapes, paper and plastic are particularly vulnerable. Cables should not rest against a hot lamp, for they can be burned up. Color media over lamps reduce the amount of air ventilating them, and themselves fume and smell when overheated, perhaps even catch fire.

Take particular care when using overrun photographic lamps (Photoflood, Nitraphot), or high-rated tungsten lamps (150 W) in domestic light fittings such as wall-brackets, ceiling lights, table lamps or desk fittings. They may overheat and damage the fitting and nearby surfaces.

Falling equipment

Light fittings can fall down or overbalance all too easily. Where possible, it is advisable to attach some form of safety bond (wire or chain) from the lamp to a secure point, to hold it (or anything attached, such as a barndoor) if it should fall.

Can anyone passing underneath a lamp hit their head on it, or move it, or burn themselves on it?

A lamp fitted to a lighting stand (floor stand) can be at hazard if it is anywhere near people. They may kick it out of position, fall over it, or knock it over!

Whenever you are using a lighting stand, it is best to place a weight on its base (perhaps a canvas sandbag, or bag of stones, even a rock) to prevent it from moving or toppling over. Very high lighting stands (over 6ft (2 m)) are extremely unstable.

Figure 4.5 Gaffer grip (gaffer clamp, clip-light)
Clamps on any firm narrow beam, pipe, door, chair.

Figure 4.6 Profiled wall plate
Tapes to any firm surface, hangs on pipes.

Figure 4.7 Lightweight stand
Collapsible extending stand used to support small lighting fixtures.

Floor cables

Remember that people can trip over cables strewn around the floor, so it is advisable to tuck all cables away neatly (e.g. near a wall), or cover them over (mat or board), or hang them (wall hooks, gaffer-taped/duct-taped) to firm non-decorated wall surfaces.

Water

Take great care when water is around. If rains falls on a lamp, it is liable to explode or short out the supply, unless the equipment is suitably designed to avoid this. Any water on the ground can cause short circuits, or electrocute the unwary, if it gets in the wrong places!

You can use the gaffer grip to clip a light to any firmly based object, such as a door, table, chair, rail, post, window or treads/step ladder (lightstand, scenic flat).

This can be a very useful compact device, enabling you to secure lamps in out-of-the-way places, when space is restricted.

4.24 Wall-plate

The wall-plate can be a very adaptable method of positioning lightweight lamps on location. It consists of a flat metal plate, fitted with a porcelain lamp support on a directional swivel.

You can hang it onto any nearby pipes, wall-fittings, etc., by its hook-shaped edges. You can even tape the plate onto a door or wall, using gaffer tape/duct tape (a plastic-faced fabric tape with a contact-adhesive coating), provided the surface is reasonably smooth, clean and dust-free.

4.25 Lightweight lamp tripod/stand

This can be a collapsible/folding type, or it may dismantle into sections for transport. How sturdy your tripod needs to be, depends on the size of the lamp fitting you are going to use and the maximum height you intend to use it at. If the tripod is too flimsy, it will be top heavy and easily upset, even by the weight of the lamp's cable. With more robust types, you can attach two or more lamps to a tripod when necessary.

4.26 Spring-loaded support pole (Jack tube, Varipole, Acrow, Polecat, Barricuda)

This telescopic fitting consists of one long tube, spring-loaded within another. When wedged between wall and ceiling, or between two side walls, or in a window-opening, it can be used to support all forms of lightweight lamps. 'Cross-tubes' ('cross-beams') can be added to interlink two or more poles.

Lamps

4.27 Camera light (video light)

A small portable quartz-light can be attached to the top of many video cameras (video light). it may be powered from a battery belt, a battery pack, the camera's supply, or an a.c. adapter (for a utility/mains supply).

Figure 4.8 Camera light
A lamp clamped to the top of the camera.

Power ratings are typically 100–350 W. A 250 W/30 volts lamp may run for 30 min from a battery supply, while a 350 W lamp would only last for around 20 min.

Its main advantage is that it always lights whatever the camera is shooting, and does not require another pair of hands. Portable lighting of this sort can provide a very convenient key light when shooting under difficult conditions, especially if you have to follow someone around as, for example, they arrive at an airport. (There may be no other solution!) And again, the lamp can provide modeling light for close exterior shots on a dull day, or fill light for hard shadows when shooting someone in sunlight.

The chief disadvantages here are that the lamp adds to the camera's overall weight, and its light is extremely frontal and so tends to flatten out the subject. Its light will reflect in spectacles and any shiny surfaces (windows, plastic) near the subject, as an intense white blob. People facing the camera may find the light dazzling.

Some camera lights have a fixed coverage, while others are adjustable (e.g. 6–35°). But the illumination is invariably localized, and when using a wide-angle camera lens, subjects may move out of the light beam. Furthermore, its illumination does not carry evenly. While anything near the camera is easily overlit, anything farther away remains virtually unlit. This can be very obvious in long shots. Some camera lights have an auto-sensor intensity control, which nominally adjusts their intensity to suit exposure and the prevailing lighting conditions. Like all automatic systems, its performance is variable.

4.28 Hand held lamps (sun gun)

A hand-held lamp separate from the camera, requires the assistance of a second person, but this can have several advantages. Apart from not burdening the cameraman with its weight, the assistant can anticipate where to point the lamp, and avoid the 'searchlight effect' that can occur as a camera-light pans around. The assistant can probably hold the lamp high (not easy for any length of time) at a better angle to light the subject and avoid direct 'kickback' reflections.

Figure 4.9 Hand-held lamp
Positioned by a second operator.

The hand-held lamp may be more powerful, e.g. from 250 W to 1000 W. It may be battery or a.c. powered. Some designs have a cooling fan; those without tend to overheat.

In daylight, a *dichroic filter* or color-compensating filter medium is used over the lamp to raise its color temperature.

4.29 Open-bulb fittings

For small scale situations, unprotected open bulbs in simple supports (clip-light, wall plate) can be quite useful. But they are very vulnerable, easily broken, and offer no protection if the bulb explodes. It is difficult to control the spread of the light and prevent it from washing over the entire scene.

An *overrun tungsten* photographic lamp typically has a brief bright life of 2, 6 or 10 hours, and uses respectively 275, 500 or 1000 W. (Their boosted light output is the equivalent of a regular tungsten lamp of 800, 1600 or 3000 W.)

An *internally silvered reflector spot lamp* can be used individually, or in multi-lamp floodlight banks. It is available in focused (hard, spotlight) and diffused forms. There are standard versions (100/300/500 W; 3200 K;

100 hours life), and overrun versions (275/375/500 W; 3400 K; 3/4/6 hours life). Their greatest shortcoming is that the light is not of even intensity overall (central hotspot).

Remember, each lamp casts its own set of shadows, so a two-lamp fitting, for instance, will produce disturbing double shadows for everything it lights.

The more robust *PAR* lamps are very widely used, individually or in banks, both inside buildings and out of doors. They have moulded heat-resistant ribbed (optical) or clear fronts, giving 'pre-focused spot' or 'flood' coverage.

There are also types with an elliptical beam shape, concentrating the light in a horizontal field, e.g. 6° × 12° to 30° × 40°. With a power range of 75–1000 W, and 5200 K or 3200 K color temperature versions available. PAR lamps offer an effective economical lightweight light source. Clip-on light shields can help to localize the illumination.

4.30 Scoop/pan

This cheap, rudimentary light fitting consists of an open bulb (e.g. an overrun photo-lamp) in the center of a large aluminium bowl. The lamp may be front-shielded, so that only reflected 'soft' light emerges. Although useful when you do have to spread light over a wide area (e.g. a backcloth, or general low-level bounce-light from a ceiling), it has few artistic merits, for you cannot really control the light coverage.

4.31 Broad

The lightweight broad (broadside) has a short trough containing a reflector and a tubular quartz light of 500–1000 W. The bulb may have a frontal shield to internally reflect the light.

Although the broad is widely referred to as a 'soft' light source, due to its small area, it produces quite discernible shadows. Nevertheless, it is an extremely useful wide-angle broad light source, that can be hung conveniently in various ways, supported on stands, or laid on the floor, arranged singly or in groups.

Two-leaf or four-leaf barndoor shutters, that can be closed to reduce the spread of the light, are often fitted to broads.

4.32 Multi-lamp sources

Several softlight sources use groups of lamps which combine, so that the shadows cast by each are 'lit out' by its neighbors.

A *strip-light* or *cyc-light* consists of a row of two to six units joined in a long trough. Each unit has a tubular bulb with a curved metal reflector. You can use the strip-light to illuminate backgrounds or translucent screens from the floor.

In a studio, strip or cyc lights are often suspended to light backgrounds from above, but they are rather too cumbersome to support in this way in a lightweight lighting rig.

Multi-lamp *banks* are excellent soft-light sources. A typical design has one to three panels of grouped PAR internal reflector lamps. Each panel can be independently switched and turned to adjust the brightness and spread of the unit. Either 650 W or 1000 W PAR lamps may be fitted, in groups of 4, 6, 9, 16 or 24.

Figure 4.10 Scoop
A basic softlight source, once universally used in studios.

Figure 4.11 Broad
Soft light source with a linear (tubular) quartz-light.

Figure 4.12 Groundrow (strip-light; cyc-light).

Part 1 A series of tubular lamps with curved reflectors, or constructed from a row of domestic tungsten lamps (150 W).

Figure 4.12 Part 2

Floodlight bank ('mini-brute').
Housing a series of switchable PAR
lamps, groups may be hinged, and
have side flaps.

**Figure 4.13 Lensless spotlight
(external reflector spotlight;
Redhead; Blonde)**
Lightweight efficient focused unit.
Light spread about 42–82°.
Light output of 800 W per unit
comparable with 2 kW fresnel spot
(3200 K).
As a keylight, typical distance 2.5–3 m.
As a backlight, typical distance 1.5 m.

The *floodlight bank* ('Minibrute', 'Maxibrute', etc.), is mainly used as a booster light for exteriors, and for large-area illumination. Large side-flaps may be fitted to restrict the light spread.

Soft-light sources that rely on internal reflection to produce light scatter, produce quite diffused light, but are relatively inefficient.

Large units fitted with a bank of fluorescent tubes are favored by some people as a cheap soft-light source. But in practice the color quality of their light does not blend well with other sources. The exception is when small fluorescent banks are used as booster-light in a store already lit by a ceiling of fluorescent tubes. They are quite cumbersome and vulnerable in use.

4.33 Lensless spotlight/open-bulb spot

This type of light fitting is very widely used in video/television production, particularly by mobile units, on location. It has a variety of names, including lensless spotlight, open-bulb spot, external reflector spot, reflector spotlight, Redhead (250 W, 600 W, 800 W), Blonde (2000 W).

The fitting is open-fronted with a plastic body, and contains a bare quartz-light (tungsten-halogen) bulb with an efficient adjustable reflector behind it. Its light beam is somewhat uneven (particularly when spotted), but this type of spotlight has many advantages.

It is extremely portable, compact, and efficient. The output of an 800 W version is comparable with a large 2 kW fresnel spotlight covering the same area. So there are many advantages where ventilation and power are limited. Moreover, it will spread over more then 80° (compared with a typical fresnel spot's 60° maximum) and that is a valuable feature where the lamp-to-subject distance (throw) is short.

Diffuser and/or corrective color filters are easily clipped to its barndoors.

4.34 Fresnel spotlights

In TV and film studios, where the lamps have to be positioned a fair distance from the subjects (e.g. over 15ft (6 m)), the large heavy-duty fresnel spotlight is universal, suspended from ceiling bars or battens. (Typical power: 2–5 kW.)

Mobile small-unit video production teams need compact lightweight equipment that can spread light over a wide area, even when quite close to the subject. So for them, the fairly restricted beam-spread of the heavier fresnel spotlight has limited use, although it has a more even light coverage, and more precise adjustment than the lensless spotlight.

Practical lighting

4.35 The general approach to lighting

● As you will have discovered earlier (Section 4.10), if you move a lamp from near the camera's position, over to the right, any prominent feature on the subject's surface (e.g. someone's nose) will cast a shadow over to the left. As you increase the lighting angle, such shadows spread across the surface, emphasizing its shape and texture. The greater the light's angle, the coarser its effect.

At the same time, the shadow of the subject itself also moves across the background, growing broader.

As you go on moving the lamp round it, less and less of the subject is illuminated, until eventually, by the time you have put the lamp right round to the side of it, only half is lit. The surface details that are caught by the light stand out prominently (a useful technique when lighting low-relief subjects such as coins).

As you raise the lamp, shadows grow downwards. Similarly, when you move a lamp upwards diagonally, shadows develop downwards diagonally in the opposite direction.

● From these basics, we can see some obvious principles to follow, whatever we want to light:

The lamp should not be *too close to the lens*. This flattens out surface modeling and causes light reflections.

The angle should not be *too steep*. It creates crude, gaunt, unattractive top light.

It should not be *too far round to one side*, unless the subject is facing that way. This can result in harsh surface modeling, and a bisected half-lit effect.

Choose the lamp direction that suits the subject and its surroundings best. And don't forget to look out for any reflections or shadow that might be distracting.

The final lamp position is often a compromise. It depends on what you are lighting, and what you want it to look like. As a general guide, if you are lighting a *person*, do not have the lamp flat-on but position it at an angle; a little to one side of their nose direction, and a little above their eyeline. Clearly, the best position for the lamp depends on which direction they are facing. If they are going to turn their head around between full-face and profile, you will need to key them roughly half-way between these two positions.

When you are lighting an *object*, you have far greater freedom of choice as to where you place lamps, for its appearance is usually less critical than when lighting people. If, for instance, you are shooting a vase inside a glass case, you might be very concerned with avoiding reflections of the light and the camera, and deliberately steepen the lighting angle, not because it shows the vase best but because it avoids the problem. You might then use an upwards reflector to relieve the shadows.

● A prominent shadow on a light surface behind a subject can seem perfectly natural, or it may cause the picture to look crudely unbalanced. If you try to 'light shadows out' with another lamp, you are likely to overexpose the background and the subject in the process. Instead, you could either move the subject farther away from the background, or raise the lamp a little to push the shadow downwards.

● As you move a lamp *farther away* from a subject, its light spreads over a greater area, but its intensity falls.

If you take a lamp *close* to a subject, you will get a higher output from it, but its light beam will cover less of the scene. You are likely to find that the subject's brightness alters rapidly if it moves at all.

Very close lamps (e.g. for maximum depth of field on close-up work, and macro-photography) are not only uncomfortably bright, but quickly overheat nearby surfaces.

For many everyday purposes, a lamp distance of around 9–15 ft (3–5 m) from the subject, suits most situations.

● Having settled on a particular lighting angle, you will find that the farther a lamp is from the subject, the higher it will need to be.

The highest you can position any lamp is often decided by the local situation, such as how high someone can reach up with a hand-lamp (stand on a box?), or the maximum safe height of your lighting stands, or even the height of ceilings (do not get too close!).

● Avoid lighting arrangements where people move in and out of light, unless this is for a dramatic effect. Lighting should generally cover the action area, plus a safety region, in case people move beyond their expected positions.

● Find out as much as you can beforehand about what is going to happen. Then set up your lighting rig to suit this action. If you can watch the action being rehearsed before shooting, use this opportunity to check your lighting treatment on camera. Do not just watch the rehearsal and *then* light the scene. Otherwise, you will probably have insufficient time to do so properly, as well as missing the opportunity to check for lighting defects.

● During rehearsal, look out for hotspots and dark areas, both on people as they move around and on the background. To adjust the lighting *balance* (i.e. the relative intensities of the various lamps) you may have to put a scrim in a light to dim it a little, or spot up another to increase its intensity.

Provided a lamp is high enough, you may be able to cut away part of its diffuser, so that the part of its beam lighting nearby subjects is reduced, while its full light falls on more distant subjects.

4.36 Shooting without lamps – in lit surroundings

● Having selected the camera viewpoint you prefer, is the lighting *intensity* right for the lens aperture you want to use (i.e. is the exposure OK)? Does the light *direction* show the subject well? Is the *balance* between lighter tones and shadows satisfactory?

If these aspects are all right, but the overall light intensity is too low, open up the lens aperture and/or increase the camera's sensitivity (gain).

● If the light direction does not show the subject well, can you angle it or move it, to catch the light better?

● Is there any extra lighting available where you are shooting (e.g. some ceiling lights) that will lift the general illumination?

● Do you have a reflector that would serve as a key (hard, polished surface) or fill light (matte white surface) to improve the shot? If you are taking a very close shot, even a sheet of paper, or plastic, or a metal tray may be pressed into service.

● Would it improve the lighting quality if you moved the camera viewpoint round towards the present main light source?

● If the background is underlit, is there sufficient light to take a closer shot of the subject excluding most or all of the background? Can you put in a dummy background (e.g. a sheet of cardboard) behind the subject to show it more clearly, or more attractively?

● You may even be able to move the subject to another place where the light is more suitable, e.g. take a statuette, standing in a dark corner of a room, outside into the daylight.

● Will the light be better or different later? Sometimes it is better to wait for clouds to pass over the sun, to reduce its intensity, than to shoot in bright sunlight with its harsh shadows and high contrast.

Figure 4.14 Using daylight
Place the subject in a good position, facing towards the light, and adjust your camera position to suit.

Figure 4.15 Using a single lamp
Place it up to 20° either side of the camera.

4.37 Using one lamp – the only light available

Whatever you are lighting, the priorities are: the subject's key light, then a fill-light to illuminate its shadows, then a backlight if needed, and finally lighting for the background.

If you have a single lamp, and this is *the only illumination there is*, you will have to use it relatively frontally.

A *single soft light*, such as a 'broad', will provide a more attractive effect than a hard light source, particularly if you use a diffuser (scrim) of tracing paper, frosted plastic, or even a fine wire mesh in front of the lamp. This will cut down its light level, but improve the pictorial effect. Although this soft light will scatter around, at least it prevents nearby areas falling into deep shadow.

If you use only a *single hard-light source*, results can be over-contrasty, leaving your subject unattractively isolated in a pool of light, within dark surroundings, or casting a strong obtrusive shadow.

4.38 Using one lamp – in lit surroundings

A lot depends on how satisfactory the existing lighting is. Your single lamp can be used in several ways:

1. As a *key light*. Your lamp can bring up the light level on the subject, to improve its exposure, or to provide clearer modeling in it, or to provide a low-intensity highlight that adds sparkle, glisten or glitter to it (e.g. eyelights).

You might let your key light flood over the background, to improve its general visibility.

Take care not to illuminate a close-up subject so strongly that you have to stop the lens down, to adjust exposure for this increased local light level. If you do this, the overall brightness of the rest of the scene will appear to fall.

Under sunny conditions, you will often achieve more attractive pictures if you shoot towards the sun, which becomes a 'backlight'. Then for closer shots, you can use your lamp (or reflector) to key the shadowed side of the subject facing the camera.

Where subjects are positioned facing across the picture, you can use a key light from the side to produce maximum modeling. This side light does not suit forward-facing subjects, but when it can be used, you will not need backlight, to separate the subject from its background.

2. As a *fill light*. A single lamp or a reflector can help to illuminate the dense shadows cast by other lighting. It is best to use soft light, so that it does not produce additional shadows of its own. But soft light rapidly falls off in intensity, with increased distance. So if you are quite a way from the subject, you may have to use hard (or softened) light to reach it.

3. As a *back light*. Sometimes you will find a subject that is perfectly well illuminated under the existing lighting, but the picture lacks that extra quality backlight can add.

Even when shooting in the open on an overcast day, a single added backlight can improve picture appeal considerably.

You may be able to position the lamp directly behind and above the subject, by suspending it, or clamping it to a sprung-bar. Or you might use your lamp on a tall stand, which could be hidden behind a chair, for example, so that it is not obvious when it appears in shot.

**Figure 4.16 Using two lamps
(facing the camera)**
Use one as the key light (5–40°
offset), the other as fill light (0–30°
offset the other side). If the head is
angled, 'light along the nose'.

**Figure 4.17 Lighting two people
with two lamps**
Several arrangements are effective.
Keys at A and B, C and D, A and
D, C and B.

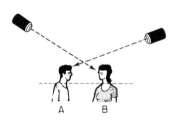

Lamps may be shared as
key A/back B, and key B/back A.
The lower part of light beams may
need diffusers to avoid over-intense
backlight.

4. As *background lighting*. Although your main subject may be well lit, you will often be able to improve the appearance of its background by careful additional lighting.

If for instance, you angle light onto items in the background, this will bring out their shapes and textures, and give the whole scene a more three-dimensional look.

Where the background has areas that are too dark to reproduce well, you can light them to make them clearer.

4.39 Using two lamps

As you might expect, when you have two lamps, the choices increase considerably. You can use them separately (e.g. as two separate key lights for two people), or combine them (as a key and a filler for one subject) in the various permutations above.

Sometimes one lamp will serve more than one purpose, and light the background as well as keying the person. A spread backlight may be angled to one side, so that it lights not only the main subject but also other subjects in the shot, and perhaps shines directly onto a side wall that will be seen later in other shots.

4.40 Using three lamps

By now, you will have realized that just because you have three light sources, you do not necessarily have to provide three-point lighting. You use the lamps according to the priorities of the situation. You might use two lamps as combined key and back lights, and the third for the background. As always, it is the effect on camera that matters.

4.41 Limited lighting

There are regular situations where you will usually need *very few* lamps:

● When you are shooting in well-lit surroundings (daylight or interior lighting) and, at most, have only to supplement the existing illumination.
● When you have only a small localized area to shoot (e.g. a tabletop).
● When you are working in a small light-toned room.
● When the camera remains still throughout the shot (all the action taking place within the frame).
● When the action does not require the camera to pan around the scene (just zoom or dolly, in and out).
● When the background is not more than about 10 ft (3 m) behind the subject. (The more you see in depth, the more you may have to light.)
● When you are working at maximum lens aperture and increased sensitivity (video gain).
● When you are lighting each shot in turn; i.e. the lighting set-up does not have to satisfy a series of shots from different viewpoints.

4.42 Using multi-lamp lighting

You are more likely to need *several lamps* to light the scene:

● When you have to provide the entire lighting for a wide shot (no other light available).
● When your lamps are of low power or have a very restricted spread.
● Where you have to light a large subject area evenly (e.g. for shots throughout an audience).

- If action moves over a wide area (e.g. dance), and people and background need to be lit throughout.
- Where a series of subjects are spread around, and cannot be lit by one lamp. (Each may need its own individual lighting.)
- If there is extensive background area (e.g. a large cyclorama or wall) that has to be evenly lit. One lamp will not cover it, and you need to blend several lamps together.
- Where backgrounds are a considerable distance behind the subject (i.e. the shot takes in a wide area).
- When there are a series of planes (e.g. one set of arches or screens behind another) which may need individual lighting treatment.
- If you want to show detail or modeling in dark background tones.
- If the camera moves around, and shows a series of background areas.
- When the subject is to be shot from several different directions.
- Where subjects are to be lit with separate patches of light, e.g. on each piece of furniture in a display, instead of one light flooding over them all.
- For lighting effects, such as patches of dappled light, light patterns, colored lighting, lighting changes (e.g. morning to night) or a series of lamps each lighting a small selected area.
- In an awkwardly shaped location, where one lamp cannot reach a series of action areas.
- When you need a considerable depth of field in the shot (i.e. the lens stopped well down).

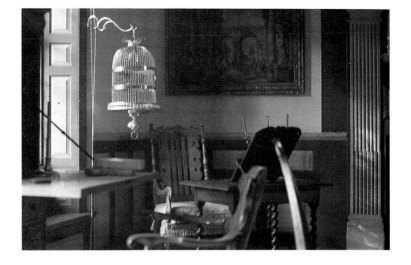

Natural light for interiors
With daylight coming in the window from exactly the right direction, the side-light creates a fine atmospheric effect.

Waiting for the right light
With a bright overcast sky, the details are clear enough, but the shot lacks appeal.

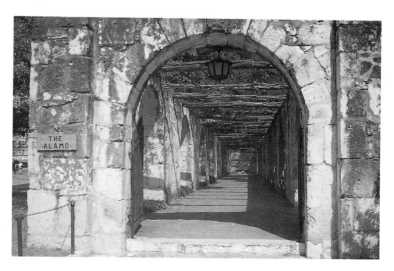

Sunlight from the side casts attractive shadows, and gives The Alamo dimension and depth.

Reflections
The cameraman is concentrating on the window display. But his audience is probably also watching what he is doing, as he stands reflected in the window!

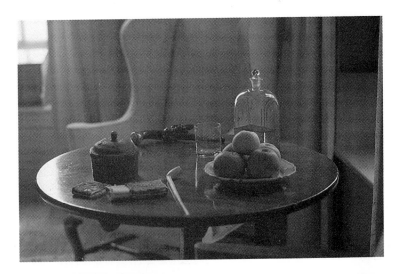

Rim lighting
These shots remind us of how effective rim lighting can be in revealing outline and texture.

By keeping the light localized, the attention is concentrated.

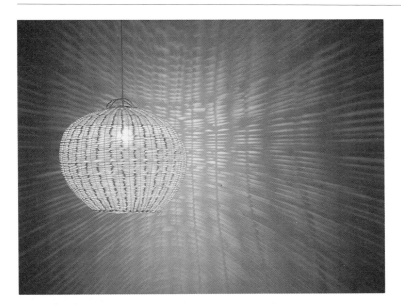

The illusion of light
The shadows from this wicker globe are falling on a flat wall behind it – yet create the illusion of curved planes. A reminder of the power of light to deceive.

High contrast in exteriors
Where contrast is high, you may not be able to expose the lighter areas and the shadows successfully.

Above: the importance of viewpoint
A feature that is almost incidental in the long shot appears impressive in a closer low shot.

Left: the audience only knows what they can see
From this close viewpoint, we see a row of charming period houses, but the shot has excluded their surroundings. Pull the camera back (below), and the effect is destroyed.

Exotic locations
When your program requires a
scene at a distant location (e.g. a
Japanese Tea House) there may be
a suitable equivalent near at hand
in a local park!
(Fairmount Park, Philadelphia).

The commentary must explain
Pictures are not always self-evident.
Unfamiliar subjects, such as these
natural formations, need an
explanatory commentary
(Pamukkale, Turkey).

Avoid overcrowded pictures
If you try to show too many things
in the picture, none will be clear
enough to see properly.

Chapter 5

Audio techniques

Audio gives your pictures a convincing realism. It makes your audience feel involved in what they are seeing. Without it, they are watching moving shadows..

5.1 The essential component

Don't underestimate the valuable contribution that sound can make to your programs. In a good production, sound is never a casual afterthought but an essential part of its appeal.

People often think of television as 'pictures accompanied by sound'. Yet when you analyze most worthwhile television and film productions, you will find that for quite a lot of the time, it is the *sound* that is conveying the information and stimulating the audience's imagination, while the picture itself is really a visual accompaniment! In a radio broadcast, we conjure up mental images of time, place and people, from just a few audio clues without any picture at all.

Sounds are very evocative. Supposing, for example, you show a picture of a couple of people leaning against a wall, with the open sky as a background. If you accompany that picture with noises of waves breaking and the shrill cry of seabirds, we quickly assume that they are near the sea-shore. Add the sound of children at play, and now we are sure that there is a pleasure beach nearby.

Replace all those sounds with the noise of battle, explosions, passing tanks . . . and they are immediately transported to a war situation! They might even appear particularly brave and unflappable, as they remain so calm in this tumult!

If fact, all we really have here is a shot of two people leaning on a wall. The wall itself might have been anywhere – up a mountain, in a desert, or a replica in a studio. The location and the mood of the occasion have been conjured up by the sound and our imagination.

As we shall see, successful audio is a blend of two things:

● Appropriate *techniques* – the ways you use your equipment,

● Appropriate *artistic choices* – how you select and blend sounds.

Both are largely a matter of know-how, combined with experience.

5.2 The nature of sound

The world about us is filled with such an endless variety of sounds that it is difficult to believe each can be resolved into a single complex vibration pattern. When several sources sound together, their separate patterns combine into an even more complicated form. Yet our eardrums, the microphone diaphragm and the loudspeaker, all follow this combined vibration; and more miraculous still, our brain interprets the result.

The simplest possible sound vibrations make a regular *sinusoidal* movement, and you hear such pure tones from a tuning fork, a flute or an audio oscillator. The faster this oscillation, the higher will we judge the *pitch* to be. Very slow vibrations (subsonic, below about 15 times a second) and extremely fast vibrations (ultrasonic, above about 20 000 times a second) fall outside our audible range. We measure the frequency or rate of these vibrations in *hertz*.

The stronger the sound's vibrations (the greater their *amplitude*), the *louder* it seems. Very slight vibrations will be inaudible, while extremely loud sounds can become painful to listen to, as they exceed our 'threshold of feeling'.

Few sources emit 'pure' sounds. Most are a complex combination of the main note (the *fundamental*) and multiples of that note (*harmonics* or *overtones*). The apparent 'quality' of a sound will depend on the proportions or relative strengths of these harmonics.

Broadly speaking, you can judge whether a particular note is being played by a double-bass, an oboe or a bassoon, by its overall quality. If the response of the audio system is not even over the whole audible range (due to filtering, or limitations in the equipment), the proportions of the harmonics can become changed. Then the quality of the reproduced sound may no longer be recognizable as the original instrument.

5.3 Acoustics

You have only to compare sound in an empty room with the difference when that same room is furnished or filled with people, to realize how acoustics alter sound quality. If you understand the basics of acoustics, you will be able to avoid many of those problems that await the unprepared.

When a sound wave hits a *hard surface* (plastic, glass, tiles, stone walls, metal) little is absorbed, so the reflected sound is almost as loud as the original. In fact, when its higher frequencies have actually been reinforced by this reflection, the sound bouncing off the surface can appear brighter and sharper.

When a sound wave meets a *soft surface* (drapes, couches, rugs) some of its energy is absorbed within the material. Higher notes are absorbed most, so the sound reflected from this sort of surface is not only quieter than the original sound wave, but lacks higher frequencies ('top', 'highs'). Its quality is more mellow, less resonant, even dull and muted. Certain soft materials absorb the sound so well that virtually none is reflected.

Where there are a lot of hard surfaces around (as in a bathroom, a large hall or a church), a place can become extremely reverberant or *live*. Sound waves rebound from one surface to another so easily that you hear

——— Direct sound   Live studio
‐‐‐‐‐ Reflected sound

Figure 5.1 Acoustics
Live surroundings. When a room contains predominantly hard surfaces, the sound is strongly reflected. Many of these reflections are picked up by the microphone, reinforcing and coloring the direct sound pick-up.

——— Direct sound   Dead studio
‐‐‐‐‐ Reflected sound

Dead surroundings. When surfaces in a room are very sound-absorbent, the direct sound waves strike walls, floor, ceiling, furnishings and are largely lost. Only a few weak reflections (if any) are picked up by the microphone.

the original and the reflected versions completely intermixed. This can cause considerable changes in the overall sound quality and degrade its clarity.

When surroundings are very reverberant, you will often hear reflections, seconds after the sound itself has stopped; in extreme cases, as a repeated echo. Whether reverberations add richness to the original sound or simply confuse it, will vary with the design of the building, the position of the sound source, the pitch and quality of the sound, and your own position as you listen to it. So there are opportunities for considerable variations here!

If on the other hand, the sound is made in a place with many absorbent surfaces, both the original sound and any reflections are quickly muffled. Under these *dead* conditions, you hear the direct sound, with few reflections from the surroundings. Even a loud noise such as a hand clap or a pistol shot, will not carry very far, but dies away rapidly.

We all know how dead the sound seems to be when we are out in the open. Because the air quickly absorbs it, and there are few reflecting surfaces, open-air sound is weak and does not travel very far. A microphone will often have to get much closer to a subject than normal, to pick up sufficient sound, especially if someone is speaking quietly.

Open-air sound has a characteristic quality that we immediately recognize; an absence of reflected sounds, combined with a lack of top and bass. This effect can be very difficult to imitate convincingly in the studio, even when we surround the subject with highly absorbent acoustic panels.

Acoustics can influence where you position your microphone. To avoid unwanted reflections in live surroundings, you need to place the mike relatively close. If you are working in dead surroundings, a close mike is necessary, because the sound does not carry well. When the surroundings are noisy, a close mike helps a voice to be heard clearly above the unwanted sounds.

However, there can be problems if you place a mike *too close* to the source. Sound quality is generally coarsened. Bass is over-emphasized. We become very aware of the noise of breathing, sibilants (*s*), blasting from explosive *ps*, *bs*, *ts*, and clicks from teeth striking together. Close to an instrument, the mike will reveal various mechanical noises such as key-clicks, bow scrape, etc.

5.4 Mono sound

In everyday life, you are used to listening with the aid of two ears. As your brain compares these two separate sound images of the external world, it builds up a three-dimensional impression from which you estimate the direction and distance of sound.

Non-stereo TV sound is not as sophisticated as this. It presents a 'single-eared' *monaural* ('mono') representation of sound in space. Your only clue to distance is loudness, while direction cannot be conveyed at all.

Many of our audio techniques are really methods of overcoming the limitations of mono sound systems. Listening to mono reproduction, we are not able to distinguish between direct and reflected sounds, as we can when listening in stereo. Instead, they become intermixed, so that the sound is often 'muddy' and less distinct. In mono sound, therefore, we become much more aware of the effects of reverberation.

Because your audience cannot easily distinguish direction and distance, you have to be careful when positioning the mono microphone that:

- You do not pick up too many sound reflections.
- You avoid a louder sound masking a quieter one (particularly in an orchestra).
- Extraneous sounds do not interfere with the ones we want to hear.

5.5 Stereo sound

Stereo sound creates an illusion of space and dimension. It enhances clarity. Because the loudspeakers in television receivers are quite close together, the effect is more limited than in most hi-fi systems. Sound quality and realism are enhanced, but our impressions of direction and depth are less obvious. Stereo can even make us more aware of the restrictions of screen size, and incompatibilities of perspective when shots change (e.g. from long shot to close-up at a concert).

To simplify sound pickup, and problems of 'stereo space', many practitioners mix central *mono* speech, with *stereo* effects and music. Where you use a stereo mike, you must be careful to maintain its direction (i.e. mike left to camera left), and to hold it still; otherwise the stereo image will move around. In a stereo system, reverberation appears more pronounced, and extraneous noises (e.g. wind, ventilation, footsteps) are more prominent; for they have direction, rather than merging with the overall background.

5.6 Microphone care

You do not need to know how various types of microphone work, to use them properly. They all convert sound waves in the air into a fluctuating electrical voltage (the audio signal). It does help though, if you are aware of their different characteristics.

Although most microphones are reasonably robust, they need careful handling if they are to remain reliable and perform up to specification. It is asking for trouble to drop them, knock them, get liquid on them, or overheat them near lamps.

5.7 Directional features

Microphones do not all behave in the same way. Some are designed to be *non-directional* (omnidirectional), and can hear equally well in all directions.

Others are *directional*, so can hear sounds directly in front of them clearly, but are comparatively deaf to sounds in all other directions.

A further design has a *bi-directional* or 'figure-of-eight' pattern, and can hear equally well both forwards and backwards; but it is deaf on either side of it.

The advantage of an *omnidirectional* mike is that it can pick up sound equally well over quite a wide area. So it is great when you want to cover a group of people, or someone who is moving around. The snag is that it cannot discriminate between the sound you want to hear (the speakers), and unwanted sounds such as reflections from walls, noises from nearby people or equipment, ventilation noise, footsteps, etc. The more reverberant the surroundings, the worse the problem. All you can do is to position your mike so that it is closer to the wanted sounds than to the extraneous noises.

When you point a *directional* mike at the sound you want to pick up, it will tend to ignore sounds from other directions, so provides a much cleaner, 'garbage free' result. On the other hand, you need to aim the directional mike carefully, and make sure that the person speaking does

Table 5.1 Copying with acoustics

When surroundings are too 'live'
To reduce acoustic reflections:
   Move the microphone closer.
   Pull drapes.
   Add thick rugs.
   Add cushions.
   Use upholstered furniture.
   Drape blankets on frames, or over chairs.
   Add acoustic-tile panels.

When surroundings are too 'dead'
To increase acoustic reflections:
   Move the microphone further away.
   Open drapes.
   Remove any rugs.
   Remove cushions.
   Remove upholstered furniture.
   Add board or plastic surfaced panels.
   Add floor panels (wood, fiberboard).
   Add artificial reverberation.

not move out of the main pick-up zone, otherwise he will be 'off-mike'. The sound will become weaker, there will probably be high-note losses, and you are likely to hear what you *are* pointing at, instead!

There are several different forms of uni-directional pick-up pattern. The *cardioid* or heart-shaped pattern is broad enough for general use, but not over selective, while the *super-* or *hyper-cardioid* response has also a limited pick-up area at its rear, to receive reflected sounds.

Line microphones such as the 'shotgun' or 'rifle' mike can be hand-held (or attached to larger cameras), and are valuable where you want to isolate a person within a crowd, or to exclude nearby noises. Around 22 in. (0.54 m) long, the shotgun mike covers a 50° angle, and is usually fitted with a foam-plastic or artificial fur wind-screen/windshield to reduce wind noise on the mike.

Finally, there is the *parabolic reflector*, a metal dish of up to 2–3 ft (0.6–0.9 m) diameter which provides a very sensitive, highly directional system (10–40°) for long-distance pick-up. Because of its size, it is liable to rock in the wind if it is not firmly secured.

5.6 Popular types of mike

Dynamic (moving-coil) microphones are pretty rugged, provide good quality sound, and are not easily overloaded by loud sounds (e.g. nearby drums). They can be hand-held without causing unwanted 'handling noise', and used in all types of microphone mountings.

Although this type of mike is sensitive in all directions (non-directional), it does tend to be quite directional at higher frequencies. In other words, anything to either side of where you are pointing the mike is liable to lack top to some extent.

Figure 5.2 Directional response
Non-directional (omnidirectional) response. Equally sensitive in all directions, generally rugged, and not too susceptible to impact shock; cannot be placed to distinguish between direct and reflected sounds, so must work close to the sound source.

Cardioid response. A broad heart-shaped pick-up pattern (e.g. 160°), insensitive on its rear side. (Better coverage of close sources than a simple half-eight pattern).

Highly directional response. Used wherever you want extremely selective pick-up, to avoid environmental noises, or for distance sources.

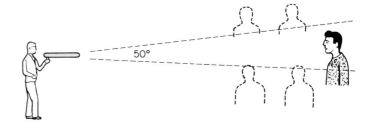

Bi-directional response. Sensitive ('live') on either face (e.g. 100° coverage for each), but deaf ('dead') at the sides. Useful for two-person pick-up, while suppressing reflected sound waves.

Electret microphones are very popular in video production. Not only are they relatively inexpensive, but they are small and adaptable. The electret mike can be used as a personal mike clipped or pinned to someone's clothing (e.g. tie, lapel or shirt), either singly or in pairs ('dual-redundancy', with one as an emergency standby). The electret capsule can also be used on a small boom or fishpole fitting, or within a parabolic reflector.

Its sound quality is good, although as you might expect, it can become somewhat muffled, when worn underneath clothing as an 'invisible mike'. The unit uses a small battery to power its tiny enclosed amplifier.

Unfortunately, the electret mike's performance (high note response; sensitivity) tends to deteriorate with time, and background hiss increases. High humidity, moisture, heat and dust can lead to failure.

The *pressure-zone* microphone (PZM) is a plate-mounted electret capsule that can be attached unobtrusively to any flat surface (table, floor or wall). Its high-quality output and sensitivity have made it increasingly popular for speech and music. However, because it is virtually non-directional, it is liable to pick up unwanted reflected sounds.

5.9 Other types of mike

The *condenser* or *electrostatic* mike produces the highest audio quality, and is ideal for musical pick-up. It can be fitted to a sound boom, a stand, a fishpole, or used slung over the action area. Its main disadvantages are that it is relatively large and liable to be overloaded by very loud nearby sounds. It also needs a special power supply.

The *ribbon* mike (figure-of-eight pick-up) again provides very high quality sound. Its main drawbacks are its size and fragility (for wind causes rumbles, and can damage it), and the way it overloads with close loud sounds.

Crystal microphones are very cheap, highly sensitive and small, but fragile. The audio quality can be quite adequate for speech, where high fidelity is not important, e.g. field interviews. They can also be used as contact mikes for some musical instruments (electric guitar).

Supporting the mike

5.10 Camera microphones

If your camera is fitted with a microphone, you will be able to pick up the program sound as you shoot, without the aid of a second person, at least in theory. A lot depends on the situation and the type of sound involved. Nothing beats a separate, high quality microphone placed in exactly the right place. However, if you are shooting on your own, or moving around in a crowded market-place, or having a series of impromptu interviews in the street, the camera mike has a lot in its favor.

The simplest form of camera microphone is a small omnidirectional *insert mike*, built in at the front of the camera itself. This picks up the sound from all round the camera, including any noises from the camera zoom lens and auto-iris, and the cameraman's grunts and breathing. With care though, this basic microphone is useful for general atmospheric background sounds (traffic, crowds), and about adequate for close speech.

With most camera mikes, you will usually find that if you try to pick-up speech more than about 4–6 ft (1.2–1.8 m) away, background noise or acoustical reflections can sound unacceptably high.

Figure 5.3 Shotgun/rifle microphone
The popular shotgun or rifle microphone (without and with its windscreen/windshield) is highly directional (50°). In a one-person unit, the shotgun mike is often attached to the top of the camera. Otherwise it is hand-held by a second operator. It can also be used in a sound boom (without the shield).

Another arrangement is the unidirectional *boom mike* fitted to some video cameras. This microphone with its surrounding foam windshield, is rather more sensitive, and attaches to a thin telescopic tube. Its 'boom' can be extended to position the mike nearer the subject, angled to keep it out of the shot.

Some types of video camera are fitted with a *zoom mike*. This ingenious unit combines electret capsules, to give it an adjustable pick-up angle. Linked to the zoom lens system, it behaves as a *non*-directional ('omni') mike when the lens is zoomed out to its widest angle, and narrows to '*ultra-uni*directional' when the lens is fully zoomed in to its narrowest angle. Nominally therefore, it matches the sound pick-up to the shot, giving close-up sound when zoomed in for close-ups, and long-distance sound when zoomed out for long shots.

At first sight, this seems a great idea. But as you know, the lens angle you choose depends on your shooting conditions, and the 'perspective effect' you want. This has nothing whatever to do with the mike coverage-angle you would use to suit the acoustics, the action spread, and the mike distance.

Let us take an example. Supposing you are shooting a person singing in an echoing church. Using an automatic zoom-mike, the long shot sound (non-directional) would be accompanied by very strong reflections – so loud perhaps, that the singer's voice is masked by them. In close shots, the sound would appear localized and relatively dead, for the narrow-beam mike is not picking up the reverberation. But what you really want is clear sound of constant quality, with just a slight change in *volume* (if any) between the distant and close shots.

However, if you are shooting unassisted, and unable to put a microphone in the optimum place, the results can be satisfactory enough for many purposes.

A further type of camera microphone uses a regular *shotgun/rifle mike* attached to the of the camera, and plugged into the camera's external mike socket. This is an excellent arrangement where you want high quality 'long-distance' sound pick-up from a subject in the picture. The main disadvantages here are the way the volume and quality of any background sounds will change as you pan around the scene, as they enter and leave the microphone's pick-up area. As always with directional mikes, you have to make sure that it is aimed accurately.

5.11 The hand mike/baton mike

Unless a microphone is designed to be held in the hand, you will hear quite a lot of handling noise (scraping, thumps, clonks) as you move it around, especially if the audio gain (amplification) has had to be increased for weaker sounds.

The hand-held mike (*stick mike*) is a familiar sight on TV, in the hands of interviewers, singers and commentators. It is a very simple, convenient method of sound pick-up provided it is used properly. Otherwise results can be erratic.

The hand mike is best held just below shoulder height, pointed slightly towards the person speaking. But don't exaggerate this pointing technique. Make it as unobtrusive as possible. If whenever you ask a question, you jab the mike at your victim, you are liable to unnerve him in no time at all!

A plastic-foam windshield (blast filter) over the mike reduces the rumbles of wind on the mike, and explosive breath-pops. But it is better

Figure 5.4 Hand microphone
The hand microphone is widely used for interviews, commentaries and stage work. If the mike has a cardioid directional response, extraneous noise pick-up is lower. If it is omnidirectional, it may need to be held closer (e.g. 9 in. (23 cm)).

Techniques:
1. Normally held just below shoulder height. Pointing the mike at the speaker improves sound quality, but can be distracting, and may place the mike too close.
2. Avoid low mike positions, as they pick up more background noise.

to talk across the microphone rather than directly into it, to avoid quality changes (particularly if the mike is directional for higher frequencies).

Some people hold the mike around waist height, to prevent it being visible in the picture, but you will generally find this results in weak pick-up, poor quality, and more intrusive background noise.

Where a hand microphone has a *cardioid* response, this helps to reduce the amount of extraneous sound overheard, so it can be used about 1–1.5 ft (30–45 cm) from the person speaking. But if you use an *omni-directional* hand mike, it will normally have to be held rather nearer, say 9 in. (25 cm).

Hand-mikes are not foolproof, and there are several points worth bearing in mind whenever you use one. Although it is fairly rugged, treat your mike gently. When you are not using it, or you need to put it down to handle something, choose a safe place where it will not roll off or get trodden on! You may able to tuck it under your arm temporarily, but this can cause loud thumps as you do so. If you put the mike in a pocket, there is every chance that the cable will pull it out. And don't be tempted in an idle moment to swing or hang the mike by its cable – this leads to broken connections!

Cables need care. If you are going to walk around holding the mike, make sure you have enough free cable to do so, and that passers-by are not liable to stand on it, or trip over it. You can often lay the cable out of sight, and use gaffer tape (duct tape) to fasten it against the floor or the wall.

As you move, hold the cable in your other hand (or under an arm, or clipped to your clothes) rather than pull it along by the mike itself. When the cable gets fouled up, don't heave on it to release it. If you cannot retake the sequence, and someone out of shot does not rescue you, just accept that you are trapped, and make the best of it!

If you are using several microphones, and want to confirm that a circuit is working ('hot', 'live'), or are checking which mike is connected to an audio mixer channel, scratch its end mesh or casing. Never blow into it, for this is liable to cause damage.

Figure 5.5 Personal microphones
Lavalier (neck mike, lanyard). The microphone is slung on a neck cord, about 6 in. (15 cm) below the chin.

Tie clip mike (miniature capsule mike – electret or dynamic). A single mike is clipped to the necktie, lapel or shirt. A 'dual redundancy' pair are used, where a standby mike is desirable. Presence filters (mid-range boost) may improve audio quality. Plastic foam windshields reduce wind-noise.

5.12 Personal mikes

Small *lavalier* (*lanyard*) microphones are designed to hang from a neckcord, at about the height of a necktie knot. Both electret and dynamic types are used. Although the audio quality and volume can vary as the wearer turns his head, results are generally very good, provided the mike is not muffled by clothing. There can be problems though, if the speaker is wearing jangly neck jewelry, or takes to thumping his chest, or hugs things to him . . .

Electret clip-on mikes (also often called 'tie-tack', or 'lavalier' mikes) are the answer to many sound problems. They are compact, unobtrusive and provide high sound quality. Provided they are clipped outside other clothing, e.g. to the tie, lapel, shirt or blouse, any noises from clothing-rub are kept to a minimum. As with all microphones, attached to the person, you can only rely on the clip-on mike picking up the sound of the individual wearing it. When you have two or more people, each has to wear his own clip-mike, connected to a separate audio circuit.

Although the lavalier/clip-on mike is itself unobtrusive enough, it does have a long trailing cable, which connects to an audio input point. (This could be the camera's external mike socket, the VCR, an audio mixer unit, or a suitable audio wall outlet in the studio.)

When a performer arrives, you have to fit him with a microphone, and arrange the cable so that it is not unsightly, e.g. concealing it beneath his jacket or other outer clothing. That's fine, provided he is not going to move from his seat.

But if performers are going to walk about, then the cable needs to be fastened to their belt or clothing, so that the microphone cannot be pulled out of position. As we discussed earlier, a certain amount of care is necessary when walking with a trailing cable. At the end of the session, remember to help the talent to detach themselves from the mike and cable.

A *wireless (radio) microphone* has no cable, so allows its wearer to move around freely. A wireless hand mike is self-contained and includes a tiny transmitter and antenna/aerial. A lavalier or clip-on mike on the other hand, has a short cable, going to a small pocket or belt transmitter worn by the performer.

The microphone's radiated signal is picked up by the antenna of a sensitive FM receiver up to 440 yards (400 m) away. Reception from its battery-powered transmitter (which may have a life of 4–6 hours) can vary. If action is located near metal structures or equipment, fading, distortion or radio blackout are not uncommon.

5.13 Fishpole mikes

The *fishpole* or *fishing-rod* mike is very widely used for video production in the field. Its collapsible aluminium pole (sometimes bamboo) is about 6–9 ft (2–2.5 m) long and carries a mike at its far end. Its cable is taped along the pole. Take care that the mike is sound-insulated from the pole (by a shock-proof fitting or foam-plastic surround) to prevent handling noise traveling along the pole, and being picked up by the mike.

When used out of doors, fishpoles are generally fitted with a *rifle mike*, covered with an artificial fur wind-gag. This is very effective at reducing extraneous noise, even in strong winds. A bass-cut too, can help to reduce background noises.

Figure 5.6 Fishpole microphone
Under-arm support. The fishpole is fitted with a mike in a shockproof cradle at the end of a pole. With it tucked under one arm, you angle the pole to place the mike near the sound source. This method is most suitable for low pick-up positions. Never hold the end of the pole in your belt; it is unbalanced and dangerous.

Above-head support. Held with fully extended arms, the mike can be positioned above the shot limits. But this is a tiring position to maintain for any length of time.

Figure 5.7 Microphone distance
You should aim to position the mike
to suit the size of the shot, keeping
it just above or below the frame
limits,
BCU 0.3 m (1 ft)
CU 1 m (3 ft)
LS 3 m (10 ft)

Figure 5.8 Small studio boom
The pre-adjusted telescopic arm
(counterweighted) is pivoted on a
column of adjustable height in a
swivel-castered tripod stand. The
boom arm can be tilted and panned,
the stand wheeled around, and the
microphone can usually be turned and
tilted. Boom stretch is typically
3–4.5 m (10–15 ft).

You can hold the fishpole with both arms well-balanced above the head
for short periods, to position the mike above the action. Or you can use
the pole tucked under one arm to place the mike in front of the speaker.
Finally you can kneel, and angle the pole upwards, to locate the mike
out of sight below the bottom of the frame of the picture.

5.14 Small booms

Occasionally, a *small sound boom* is used for video production, to
position the microphone over the action area. It consists of a pivoted
telescopic rod (in principle, rather like a fishpole) balanced on the
column of a castered tripod. It is usually possible to turn and tilt the
microphone, with the boom preadjusted to stretch some 10–15 ft
(3–4.5 m) towards the action. Although the base can be wheeled, the
whole contraption tends to be rather top-heavy and to have a will of its
own, even when the floor is smooth and level.

Figure 5.9 Desk microphone
Desk fitting. Fitted in a small stand, the mike
can be used for people seated at a table.

Position. Typical mike positions are
about 1.5–2 ft (0.3–0.6 m) from the
speaker; 3–4 ft (0.9–1.2 m) between
mikes.

Shock. A foam pad under
the desk mike will insulate it
from thumps and vibrations.

Figure 5.10 Stand microphone
The stand height is adjustable, and angled extensions can be fitted. A quick-release head allows the mike to be removed easily and used as a hand mike. Lightweight stands can be very unstable.

Figure 5.11 Hanging/slung microphone
Useful for area pick-up (audience applause, choir). But problems arise when people move around, or are at different distances from the mike (e.g. seated and standing).

5.15 Desk mikes (See Figure 5.9 on page 97.)

Where you have someone seated behind a desk or table, you can clamp the mike in a small support-stand in front of him, resting on a foam-plastic pad. (This helps to isolate the mike from any shocks if the speaker happens to kick the desk, or thumps its top). If necessary, tape the fitting to the desk to prevent its being moved accidentally, and tidy its cable away neatly, taping it where necessary.

5.16 Stand mikes

There are several types of microphone stand, from robust bottom-weighted telescopic forms to unobtrusive versions with thin flexible or curved tubing intended for miniature mikes. Some have quick-release tops, allowing the mike to be removed and hand-held if necessary.

The stand mike is a useful general-purpose arrangement, when you do not mind the fitting appearing in shot, e.g. for center-stage announcements, a singing group or for miking musical instruments.

It has its disadvantages though. If people move around much, they easily get off mike. You have to rely on performer's getting to the right place and keeping the right distance from the mike. It is a good idea to give them taped foot marks on the floor to guide them. And of course, there is always the danger that they will kick the stand or trip over the cable. Floor tape the cable if need be.

Hanging or slung mikes

Sometimes the best solution to locating a microphone near enough to the sound source is to suspend it over them, e.g. above a choir, or part of an orchestra or an audience. Do not hang the mike by its own cable, but rig it securely with line (cord), using extra safety lines in case anything comes adrift and it falls down.

The hanging mike has several limitations. The mike will be visible in long shots (this may not matter). It usually has a fairly localized pick-up area (people may inadvertently move out of it). Its position cannot normally be adjusted during the production item. It may pick up quite a lot of extraneous noise. Its coverage of individual speakers in seated groups is poor. It can overheat and pick up hum from nearby lamps. It may cast a distracting shadow on the background.

5.18 Hidden mikes

When other methods of sound pick-up are difficult, a hidden microphone may be the solution to your problems. It can be concealed among a bunch of flowers on a table, behind props, in a piece of furniture, etc.

This idea too has its limitations. Although you can hide the mike, it may not be easy to prevent its cable being seen. Sound quality may be affected by nearby reflecting or absorbing surfaces. Because the mike covers a fixed localized area, you have to rely on a performer playing to the mike and not speaking off-mike.

Controlling dynamics

5.19 Dynamic range

Everyday sounds can cover a considerable volume range. Fortunately for us, our ears are able to readjust to an astonishing extent to cope with these variations. But audio systems can't do this. If audio signals are larger than the system can accept, they will overload it and become badly distorted. If on the other hand sounds are too weak, they get lost in general background noise. So if we want to reproduce audio clearly, with fidelity, it has to be kept within the system's limits.

A lot of sounds pose no problems at all. They don't get particularly soft or loud; that is, they do not have a wide dynamic range. When you are recording sound of this sort, there is little need to alter the gain (amplification) of the system, once it has been set to an appropriate 'average' position.

But one has to record sounds that vary in volume from a whisper to an ear-shattering blast. And the latter will certainly exceed the system's handling capacity, unless you compensate in some way. The obvious thing to do is to turn down the system's audio gain so that the loud parts never reach its upper limit. But now the quiet passages may be so faint that they are inaudible.

So somehow or other, you need to control levels, unless the sounds happen to have a limited dynamic range.

5.20 Automatic control

As you saw earlier when looking at video cameras, equipment today often allows you two options – either you can let it adjust itself *automatically*, or you can control it *manually*.

Audio systems and VCR's often include *AGC* (*automatic gain control*) circuits to hold back very loud sounds and prevent overload distortion. You plug your microphone in, and the circuitry looks after itself.

This is quite an effective way of dealing with the odd sound peak. If however, the sound is so loud that it is continually 'hitting the limiter', the result can be an unpleasant strangled effect.

This system does not compensate though, for sounds that are undesirably quiet. So you have to make sure that the gain control is set high enough to amplify the quietest passages sufficiently.

Figure 5.12 VU (volume unit) meter
Lower scale shows percentage modulation, where 100% is system's maximum limit. Keep your sound peaks in 80–100% (12–0 dB), only occasionally over (+1 to +3 dB) in the red area. Readings are unreliably low for loud transient sounds (e.g. percussion). The upper scale marked in decibels (dB), is used for calibration and line-up (with steady tone). Normal range is –20 to 0 dB.

5.21 Manual control

The other method of controlling the audio level is to listen continuously to the program ('monitor' it), while watching a *volume indicator*, or *audio level meter*. As you watch, you re-adjust the system's gain (amplification) whenever necessary, to suit the incoming audio signal. That does not mean of course, that one should iron out the dynamics, by making all the quiet sections loud, and holding back all the loud passages. 'Riding the gain' in this way can ruin the program.

Instead, if you know sounds are going to be weak, you anticipate by gradually increasing the gain, and conversely, you slowly take back the gain before loud passages. Then the listeners are unaware that you are making changes to accommodate the audio system's limitations.

How quiet you allow the softest sound to be, can depend on the purpose of your program. If, for example, you are making a videotape that is to be used in noisy surroundings, or shown in the open air, it may be best to keep the gain up to prevent quietest sounds from falling below –15 or –20 dB. If you are shooting a piano performance, to be heard indoors, take care not to over-control the music's dynamics, and use the system's full volume range.

Because, unlike auto circuits, you are able to anticipate and make artistic judgments, the final effect can be far superior. The drawback to manual control though, is that you have to be vigilant all the time, ready to make any necessary re-adjustments. If you are caught out, results may be less satisfactory than the auto circuits would have produced!

There are several types of volume indicator, but the commonest on video equipment take the form of *visual displays* using bargraphs of LEDs (light emitting diodes) or *VU meters*.

A bargraph has a strip made up of tiny lit segments. This varies in length with the audio signal's strength. Calibrations vary, but it might for example have a decibel scale from –50 to +10 dB, with an upper working limit of about +2 dB. You simply adjust the audio gain control so that the sound peaks reach this upper mark.

The VU meter is a widely used volume indicator. It has two scales: a 'volume unit' scale marked in decibels, and another showing 'percentage modulation'. Although accurate for steady tones, the VU meter gives deceptively low readings for brief loud sounds or transients (e.g. percussion). So one could accidentally let the system overload.

Maximum signal coincides with 100% modulation /0 dB. Above that, in the red sector, sounds will distort, although occasional peaks are acceptable. The normal range used is –20 to 0 dB, typically peaking between –2 to 0 dB.

A further type of indicator, the *PPM* (*peak program meter*) is used only on certain professional audio equipment. It has a seven-section scale (4 dB per division), using 2–6 as its normal range.

We might summarize the situation by saying that if you need the audio system to look after itself, because you are preoccupied with shooting the scene, or are coping with very unpredictable sounds, then AGC has its merits, for it will prevent loud sounds overloading the system. If you have an assistant who can monitor the sound as it is being recorded, and adjust the gain for optimum results, then this has artistic advantages.

There are special electronic devices, called 'limiters' or 'compressors', that automatically adjust the dynamic range of the audio signal, but these are only found in more sophisticated systems.

5.22 Monitoring sound

Monitoring sound for a video program involves

- *watching:* checking the volume indicator, and seeing that the mike does not pop into shot inadvertently,
- *listening:* on high-grade earphones or a loudspeaker, to check sound quality and balance, and detect any unwanted background noises.

If you are going to tape a performance straight off, without rehearsal, as with an interview, you should ask a performer to give you a few words before they begin, as a *voice-level* or *level-test* at the volume they are going to use during the taping. Alternatively, if they have a preliminary chat with an interviewer, you can normally 'take a level' then instead. Otherwise, you can judge the volume and dynamics from a rehearsal.

As you monitor the sound, get an impression of its possible dynamic range, while watching its peak on the indicator. (Even if the system is using AGC, there is often an indicator to prevent your 'undermoding' by having the audio gain setting too low.) If the results are not satisfactory, you may need to ask the speaker to talk louder or more quietly, or to reposition the mike. Finally, on a prearranged hand signal, when the recording has started, you cue him to begin.

Figure 5.13 Portable audio mixer
Used in the field, to mix up to three mikes, the overall output is controlled by a master fader. An optional bass cut can be switched into any channel (to cut wind-rumble and improve intelligibility). A VU meter provides a volume indicator. This mixer includes a limiter, to prevent audio overload. A phones check-jack monitors the audio.

5.23 The audio mixer

You need an *audio mixer panel* whenever you have a number of sound sources to select, blend together and control (e.g. a couple of mikes, audio tape, disc, VCR audio output, etc.). The output of this unit is fed to the VCR.

On the front panel of the audio mixer, are a series of rotating knobs (or sliders). Each of these 'pots' (potentiometers) or 'faders' can adjust its channel's volume from full, down to fade-out (silence). In some designs, you can also switch a channel in or out ('key it') on cue.

When you plug the sources into the patch panel (connector strip) at the rear of the unit, you can choose which pot controls which source. Some mixers also include *channel selector switches* that allow you to reselect the channel controlled by a particular pot (e.g. either mike-1 or mike-2).

In a larger panel, as well as these individual channel pots, there may be *group faders* (group masters, submasters). Each of these group faders controls the *combined* outputs of several channels, and it may have its own group volume indicator. You could, for instance, use one group fader for all the mikes on an audience.

Finally, there is generally a *master fader* that controls the overall audio strength being sent to line (e.g. on the VCR). This can be used to fade the complete mix in or out. A master volume indicator shows the combined strength of the mixed audio.

Larger audio mixers include a *cue circuit* (audition, pre-hear), that enables you to listen 'privately' on earphones or a loudspeaker to the output of any individual channel, even when its pot is faded right out. So you can hear to set up a disc or tape at exactly the right spot, ready to be started on cue, without this being overheard on-air. You can also use the facility to identify circuits, making sure that the person at the other end is ready with their contribution.

The larger mixer panel will also include an *intercom* (production talkback) circuit that allows the sound man to talk to his assistant(s), and the director to communicate with his production team on headsets.

5.24 Using the mixer

When the sound man sits at the mixer controlling the audio, he is doing a number of things:

1. cueing sources in and out,
2. maintaining program continuity,
3. creating a sound balance,
4. controlling the sound level and the dynamic range.

Let's look at these operations in a little detail.

1. Cueing in and out. It is normal practice to cue a sound source, fade it in just before it begins (to the appropriate pot setting), and fade it out when it has finished.

If all the channels you want to cue are linked to a group fader (e.g. several mikes on a choir), this will control them simultaneously.

You can fade a source or a group in and out gradually (sneak in, fade-away) or rapidly (a straight fade-in, fade-out), whatever is most appropriate.

You should never leave a mike 'open' (live) when it is not in use. Apart from accidentally recording overheard remarks ('Was that all right?') and other unwanted sounds, it may pick up someone who is on another mike. Then you will have the sound from their mike, mixed with the 'off-mike' sound from the original microphone, which will produce an unpleasant echo effect.

2. Program continuity. Here we are concerned with selecting and introducing the right source at the right moment, and cutting each contribution as it is completed.

You can use either the channel pots for individual sources, or the group faders for a pre-balanced group.

Let's take an example. You might have a scene in which music from a radio (actually a disc) plays quietly behind the foreground speech (from a live mike), a phone rings nearby (fade up effects tape), and the performer turns off the radio (fade out disc) and picks up the phone (tape insert stops). A continuous background of bird-song is left at a low level throughout. This would all be done on individual channel pots.

3. Creating a sound balance. If you are combining several sound sources, you will seldom want to add them all at their full original strengths. You will want to blend them for a particular overall effect.

Supposing you use a single microphone to pick up the sound from a musical group. With experience and good acoustics, this could work. But the chances are that it would pick up certain instruments much better than others. Loud ones would dominate; quiet ones would be lost. The overall balance would be poor.

Instead, you could use several microphones, devoted to different parts of the group. Then you would be able to increase the volume of weaker instruments (e.g. a flute) and hold back the louder ones (drums). With care, the result would sound perfectly natural and have a clearer overall balance.

Sometimes you will want to adjust the relative volumes of sounds to create an illusion of *distance*. If the sound of a telephone ringing is loud, we assume it is nearby; if it is faint, it must be some distance away.

You might deliberately *emphasize* sounds, e.g. by re-adjusting the pot controlling the crowd noise, to make it louder at an exciting moment, and give it dramatic impact.

The final balance you decide on is always a blend to suit your production.

5.25 Sound complexity

Preparing program sound can be simple and straightforward, or a highly complex business. It depends on the type of program you are making, how you decide to treat it, and how you go about the job. If you want to point your camera with its attached mike at the scene, and edit in camera, to get a finished product, you can do so, within certain limitations. But this is a very restrictive technique.

You do not have to have expensive, sophisticated audio equipment, to develop an effective, interesting soundtrack. With a certain amount of imagination, patience and careful organization, you can often achieve impressive effects cheaply and successfully with everyday facilities. But it is liable to be a longer and more laborious process. That is the price one has to pay.

5.26 Live sound

Practically speaking, there are really two live sound pick-up situations:

- The *repeatable performance*, in which you can re-record a sequence until it is just as you want it.
- The *once-time event*, in which you have just the one shot and must get it right first time.

The latter is the time when it may be wise to have a second microphone and a duplicate audio recording. If for example you are taping an important once-only speech, you could always at a pinch use track from the standby audio recorder together with audience shots ('cutaways'), rather than have an embarrassing gap in the program at the moment someone knocked the camera or pulled the main mike cable!

When you are recording an item 'live', as it happens, you need to monitor the program carefully, keeping a lookout for any errors or defects. It is too easy for something to go wrong, and remain unnoticed until afterwards. A fault that may be easily corrected at the time can be impossible to gloss over later, if you discover on replay that the sequence is unusable!

5.27 Recorded inserts

The great advantage of recorded material is that you know exactly what is in it – its contents, quality and durations. Even when there are unwanted sections, you can usually avoid them.

It can be more convenient, and a lot simpler, to audio tape an item beforehand ('pre-recording'), than to wait and include it live in the main taping session: piano music, for instance, played in the background of a scene.

Apart from various sound effects, recorded audio inserts have some less obvious uses too. In a drama for instance, you can play audio tape, to provide the voice of 'someone speaking in the next room', or at the other end of a phone 'conversation', and avoid using an extra microphone to take just those few words live in the studio. Audio tape can provide the 'voice-over' of a commentator or an announcer. Your audience will not notice the difference, whether the inserts are live or pre-recorded.

It is possible to manipulate recorded sound in many ways. You can cut bits out, play only selected portions, change the order of sections – even alter its speed or play it backwards if you really want to! And of course, you can add filtering, echo and distortion with a full knowledge that if anything goes wrong, you still have the original recording to go back to and try again.

There are several tricks you can play with recorded effects, to enable them to fit your particular needs. For instance, if you want to insert a recorded sound effect, but find that the version you have is too brief, you may be able to extend it by re-recording it several times in succession; so you could extend the drawn-out sounds of wind, seawash, a mob, machinery, traffic, etc. But watch out for any easily recognized feature though, such as a shout or the bleep of a car horn, that would become repetitious if repeated over and over.

You can create an illusion quite economically, by mixing suitable sound effects together. For instance, wind + rain + thunder + an automobile engine, can suggest that the car is traveling through a storm, although all the audience can see is the people inside it, and water on its windows.

By taking small parts of several effects, and joining them together, you can create the sound of something that does not exist! Thus you might combine the sounds of several different kinds of machinery (jet engine, sewing machine and slowed-down truck) to make the sound of a 'time machine'. A prehistoric monster might be contrived from the sound of several wild animals blended together, reversed, with speed changes.

5.28 Sync and non-sync sound

If the sound coincides exactly with the action in a picture, it is said to be *synchronized*, or 'in sync' with the action. This effect is most apparent when you can see anyone's lips as they speak, or their finger movements as they play an instrument, or watch actions that create noise (hammering or footsteps).

If after the picture and sound are recorded, they become 'out of sync' for any reason, the effect is usually distracting, annoying or comic.

When you cannot judge cause and effect in this way, there can be no sync problems. For example, if the picture shows someone with his face turned away from the camera, or a performer's finger movements are hidden as he plays (e.g. a through-the-lid shot of a pianist), or a person's legs are not seen as he walks, sound and picture do not have to match accurately, for we cannot see whether the sound is perfectly synchronized with its picture or not.

In fact, what we see and what we hear in the final program need not even be related! The back-of-head-shot may be a 'cutaway', and the person at the piano may only be pretending to play, as the music comes from a disc.

Why alter the soundtrack?

If you are shooting someone making a formal speech, the most appropriate technique may be simply to make a straightforward recording of what is taking place. But for many types of programs, this approach would be far too austere and ordinary.

You want to make your subject interesting, hold your audience's attention, give it a persuasive, convincing quality. And to do this, you may need not only attractive, well-chosen pictures, but carefully selected sound effects and music.

Let us take a dramatic example. Supposing that, at the time you were shooting a night scene, the location was disappointingly silent. Rather than leave the recording that way, you could make it more effective by introducing the sounds of night creatures such as owls, frogs, crickets, or even a quiet wind to build up a suitable atmosphere. Depending on what you choose, the same picture could be made to convey peaceful rest, anxiety, even impending doom – whatever is dramatically appropriate.

There are situations where, by altering the soundtrack, you can remedy what would otherwise be a disaster. Imagine shooting a documentary on the seashore, and finding that the speaker's words are regularly interrupted by persistent blasts from a nearby foghorn. The program seems ruined.

But all is not lost! You could take the videotape, and omit any shots that show the speaker close enough to reveal moving lips. You then get him to re-record his lecture (perhaps using the original videotape soundtrack to derive a script). Add the general, unsynchronized sound effects of sea-wash (without foghorns!), and use this new version to replace the original soundtrack. You now have a complete, unblemished program.

If you are showing a series of pictures that are really somewhat disjointed – various views around a city perhaps – you can link them together, and create a sense of continuity, by having the same background of sound effects or music behind the entire sequence.

5.30 Making the changes

If you are making a video program in a studio, it is customary to mix in any recorded inserts with the live pick-up from microphones, as you shoot a scene. This has the advantage that you finish up with a complete soundtrack on the video recording at the end of the taping session.

But if, later, you decide to edit this program, you will interrupt its *combined soundtrack*. So a piece of music accompanying dancers would change abruptly, if you later cut out the bit where the camera lost focus, or you put in an extra shot! Therefore many directors prefer to keep their options open, and wait until they have finished editing the pictures before finalizing the soundtrack. And that results in a detailed post-production editing session.

However, where you *do* need to picture-edit a videotape program that already has a soundtrack with its pictures, there are two basic methods of doing this:

1. The simplest is to make a modified copy (a *dupe* or *dubbing*) of your program on another VCR.

To do this:

(a) Cable the *video* output of the replay machine to the video input of the record VCR. That will enable you to copy the original picture.

(b) You also feed the *audio* output of the replay VCR to an *audio mixer*. Other audio sources carrying effects or music are plugged into the audio mixer too.

(c) The output of the mixer is taken to the *audio* input of the record VCR. This will be carrying the original soundtrack, blended with the sound effects/music you are adding.

(d) Now you are ready to begin. Start the replay VCR, and the recording (dubbing) VCR, and introduce the extra audio sources as you go.

It is an easy, foolproof method, and if at first you do not succeed you can try again. The result is a *second generation* copy of the original pictures, and a new composite soundtrack.

Because no copy can ever be as good as the original recording, the picture quality on this version will inevitably have deteriorated somewhat during the copying, but it may not be apparent. However, you still have the original videotape with its 'first generation' picture and sound should you need it.

2. Another method of changing the soundtrack uses a facility called *audio-dub* on the VCR. This allows you to replace the original soundtrack on a videotape, but leaves its pictures untouched.

You *lift off* the original soundtrack, make a new version, then *lay this back* in place of the old one, as follows:

(a) First you play your videotape program, making a copy of just its soundtrack, on an audio-tape recorder (from 'audio out' on the VCR).

(b) You then replay this audio-tape copy, through a mixer, blending it with the effects and music recordings you want to add. From the mixer's output, you record the new *master audio track*.

(b) Check this new track.

(c) When you are satisfied with the result, you load a VCR with your original videotape (set back at its start), and switch the VCR to *audio-dub*.

(d) Now you simultaneously play the new master audio track and record on the VCR. This will only affect the soundtrack of the original videotape. The result will be your new composite audio recorded alongside the original pictures, in place of the old sound.

The great advantage of this technique is that you have the original picture. So if you want to make copies of this program for distribution, you will get the best possible picture quality. (However, unless you keep an audio copy of its original soundtrack, you will have lost it during the 'audio-dub' process).

There is a major snag though, if the program sound needs to synchronize exactly with the picture, e.g. close-up of people talking. Unless you are very careful(!) to ensure that the composite track starts at precisely the right moment, as you lay it back, you will get sound-sync errors.

Fortunately this situation is not as discouraging as it seems, for a surprisingly large number of programs do not contain (or can avoid) accurate sound sync.

At stage (b), instead of using a further audio recorder, you could have dubbed the mix straight back over the videotape's old audio track, but the method outlined is more flexible.

5.31 Discontinuous shooting

Most video programs are made up of a series of shots, taken in whatever order is most convenient, and edited together later to form the final program. This approach has both advantages and drawbacks. As far as the program sound is concerned, there are several complications.

First of all, although the various shots in a sequence have been taken at different times, you really want their quality and volume to match when they are edited together. Otherwise there will be sudden jumps whenever the shot changes. If, for instance, you take a shot of a person walking down a hallway, using a close mike, and then a side view of the same action using a more distant mike, the difference in the sound, on cutting from one viewpoint to the other, could be quite noticeable. The overall effect would draw attention to the editing.

When you are editing together a sequence of pictures shot at different times you may find that their background sounds do not match. Supposing we stop shooting for a few minutes to reposition the camera, adjust a light or to retake the action. Background noises often change quite considerably, but we do not notice for we are busy with the job in hand. When we start again, they are now different.

So sounds that we became accustomed to while shooting the scene, such as overflying aircraft, farm equipment, hammering or typing, can have a nasty habit of instantly disappearing and reappearing when the shots are joined together.

When you are on location, it is a good habit to record some general background noise on a separate audio tape during the shooting session. It is surprising how often this unsynchronized *wild track* comes in useful during audio editing, for use as background sounds.

Even when you are shooting under what seem to be quiet conditions, there is a certain amount of background noise from air-conditioners, equipment hum, etc. A wild track of this *atmosphere* ('atmos') can be used later, to cover any moments where there is a break in the sound-track during editing.

There will be times when you decide that the sound you are getting on location is not really suitable for your particular program. It may be too noisy, too quiet, or you may find that you cannot get good sound pick-up. In these situations you may decide not to record it (to shoot 'mute'), or to replace the available sound with others you have recorded at some other time. A suitable wild track can be extremely useful here.

Perhaps, for example, you have shot scenes in a street market, and find later that instead of a general atmospheric hubbub you want to go behind (lay under) a commentary, your sound track is dominated by a few intrusive noises. You can replace the original sound with more appropriate wild track instead.

Wild track can help during those awkward moments when background sounds in successive shots do not match. It can serve as a bridge to disguise when silent and sound shots are intercut.

You might be cutting from someone speaking, to a silent shot ('mute') as they walk away. Wild track behind the entire sequence would give it continuity.

Even when the shot contains action that would seem to need synchronized sound (e.g. people walking around in the booking hall of a bus station), a wild track recording made at different time (or a different bus station!) will be quite convincing.

When we see and hear the finished results of all this trickery, the whole thing appears quite real and natural.

Getting organized

5.32 Preparations

So far we have been considering the nature of sound pick-up, and what you are aiming to do. Now we come to the very practical business of organizing exactly how you are going to tackle the job in hand. Even if your video program only involves one seated person speaking to camera, it is as well to anticipate, before you go ahead.

5.33 Working single-handed

If you are program-making single-handed, and have to operate the camera *and* arrange sound pick-up, you cannot control the sound manually. But the AGC circuits of the video recorder will prevent the soundtrack from being overloaded ('over-mod'). Where you have an audio gain control, take a sound level test beforehand, and check on the volume indicator.

Whether you are using a separate VCR or a camcorder, you can check the audio as you shoot with an earpiece plugged into a monitor-socket on the camera. (In some designs, there is a small in-built monitor loudspeaker in the side of the camera unit.)

As to the method of sound pickup you use, a lot depends on whether you are shooting continuously or discontinuously (intermittently); whether you are editing the recording or not; and whether the talent remains still or is moving around.

If you are going to break the action down into a series of separate takes, and shoot *discontinuously*, you can obviously reposition the camera and the microphone to suit each shot, editing either in camera or afterwards. When you are shooting *continuously* though, sound pickup may pose some problems – but there are several solutions.

5.34 Practical methods

A *camera mike* provides a very easy approach to sound pickup (section 5.10). But where there are strong sound reflections or background noises, you may need to get rather closer to the subject than you would have wished, in order to avoid them. Then, to prevent the shot appearing too close, you would have to widen the lens angle.

If the talent is moving about, it might be advisable to ask them not to talk while moving, particularly if they turn away from the camera while speaking, perhaps to point out something on a nearby map, for the volume and quality of the sound can fall as they get 'off mike'.

A properly positioned individual microphone will usually provide much better sound quality than a camera mike. And where you have an experienced interviewer using a hand mike well, sound pick-up clearly presents few difficulties (section 5.11). However, do not assume that you will get equally reliable results if you give a hand mike to an inexperienced person. Typically, they will feel ill at ease, and hold it incorrectly. You will usually see a similar response if you place them in front of a stand mike. Remember, standing with a hand mike, or at a stand mike, is a very artificial, 'staged' situation, and in fact, this approach will not always be the appropriate solution.

A *desk mike* is often the best form of sound pick-up where someone is seated at a table or desk (although rather less effective if they are standing). Whether you leave the mike clearly visible, or hide it behind something on the desk-top, is up to you. Be warned though, against putting the mike *inside* anything lying on the desk, for it will reduce the top (upper notes) and degrade the sound quality. If the speaker is going to turn to side, as well as face the camera, place the desk mike mid-way between the head directions, so that the sound is similar for both directions.

As we saw earlier (section 5.12), a *personal mike* is a very convenient method of picking up the sound for people who are not going to move around to any extent. It is best clipped on the clothing (tie, lapel or shirt front) whichever side the person is most likely to turn.

A cable can be a menace if he is going to do anything energetic, or move in and out of a series of obstacles, e.g. within various pieces of sculpture in an art display. A wireless mike overcomes this dilemma, but of course it is a much more costly solution.

Whereas you can place a desk mike in position beforehand, you have to wait for the speaker to arrive to fit a lavalier/tie-clip mike. People who are unused to personal mikes may feel awkward and tied down by this unfamiliar appendage.

If someone is moving around over a wide area, you will not be able to cover him effectively with one static microphone. A very directional microphone, that is carefully aimed, could be successful, but this would involve a separate operator. So for the lone program-maker, the best solution may be to use two microphones, one for each action area. These are cabled to a small belt-worn audio mixer, and you fade from one to the other as the talent moves over to the respective mike.

5.35 Variations on a theme

As you will have realized by now, we need to be *adaptable* when deciding how to tackle a particular situation. If circumstances change, our method will often change too.

Supposing for example, there are to be a series of *live* events in a large hall. If you are shooting discontinuously, you could record the first, stop the recording, then reposition the microphone and camera for the second. When you are settled, you would recommence recording. This way, you could have a clean cut between the two shots.

Alternatively, to save time, you could keep the recording running, and relocate the shot and mike on the second event, and cut out the pause during post-production editing.

You can avoid editing altogether. At the finish of the first item (in sound and picture), you could widen the shot to reveal the new action area, where the performer appears busy preparing (mute). Move the camera in to him, and when the camera and mike have arrived, he can speak on cue.

5.36 Working with assistance

The entire situation changes when you have an assistant who can concentrate on the the sound pick-up, handle various preparatory jobs, such as positioning mikes, running cables and fitting/removing personal mikes, etc.

If he is using a fishpole mike or a shotgun (rifle) mike, he can continually reposition it for the best sound quality. Because the mike is independent of the camera (although perhaps cabled to it, using its 'external mike' audio socket), it is better able to follow the talent.

5.37 Action

You need to have a reasonable idea of the action in advance, in order to decide how to arrange its sound pick-up. Clearly, if you begin to shoot a scene with your sound assistant standing to the left of the camera with a fishpole mike, and then the subject moves over to a table on camera right, it can be embarrassing to say the least. Yet such things do happen!

The sound assistant wants to know: when the talent is going to move (an action cue), where they are going to, and how quickly. If the talent is fitted with a lavalier mike, the trailing cable's route needs to be anticipated.

If the sound assistant is going to follow them with a fishpole or small boom, can it turn or reposition quickly enough, and will the mike be pointing in the right direction to pick them up in their new position?

As well as position changes, you need to be prepared for any *loud noises* that are likely to arise during the action. One of the worst dilemmas is when someone who is quietly spoken stands by a noisy machine, explaining how it is used. If you hold back the audio gain to accommodate the machine-noise, they become inaudible. A friendly word beforehand, asking them not to speak while the machine is on, may solve the problem.

Another approach would be to shoot the action, then record the voice of the demonstrator separately afterwards as he watches a picture replay. You could tape this speech on a separate audio recorder, and mix it with a lower-level version of the machine sounds to form the final soundtrack, and use 'audio-dub' to place it beside the videotape pictures.

It is very hard to avoid unexpected noises interrupting the wanted sound at some time or other, and either over-peaking and distorting, or shattering the viewer's concentration. Even apparently inoffensive actions can sound very exaggerated, when picked up on a close microphone. All you can do, is to warn people in advance if they are likely to be hammering (lower the audio gain at that point), or ask them not to clatter kitchen-ware, etc. If the result is unacceptable, you may be able to retake the shot, or even cut it out of the soundtrack, if the worst comes to the worst.

5.38 Facilities

It might be argued that the more facilities you have, the greater your opportunities to do more sophisticated things. But many a hi-fi enthusiast has sufficient equipment to produce an interesting soundtrack for a wide variety of programs. And of course, with a little ingenuity, you can devise extra, useful facilities.

The same small electret microphone may be used in various ways:

- It can be clipped onto your subject, as a personal mike.

- As a table mike, its base can be inserted into a block of foam plastic if you do not have the right support.

- Attached to a thin vertical aluminium tube (isolated via a flexible joint) with a simple bottom weight, you have an improved stand mike.

- Held in a foam-plastic collar, clamped at the end of an aluminium pole, you have a 'fishpole'. (A monopole, or even a hand-held extended car radio antenna, has been used as an emergency fishpole, to hold the mike closer to the action.)

- Fix the electret mike facing into the center of a parabolic dish, and you have a narrow-angle reflector mike.

5.39 Audio dubbing

Dubbing, or recording an existing recording (i.e. making a 'second generation'), is a regular way of creating more elaborate background sounds. Now although sound quality will deteriorate to some extent whenever you make such a copy – and will worsen further if you go on and make a copy of that copy ('third generation') – things are not as bad as one might imagine in practice. With modern audio equipment and tape, these losses need not be great, especially if increased tape noise is lost in the background effects.

So we can advantage of this fact, and by multi-dubbing, create quite complex soundtracks with modest equipment.

As you know, the soundtrack accompanying video programs, is generally *mono*. Now many audio stereo recorders have the useful facility that they can be switched from 'stereo', to record two independent tracks of 'mono' sound side by side instead. Using this facility, you can prepare a different sound effect on each track of the audio tape. When you replay the tape (in 'mono replay' mode), the two tracks will combine, in sync, and give you a composite mono soundtrack.

Some audio stereo recorders also allow you to dub from one track to another, as you play the tape and mix the sounds into a composite. You can then transfer this composite track, mixed with a further sound, back onto the first track, and so build up a detailed composite on one machine. All this takes time, but where you do not have several audio tape machines and an audio mixer, it does enable you to create very successful results nevertheless.

5.40 Anticipating sound editing

When you are shooting a scene, how can you anticipate and overcome the problems of sound editing?

- *Continuity*. Try to ensure that the quality and level of successive shots in the same scene match as far as possible.
- *Effects*. Keep a small audio recorder handy when you are shooting. It is good habit to record some general 'atmos' track, and typical background sounds (wild track) in case you need these later.
- *Sound effects*. If you have time, record any sound effects that crop up unexpectedly, that might be a useful addition to your effects library. Although you may be shooting a program on crops, any unwanted sounds of a passing fire engine, a police car, a dog barking, children playing, a shopping crowd or thunder, could all be used at the right moment in another program.
- *Question*. When you are shooting an interview, and the single camera and microphone are concentrating on the guest, the questions of the interviewer may not be audible on the videotape. So use your audio recorder to tape an interviewer's questions. These can be 'dropped into' the final soundtrack at the right moments, during the audio dubbing session.

This idea can be used too, to ensure sound continuity for *pickup shots*, where a speaker moves from one location to another during unscripted speech.

Let's take an example of this last point. A lecturer has been telling us about the birthplace of a celebrity: '. . . he lived down there, at the bottom of this hill'. The scene changes, and the camera is now relocated inside the house. But in reality it took us half an hour to move the camera to the new location, and set up the lights. What were the lecturer's last words in the previous shot? Quicker than reviewing the videotape, we have the answer immediately on the audio recorder. When we are ready, the new shot begins: 'and in the kitchen of this house . . . '. Obvious enough perhaps, but a good way of ensuring that you do not later find yourself trying to edit together scenes that have no speech continuity.

5.41 Music and effects track

When your program is to be seen by audiences who speak different languages, it is worth taking the trouble to make a special 'music and effects' (M&E) audio track. This includes all atmospheric sounds, effects and music, but no speech. Commentary or dialogue in the appropriate language can then be added to this track as required.

If the video recorder has stereo facilities, you can tape a mono version of one language plus the M&E on one audio track of the videotape, and a different language combination on its other audio track.

5.42 Filtered sound

You can make considerable changes to the quality of sound by introducing an *audio filter* into the system. It can be adjusted to increase or decrease a chosen part of the audio spectrum, to exaggerate or suppress the higher notes, bass or middle register, depending on the type of filter system you use, and how you adjust it.

The simplest 'tone control' progressively reduces higher notes during reproduction. A more flexible type of audio filter has the various names of *audio baton*, *octave filter*, *shaping filter* or *graphic equalizer*. This can boost or reduce any segment(s) of the audio spectrum by changing the positions of a series of slider pots. The outline of these sliders shows the system's effective response.

Here are typical ways in which filtering can enhance the subjective effect of the sound:

- Cutting low bass can reduce rumble or hum; improve speech clarity; lessen the boomy or hollow sound of some small rooms; weaken background noise from ventilation, passing traffic, etc. Overdone, the result sounds thin, lacking body.
- Cutting higher notes can make hiss, whistles, tape noise, sibilant speech, and other high-pitched sound less prominent. However, if you cut them too much, the sound will lack clarity and intelligibility.
- If you cut bass and top, the sound will have a much more 'open-air' quality – a useful cheat, when shooting an 'exterior' scene in a studio.
- By slightly increasing bass, you can increase the impression of size and grandeur of a large interior.
- You can improve the clarity and 'presence' of many sounds, making them appear closer, by boosting the middle part of the audio spectrum (e.g. 2–6 kHz).
- Filtering can make the quality of sound recorded in different places more similar (e.g. shots of someone inside and outside a building). It can helps to match the sound quality of different microphones.

5.43 Sound effects

What sort of sound effects you need, and in fact whether you need them at all, will depend on the kinds of programs you are making. Even the effectiveness of a volcano diagram in a geography lesson, may be enhanced when accompanied by 'subterranean rumblings'!

You can obtain or create your sound effects in various ways:

- Record the original sounds (e.g. a person's footsteps).
- Substitute identical sounds for the original ones, (e.g. sound of your own footsteps, keeping in time with their movements).
- Use a sound effect from a commercial audio effects library (available on disc, tape or CD).
- Use an imitative sound effect (e.g. musical, or computer generated).
- Process an existing sound (filtering, speed changes, reverse, etc.)

Sound samplers are increasingly used to create synthetic sound effects. The system records a brief burst of sound, and replays it at various pitches, using a 'piano keyboard'. The recorded sounds can be shaped, stretched, increased or decreased in duration, their volume and quality altered, and edited, in endless variety.

In this age of sophisticated electronics, you should not overlook some of the traditional methods of creating sound effects. Basic but effective! Here is a wide field for experiment: the sounds of pouring sand, crumpling paper, plucking a stretched rubber band, flapping an umbrella. . . Played slowly and/or backwards, filtered, they offer many surprising opportunities.

Why not try out the following?

Hollow muffled sounds. Either speak into, or use a small loudspeaker directed into, an enclosure such as a tumbler, basin, pan, tin box, plastic pipe, oven or cupboard.

Echo. Replay sounds into a tiled bathroom or empty room, re-recording them on another machine.

Fast repeat sounds; echoes. On many audio recorders, a separate replay head lets you check the track as you record. (Others only have a single dual-purpose head.) There is a brief time lag as the tape moves past the record head to the replay head. So if you mix a little of this replayed sound with the incoming sound that is being recorded (i.e. 'Replay out' to 'Record in'), you can get effects ranging from an 'echo' to a 'stutter'.

Low-pitched powerful voices. If you are using a multi-speed audio recorder (reel-to-reel), a further range of effects becomes possible through speed changes. Make an audio recording, speaking quickly, and replay the tape at a slower speed to create the voices of giants, monsters, etc.

High-pitched 'miniature' voices. Make an audio recording, speaking slowly and distinctly, and replay the tape at a faster speed to create the voices of tiny creatures, chipmunks, etc.

Threatening rumbling, thunder. Experiment with playing low-pitched taped music slowly backwards or disc slowly rotated by hand.

Low metallic gong-like sounds. Hold a suspended metal sheet, metal coat-hanger or fork against the microphone, and tap gently. (Perhaps replay the recording at a slower speed).

Chapter 6

Backgrounds

The background is much more than 'whatever happens to appear behind the subject'. It directly affects the success of your presentation, and you need to select and control it with care.

6.1 The importance of the background

Video programs are shot in an extremely wide range of locations; people's homes, offices, factories, classrooms, halls, public buildings, campus studios, out in the streets, and the wide open spaces. Where we shoot the program may be vital to what we want to tell our audience, or it can be merely incidental.

To some extent, the importance of the background, depends on you; on the way you approach your subject and the style and form you adopt. A dramatic play can be presented successfully in front of black drapes, and shooting the same play on location, or in a built setting, might add little to its emotional appeal.

Shakespeare's plays were originally performed on an open stage with no scenery. It was in the imagination of his audience. Today, broadcast documentary programs whisk a speaker around the world, one exotic background following another in rapid succession. Yet this kaleidoscope of pictures often contributes nothing to our understanding of the subject. It just gets in the way of the words! Effective backgrounds are more a matter of making wise choices, than having a big budget.

6.2 The impact of the background

Most programs are about *people* – what they are saying and what they are doing. But the *background* for the action can play an essential part in a program's appeal.

Surroundings have a considerable influence on how we feel about what we are seeing and hearing. It is not just a matter of choosing a background that looks appropriate or attractive, but determining whether its audience-impact is right for the particular points you are making in your program.

We often overlook the considerable influence the surroundings have on how we feel about what we are seeing and hearing. The background we choose for our action, and the way we shoot it, can affect how persuasively points are put to our audience. It is one thing to see a person in a street market, recommending a type of medicine, and another when we see them wearing a white coat in a laboratory. The surroundings have swayed our reactions; yet they have nothing to do with the true quality of the product.

Having gone to a particular location, your camera cannot avoid being selective. You could, for example, take it to an off-shore oil rig, but depending on which parts of the structure you shot, you would give quite different impressions of the life there. The final emphasis could be on its huge geometric structure; the isolation of this group of workers in treacherous seas; it might appear as a scene of endless noise and tense activity. In the end, it is your shot selection and editing that will build up a concept in the minds of your audience. The result may be a fair cross-section of life there, or it could be over-selective. Much depends on the point of view you adopt.

6.3 Real and unreal backgrounds

To your audience, it is quite unimportant whether the background behind the action is real or the result of ingenious trickery. It is the effect that counts. But it is worth remembering that you can derive a background in a number of ways:

- *Use of actual place.* The action is really shot in the Sahara desert.
- *Use of substitute.* Shoot the action in a convenient home location that looks sufficiently like part of the Sahara desert.
- *Use of scenery.* Build scenery in a studio, that resembles the real thing.
- *Suggested location.* The camera shows location shots of the Eiffel Tower (part of a picture postcard), intercut with shots of someone standing against a brick wall. Thanks to sound effects of traffic, etc., the viewer assumes that this is shot in Paris.
- *Electronic insertion.* It is possible with various optical and electronic devices to insert the person standing in front of the camera into a separate background picture. With care, it can be done absolutely convincingly.

6.4 The neutral background

There are times when we want the background to provide totally *neutral* surroundings for the action.

In the extreme, this background could be just a blank white (*limbo*) or black (*cameo*) area, for we are concentrating on the performers.

However, we usually want something rather more interesting to look at than a plain area of tone, and TV solved this problem by creating the *neutral setting*; a background that is visually attractive, without actually reminding us of any specific style, period or place. You will see this sort of setting in broadcast talks programs, studio interviews, discussions; or in their more jazzed-up versions, for panel games and quiz shows.

Basically, neutral backgrounds are usually made up from scenic units, positioned in front of a *cyclorama* or *cyc* (pronounced 'sike').

The cyc provides an extremely useful general-purpose background surface for studios of all sizes. Whether you are improvising in a room, in a large hall, on a stage, or in a custom-built studio, the cyclorama can be the basis of a wide range of program backgrounds from the mundane

Figure 6.1 The cyclorama

Part 1 The cyclorama serves as a general purpose detailless background.

Part 2 A ground row of cyc lights can be used to illuminate the cyclorama from below.

Figure 6.2 Paper cyc
Background paper can be hung or draped along the floor.

Figure 6.3 Open setting
A minimum amount of scenery or furniture, positioned in front of the cyc, creates a 'setting'.

to the spectacular. It can be scaled to suit your needs: anything from a few feet long to a complete wall around the staging area.

A cyc is usually made of a plain cloth, hanging from a batten, and stretched taut to form a smooth featureless surface by a further batten or pipe along its bottom edge. It may be straight or curved, vertical or slightly off-vertical. A simple horizontal board (*ground row*) will hide a row of strip-lamps to illuminate the cyc or back wall from below.

Typical materials for cycs include duck, canvas, filled gauze and sharks-tooth scrim. Ideally, the surface should appear seamless, but if necessary you can hide the seams with a decorative strip, a column or a lightweight structure of some sort. Colors range from off-white, light gray, mid-gray, black, light blue, dark blue, to chromakey blue. Of these, light to mid-gray are probably the most adaptable.

The cyc is a very versatile facility. You can adjust its overall tone by lighting, project light-patterns onto it, hang lightweight cutouts in front of it or rear-light it to produce silhouettes. It can appear as infinite space.

Try to avoid tears, blemishes, creases or dirty marks on the background, for they can be surprisingly prominent, even in longer shots. If this problem does arise, you may be able to avoid shooting that area, rearrange the cyc, or hide the offending blemish with foreground scenery.

For smaller areas, seamless paper can form an effective background, with the roll fixed to the top of the wall and the paper curving onto the floor to form a continuous plane. At a pinch, any hung cloth sheeting can serve as a background.

6.5 Economical settings

If you are working on a tight budget and with limited storage facilities, you will have little opportunity to build much scenery. But that need not be a major limitation, for it is possible to develop very attractive scenic effects, simply and economically, by using just a few multi-purpose scenic units in front of a cyclorama or a background wall.

● *Lighting* alone, can change the appearance of a background to a remarkable extent, whether it is a plain wall or a cyc. You can light it evenly, shade it (bottom-lit from a ground-row), light it in blobs or dapples, project shadows or patterns on it, or use plain or blended color areas.
● You can form an *open set* by carefully grouping a few pieces of furniture in front of the cyc. Even as little as a sofa, low table, table lamp, potted plants, a screen, chair and stand lamp, can suggest a real complete room.

For training purposes, when one is concerned not with creating a realistic effect, but with the mechanics of production, quite a lot can be done using a few folding tables and chairs and a little imagination. A couple of tables side by side form a bench. A row of chairs become a sofa.

To suggest a doorway, a pair of upright poles on a wooden base is useful (bottom-weighted with sand or stoned-filled bags). Or you can use a hinged lightweight panel on a timber frame.

● Open *support frames* are quite simple to construct from lengths of tubular or angled aluminium or timber. They can be dismantled or folded, are easily transported, and require little storage space.

● Various materials can be stretched across these support frames to make *decorative screens*, and taped, wired, clipped or stapled on. Many materials can be used, including mesh, trelliswork, scrim, netting, cord, perforated board, wall-coverings, translucent plastic sheet, etc.

Figure 6.4 Support frames
A basic metal or timber frame can be used to support decorated surfaces, patterns, cutouts, perforated screens, etc., and drapes.

- You can attach *hang-on boards* to these frames, decorated in endless different ways, with surfaces selected to suit the program. Among a wide variety of possible materials are matt-black chalk boards, flock paper, thin painted board or plastic laminate and cardboard/strawboard.

These boards can be single- or double-faced, in light, medium or dark tones. Even a small selection can be rearranged in many different ways, to form single-tone, multi-tone or graded layouts. And of course, the units themselves can be positioned singly, in groups, or side by side, to form a complete background.

- The same support frames can be used as *drape frames* to display cloth or plastic drapes, arranged in pleats, folds, swags or stretched.

- To *decorate* these units quickly and cheaply, you can stencil or color-shade them with aerosol spray paints, form lines/patterns with color tapes, or add adhesive motifs (Christmas, Halloween, and similar decorations).

- *Modular units.* If you are constructing scenery that is only to be used on one occasion, then you can use cheap flimsy materials (e.g. cardboard shapes), and improvised units (e.g. paper-covered or painted cardboard boxes). The results need not look at all primitive on camera.

But for regular scenic units that can be transported, stored, and re-used, more substantial modular types are a must. These can be used singly or together, to form interesting variations, and are mostly demountable. The main units are 'box units', 'shell units', 'frameworks' and 'scenic flats'. You will see details of these modular units in Figure 6.5.

Figure 6.5 Modular units
Open frames with clip-on surfaces can be adapted to a very wide range of purposes. They can be re-structured to form display units, benches, desks, platforms, etc.

6.6 The location as a background

Location backgrounds make action look real and genuine in a way that it is hard to imitate in any studio.

But remember, all your audience knows of the location background, is what *you* show them. It is possible to go to an exotic place, and shoot someone against a tree that looks just like one back home! If you are on location, make good use of it. Ensure that there are sufficient visual clues for people to benefit from the particular atmosphere of the place.

6.7 Keep a lookout

When you are busy shooting action, it is so easy to overlook things in the background that can become a nuisance in the final picture. On the spot, you just accept them as part of the scene. In the picture, they distract one's attention. Even major movies often have a microphone sneaking into shot at the top of the picture, or a shadow of the camera crew, or prominent lighting cables, in spite of all their vigilance.

Sometimes these odd things are puzzling or disturbing; at others they look funny – e.g. someone standing with a flagpole 'growing out of their head', or a circular ceiling light hovering like a halo. You may not be able to avoid them anyway, but they are worth looking out for. So here are some reminders of typical things that can spoil the picture.

Windows can be an embarrassment when shooting interiors. A large patch of sky in shot will push the exposure down if you are using auto-iris. Even if you expose the interior properly, this bright blank area still takes the eye.

Although you can use a corrective filter to compensate for the high color temperature of the daylight, its intensity can easily overwhelm your interior illumination and prevent you from getting a good tonal balance.

In addition to all that, if your audience has a good view of what is going on outside the window, there is always the chance that they will find this more intriguing than the real subject!

The simply remedy is to keep the window out of shot, or close the shades.

Reflecting surfaces in the background are difficult to avoid. But glass, plastic, even highly polished furniture, can be very troublesome. They can even reflect the camera and its crew. So instead of admiring the gleaming new automobile, your audience watches these interesting reflections in its door panel.

Worse still, shiny surfaces reflect lamps! If you are using a camera light, its beam will bounce straight back into the lens. When you move the camera, the blob of light will move with you, often leaving a long comet-tail trailing behind it.

Low-intensity reflections give sparkle and life to a surface. Strong light reflections are a pain, both technically and artistically. Apart from avoiding shooting straight-on to such surfaces, or keeping them out of shot, the quick solutions are to change your viewpoint, cover them up (e.g. position something or someone so that the highlight is not reflected), or angle the surface. You may be able to dull it down with a wax spray.

Any strong lights directly visible in the background, can be similarly troublesome. But unless you can control their intensities, or keep them out of shot, you will usually have to accept the results.

Flashing signs, prominent posters, direction signs and *billboards* are among the visual diversions that await the unwary cameraman. They are all part of the scene, but if you have a dramatic situation taking place anywhere near an animated advertising sign, do not be surprised if part of your audience's attention is elsewhere!

Even if you are shooting in a busy spot, it is often possible to find a quiet corner, where there are not too many interruptions. Try to avoid including a door or busy throughway in the background, or similar hurry-spots with a continually changing stream of people, for there will be constant distractions. Passers-by staring at the camera, and bystanders watching (particularly the hand-waving types!) are a regular problem, and there is little one can do, except try as far as possible to keep them out of shot.

Low camera viewpoint   Average camera height   High camera

Figure 6.6 Camera height
Low viewpoint. The camera's height affects the impression it gives. From a low viewpoint, the floor space is foreshortened; even small foreground objects appear large and may mask the shot. Space appears compressed. A lot of ceiling may be visible, or the camera may shoot over scenic backgrounds ('shoot off').
Normal viewpoint. From normal eye-height, we get a natural impression of size and distance. Small foreground items below chest height are unseen.
High viewpoint. From a higher camera position, the floor area becomes more prominent. The camera can see things on tables, etc., more clearly. It can shoot over quite large foreground items or obstructions, which are therefore not seen in the picture.

6.8 Camera height

The camera's height has a considerable effect on how much of the scene is visible in the shot. From a lower viewpoint you will see less of the middle ground, and this reduces the feeling of space and distance in the picture. Things nearer the camera become more prominent – perhaps overprominent.

When you see a very low viewpoint, even quite small foreground objects standing nearby can obscure the shot. But raise the camera just a little, and not only will it shoot over them but your audience will not even realize that they are there!

As you increase the camera's height, more of the middleground comes into view, and we get a greater impression of space and distance.

However, if you shoot a scene from a very steep angle, or use overhead shots, your audience will no longer feel that they are *within* a location, but will find themselves looking down, inspecting it instead.

6.9 Foreground pieces

You can *deliberately* arrange objects in the foreground of a picture to improve its composition, to increase the impression of distance, or simply to hide something in the scene.

You must have seen many an exterior shot with foliage hanging into the top of the frame. It is almost a visual cliché. But the cameraman has done this because the picture looks more complete, and gives a better sense of scale, than if there was just blank open sky. With this border, the picture tends to look more balanced, and no longer 'bottom-heavy'. When there does not happen to be a handy overhanging tree to shoot past, you can always hold an odd piece of tree branch above the lens so that it does the job instead! The effect is such an improvement, and your audience will never know!

Although the TV picture itself has a fixed horizontal 4 × 3 format (aspect ratio), you can use a foreground window, an arch, or a similar opening, to provide a border that alters the apparent *shape* of the picture.

By carefully framing foreground objects, you can hide all manner of things in the background that you do not want to see in the shot. They might be unattractive, or perhaps they would distract your audience. They might spoil the shot in some other way. If you are re-enacting an historical scene in a drama, it is very convenient to say the least, if a carefully positioned gatepost, bush, or even a standing person in the foreground, hides the modern signs, TV arrays, power lines, etc.

A shot through a castle gateway shows us the site of the ancient battle-field beyond. But because you have cunningly arranged for the gateway to form a border to the shot, your audience does not see the heavy trucks roaring along the major highway nearby. Instead of using the inappropriate sound from this location, you can lay down an effects wildtrack of birdsong or music, and the illusion is complete!

6.10 The location as the subject

We have talked about using location shots as the background to action. But supposing that, instead, you are making a documentary in which *the location itself* is the subject of your program?

There are interesting differences. Streets that were previously an incidental, unobtrusive backdrop, now become atmospheric opportunities to be explored with your camera. You will be drawing your audience's attention to various features: a window display, a quaint sign, the tourist sights, the people who live and work there. Your aim is to create a real living place in the minds of your audience.

You can approach this subject in a number of ways:

● You can have a guide who appears in most shots, and takes us around, explaining as we go.
● Alternatively, you can have a commentary spoken over the edited pictures, by someone who never appears.
● In place of a written commentary, you could insert the audio-taped voices of citizens and travelers you have talked to (before or after shooting).
● Lastly, you can rely on pictures and background sounds alone, to create an impression.

Each scheme has its appeal. You could combine them. The first somehow seems more personal, as someone guides us around, showing us the highlights. The audience feels involved in what is going on. We take any odd comments, observations, criticisms, as our guide's opinions; as part of his personality.

However, there are certain inherent difficulties in making the show this way. Moving about with your camera, and coping with people and traffic as you go, sound pick-up conditions may vary considerably, and it may be difficult to achieve reasonable sound continuity.

Occasionally, in particularly noisy surroundings, you may deliberately use long shots or over-shoulder shots of the guide, to avoid showing his lip movements. You record his words at a more suitable moment, and insert them during editing.

The 'commentary over' approach on the other hand, is much simpler. But there can be subtle differences. For example, a critical observation made to the camera with a grin or a shrug can appear like friendly banter, but the same remarks from an unseen commentator may seem sarcastic or fault-finding.

The method itself is very straightforward. You can shoot the pictures mute or with wild track, in any order you choose. Later you edit them together, and add commentary and effects at leisure onto the videotape soundtrack using 'audio-dub' facilities, either directly or via a prepared audio-tape.

Even for the broadcaster, it is not always practical or economic to shoot new material for every minute of every production. He regularly draws on *library shots* (*stock shots*), that have been excerpted from previous programs and retained for later re-use. You can follow this idea too, and explore still photographs or slides with your video camera when it is not practical to go out and shoot the real place, or when shooting conditions are difficult. But take care that you do not let a succession of animated still pictures degenerate into a 'moving slide show'.

6.11 Versions of 'reality'

As you will have already gathered by now, the camera does not 'tell the truth'. It *interprets*. Each aspect of the picture and the sound influences how your audience responds to what they see and hear. A slight change in the camera position can entirely alter the picture's impact. If the sun comes out, what was a drab threatening block of building can become transformed into an attractive, interesting piece of architecture. In winter, we see a dull-looking street planted with stark, lifeless skeletons of neglected trees. In spring, it becomes a charming avenue, where sidewalks are dappled with shade.

With this in mind, it is not difficult to see that you can present most places to convey the type of image *you want them to have!* Admittedly, there are places it would be difficult to make attractive. But it is possible to make a garbage heap look interesting, even beautiful, by using low shots, a diffusion disc over the lens, strong backlight, misty atmosphere, dreamy music, mysterious shadows, patches of color and interesting silhouettes against a sunset sky.

It is equally possible to make a beautiful situation look plain and tawdry, just by the way you shoot it, the way you edit the shots, and the sound accompanying them (hard top lighting, high-angle shots, sharp shadows cutting across attractive surfaces, no fill-light, crude mixtures of colored light, emphasize the ugly and the decaying, avoid the elegant).

You can shoot a location so that your audience envies its inhabitants, or pities them for having to live there. It can appear a fine place, or an eyesore. It's all a matter of what you choose to include, and what you omit; what you emphasize, and what you suppress.

Sound-effects and music can alter the feeling you convey. Use loud, harsh, discordant sounds, and you can build up an impression of noise, aggravation, confusion and antagonism. Fast sounds suggest hurry and bustle. On the other hand you can use quiet sounds, soothing, happy, pastoral, associated with good things, and the overall effect is peaceful and contented. You can accompany a picture of children playing with joyous laughter, or angry screams and shouts, and suggest quite different things.

As the camera moves around, it can dwell on busy purposeful bustle, as people go to work, or it can linger on those who appear to be lounging around with nothing to do. (In reality, they might be waiting for a bus, but at the moment the camera captures them, they are 'aimlessly inactive'!)

You can suggest spaciousness by shooting with a wide-angle lens. Use a narrow-angle lens instead, and the same streets can look congested.

Under dull overcast skies and rain, a location can look a drab, miserable, unwelcoming place. Harsh, overhead sunlight with sharply cut shadows can produce a crude, hard appearance.

In most cities, one can find litter, decay, graffiti; but conversely, there will be signs of prosperity, attractive buildings, green spaces, fountains, wildlife, things that are amusing, others that are touching. How you select and relate the kaleidoscope of potential images will influence how your audience interprets the scene.

6.12 What can we do about the background?

If you are shooting in a studio, and the background is unsatisfactory for any reason, you can usually improve it in some way or other. But what can you do on location, if the background proves to be troublesome or unsuitable?

If you are a guest in someone's home, the answer may be disappointingly little. So much depends on the people involved, and on your own diplomacy. If they are not accustomed on appearing on camera, they will probably be disturbed if you suggest altering things around to any extent. They may even feel uncomfortable if they are not sitting in their customary chair. There is little point in doing things that will jeopardize the interview you are there for. But there are various little things you can do unobtrusively to improve matters:

- If you can use natural lighting, rather than introduce lamps, the person you are talking to will probably feel more at ease. But additional lighting cannot be avoided in most interiors if you are to get good pictures.

- Although you cannot change tones in the surroundings, you may be able to shade your lamps off a light-toned surface to prevent them appearing too bright (using a barndoor, flag, or partial diffuser). And you may also add a little illumination in dark corners.

- If there are reflections in a glass-fronted picture, and you cannot move your lamp or the camera to avoid them, slightly angling the picture may cure the dilemma. A wall picture or mirror can often be tilted up or down a bit by wedging a bunched-up tissue behind it. To avoid seeing the camera in a glass-fronted bookcase behind a speaker, you might slightly open its doors.

- Closing, or partly closing, the room drapes may help to adjust the lighting balance in a room.

- If you have to shoot a corridor or hallway, it can help if doors in a side wall are opened enough to let extra light in.

- Even if you are shooting in daylight, it may provide more interesting pictures if you have table-lamps or other room-light fittings on.

- You may be able to conceal low-powered lamps behind furniture or wall angles, to illuminate distant parts of the room; but take great care that they do not overlight, or even burn-up nearby surfaces.

6.13 Rearranging the background

If you are commissioned to make a program, it is much more likely that you will be able to alter the background to achieve the best effect. Again, this has to be done diplomatically, but if you gain the confidence of the people involved, and seem to know what you are doing, there should be no difficulties.

The simplest changes just involve moving around what is there already, to avoid any unnecessary distractions or unwanted effects in the picture.

Make it a regular routine to check that nothing is going to appear to be growing from the top of the speaker's head, or balancing on it, and that no vertical or horizontal lines cut through the center of the head or across the shoulders. These visual accidents can make the picture look contrived or comic.

Look out for reflection, ugly shadows, items that catch the eye (especially brightly colored objects that will be defocused in the shot) and anything that gets in the way of the shot such as a lamp or a vase of flowers on a desk. If there are books, posters, etc., in the back of the shot that might attract attention away from your subject, perhaps you can move or cover them to improve the picture. Otherwise you may be able to restrict the depth of field (larger lens aperture) to defocus them a little.

If you are shooting someone in an office, who is seated in front of a bright window, you may get better results if the window-blind is partially or completely lowered, or the drapes closed. Very occasionally, you could try moving the desk to the corner of the room or another wall, where the lighting is better, or there are no background problems.

6.14 Altering the background

You may want to improve the appearance of a room you are using, to make it look more attractive on camera.

A certain amount of tidying-up and neatening is helpful, to prevent a place from looking too muddled and disorganized. But do not get to the point where everything looks over-tidy and unlived-in. Neat precisely positioned papers and magazines, decorative ornaments placed exactly in the middle of shelves, can ring a false note.

'Improvements' can easily get out of hand, as too many photographs of 'designed interiors' for houses, show! You find that all manner of bric-a-brac has been 'artistically positioned' in the kitchen, to produce an effect that no self-respecting cook would tolerate for a moment in their workplace! The result is pretentious and artificial.

But it is possible to enhance the feel of a room considerably, by making a few modest changes; adding a group of flowers here, an extra chair there, replacing a wall-picture perhaps. If you are not careful though, the place could become 'different' rather than 'better'.

If you really need to change the appearance of an interior considerably, to make it look like *somewhere else* (for a dramatic production perhaps), there are a number of quick, cheap and simple things you can do – successfully enough at least, to fool the camera:

- Rearrange furniture positions.
- Replace furniture with other pieces from nearby rooms, or lightweight portable units you have installed.
- Add or remove rugs.
- Hide a doorway with a folding screen, a vertical notice-board, or a drape on a frame.
- Tape lightweight drapes over the window or room features (niches, recesses, existing notice boards).
- Attach display posters to the walls.

- Insert a panel of heavy cardboard or laminate into a window opening, to provide a 'notice-board' or a dummy bookcase.
- Rows of dummy books come in forms ranging from printed card sheets, to actual book-backs attached to plywood. These can be used to provide an 'instant library'.
- Position indoor plants (e.g. ferns) to break up the background.
- Introduce notices and signs on walls, doors, etc.
- Add portable light-fittings (table lamps, stand lamps) – either 'non-practical' (not working), or 'fully practical' (working, and switched on).
- Add a dummy 'doorway' made from timber-finished laminate sheet, with a plastic-strip surround, attached to the wall with double-sided adhesive tape.
- A dummy window made of drapes on a frame, can be held against a wall behind an existing low bookcase.
- A wall-clock can be imitated by a clock dial (painted or attached hands) stuck to the wall with double-sided tape or plastic putty.

To be even more ambitious, it is possible to get extremely realistic, three-dimensional moldings in the form of thin plastic PVC shells, that you can paint and attach to suit your needs. Low cost, featherweight and re-usable, they range from decorative pieces (e.g. shields), display panels (shields, guns, pistols, fish, wood carving), armor, wooden paneling, to stonework, brickwork, tiling, beams, rock-face, etc.

If you are shooting out in the open, there are relatively few things you can do cheaply and easily to change the background. It is possible of course, to carry around your own area of brickwork or stonework (plastic shell) to put in the foreground to hide unwanted bits of the background, or to introduce the odd foreground bush or branch. You might position a car, so that it hides an inappropriate building in the distance. But anything more than adding the odd sign to sticking a new shop name over an existing one, or scattering peat or sand over the road to cover markings, is usually out of the question for small-unit video on a tight budget.

6.15 Auxiliary backgrounds

Sometimes you will want to make changes to improve the *clarity* of the picture.

An arrangement within an exhibition or a museum, that looks excellent if you were walking around, seeing it from all angles, can look cluttered and confused in the camera's two-dimensional picture. Careful lighting can help, but it is seldom the complete answer.

If the subject you want to demonstrate or display is surrounded by a number of others (e.g. one bowl within a group), it will help your audience to concentrate on that particular piece if you are able to isolate it in some way.

Can you get a close-enough shot of the subject to exclude the rest? Would you be allowed to move the subject, and display it separately? Would it help if you restricted the depth of field, to defocus the other subjects into a blur?

The best remedy may be to introduce your own carefully positioned background. If for instance, you are shooting items that are inside a glass-sided showcase in a display area, you might attach a neutral-toned backing to the far side of the case to hide other items nearby. Similarly, by placing a board behind a group of flowers, you can isolate them from others in the vicinity.

You can often place portable lightweight screens round larger subjects, to block off their surroundings. Naturally, the number you need will depend on the area you are shooting and the camera position. Close shots only require a small backing.

If you are shooting at an angle to your background (e.g. at greater than about 50°), you are liable to shoot past its end, and see whatever lies beyond ('overshoot', 'shoot-off'). Rather than extend the background, it is better to curve it round or place 'wings' at its end.

It may not matter if you do overshoot, particularly if the rest of the surroundings are in darkness, or lit to a much lower intensity, but it is as well to check.

Sometimes, when you are shooting at night, you can avoid the need for extra backings, by lighting just the localized action area and letting everything else merge into darkness. In a factory, warehouse or similar large enclosure, this avoids the audience seeing empty areas in the back of the shot. The overall result may not be as bright and interesting as you can get by using light-toned screens, but it can take less time and trouble.

6.16 Partial settings

This is a strategy for convincing your audience that a very modest setting is not only the real thing, but is much more extensive than it actually is. Yet the cost and effort involved are minimal.

If your camera does not move, it can only see a limited amount of the scene in a mid-shot or a close-shot. So with partial settings, you concentrate on building up a section of the scene, just big enough to suit the camera's shot, and no more. Within the scene, you include enough features to allow your audience to interpret where the action is supposed to be taking place.

Do not underrate this idea. It has been used successfully in film and TV for many years. The result need not be at all crude or amateurish, for if you are only showing a scene width of around 9 ft (3 m), just a few items will quickly furnish the shot. Add a garnish of associated sound effects, and the combined image can be indistinguishable from the real thing.

Figure 6.7 Partial settings
A few items can suggest a complete setting if the shot is fairly restricted.

6.17 Typical examples

You can create an 'instant store' by putting the appropriate sort of merchandise on a foreground table (the 'counter'), an advertisement or two on the back wall, and a shelf behind the salesperson, holding some more products.

Sometimes even a single feature in the picture can suggest an environment. A stained-glass window and organ music become a church interior. (The window could be a projected slide.)

You can form a convincing 'room' in a studio, with just a couple of flats or screens and a chair. Add an extra item or two, such as a side-table with a potted plant, a picture perhaps, and it begins to take on a particular character. If you hang a drape over part of the wall, one assumes a window there. Whether it is interpreted as being someone's home, or a waiting room for instance, largely depends on the way people in the scene behave. Lying back casually dressed, reading a paper, it is obviously their home. In outdoor attire, sitting upright and anxious, they are waiting.

Replace the plant with a typewriter, and the picture with a framed certificate, and magically, the setting has become an office.

You can ring the changes as simply as this in a real room of course, and make striking alterations at little cost, provided you keep your shot reasonably localized, using only a corner of the room or part of one wall.

Out on location, the same idea is still useful, i.e. restrict your shot, and 'doctor' the background. Suppose you are shooting a scene in a 19th century drama, where somebody visits their lawyer. You have found a house exterior of about the right period, but the rest of the street is so obviously a busy modern thoroughfare. Fortunately, all you need is a shot of the house doorway with a suitable name-plate alongside, and the picture explains itself to your audience. So you attach a name-plate to the wall for a few minutes, have the actor go up to the door, or pretend to leave the house, and your audience immediately accepts the location as the lawyer's office. It only needs the sounds of horse-drawn vehicles to replace modern traffic noise, and the period illusion is complete.

With a little care and imagination, you can create the impression of a particular location from a minimum amount of scenery. Paint a surface dull black, give it a pattern of rivets and a little rust-staining, set down a large coil of rope, and reflect light from a trayful of water, and you have a quayside scene that can be intercut with location shots. Add sounds of water lapping, sea birds, hooting tugs, and the effect can be really authentic.

If a scene is brief and the action limited (especially if it is a night shot), you can often get away with remarkably little scenery. Against a black background, even a few tree branches can convince your audience that they are seeing a wood. A person backed by black, lit by localized light, can appear on screen to be under a street lamp in a sleazy alley. Leaning on a horizontal pole against a light-toned background, someone is at the rail of a ship, if you build up the right expectancy in your audience and include appropriate sound effects.

It is incredible how seemingly trivial tricks can give a totally convincing effect on camera:

- The camera rhythmically tilting up and down that sells the illusion of *a ship at sea*.
- The *wafting breeze*, that is really the result of an assistant waving a piece of board.

- The shuddering camera accompanied by things falling to the ground (pulled by unseen fishline), that implies an *explosion* or an *earthquake*. A hanging lamp swings alarmingly – tugged by an out-of-shot cord.
- The flickering flames of a nearby *fire* – that comes from a stick of rag-strips waved in front of a ground lamp.

These are just a few examples of how little ingenuity can apparently achieve the impossible, and create a strong impression in your audience's minds.

6.18 Creating depth

To get even more from your limited background, you can include foreground masking pieces (see section 6.9). If you shoot through a foreground bookshelf (a few books on a propped up board) to see just beyond, a table with piles of books and distant shelves of books (strips of printed book-backs attached to the wall), the result is a plausible bookshop. Keep the lighting shadowy and confined, to suggest an interior.

You can create an impressive sense of distance by using a series of planes between the camera and the background. If you can position larger items in the foreground, and small pieces in the distance (small pictures on the walls, small vases of flowers), the illusion is enhanced, particularly if you shoot the scene on a wide-angle lens.

6.19 Permanent sets

Many small studios use a combination of *temporary settings*, that are designed and erected for a specific production, and *permanent settings* that remain in the studio for a long period.

A 'permanent' set has the advantage that it can be:

- erected (assembled; fixed together and firmly supported),
- dressed (various properties and furnishings added),
- lit (lamps arranged and adjusted),

and then left in position, while manpower and resources are concentrated on other jobs.

When a studio is regularly staging a certain type of program, it may have a permanent setting installed, such as a kitchen, a laboratory, an office, a lounge or a news-desk layout, designed to suit these productions.

Another approach is the adjustable permanent set, which can be revamped to suit a wide range of productions: demonstrations, interviews, lecture, talks, documentary and travel programs, etc.

6.20 Adjustable permanent setting

The features of this type of setting can be altered in an unlimited number of ways:

1. Panels can be added and removed as necessary (hooked on, or slid along grooves). Double-sided, to give greater variety, they can have a range of tones, shades, textures, shapes, with different surface patterns, added contours, etc.

Sections can be prepared for use as chalk-boards, magnetic graphics (magnetic plastic sheet motifs, adhering to a steel surface) or as chroma-key screens (see section 12.13).

2. Wherever these panels are removed, the camera can see a set of permanently fixed screens, made of translucent frosted plastic sheet. You can use these screens decoratively in endless permutations.

Lit from below at the rear, by trough/strip-light/cyc lights, you have a shaded background. Use a sequence of red, green, blue filters on these lights (and separate dimmers for each color), and you can blend them to provide a very wide mixture of hues.

Add a corresponding series of overhead light-battens, and you can illuminate the screens evenly overall. Switch in only the blue circuits, and you instantly have a useful chroma-key surface.

Suspend perforated, openwork or cutout panels in front of, or behind, the lit screens, and you have silhouetted shapes.

You can also use the screens to display rear-projected patterns. These are produced quite simply, by placing a piece of stenciled foil sheet a short distance in front of a ground spotlight, or by bouncing light off crumpled kitchen foil. Projector lanterns can be used, but require a greater distance ('throw') behind the screens, to project large-area patterns.

Also, of course, you can rear-project slides onto the screens, to provide pictures illustrating a program or to produce patterns. If the images from several projectors are combined to form a multivision/multiscreen presentation, with a series of adjacent displays, very large effects become possible.

3. Drapes (reversible) can be suspended at the front of the structure, and used fully stretched or pleated, in sections or overall.

4. Pull-down blinds can also be fitted to the structure to display program logos, station identification and similar material. A blue pull-down blind provides you with a local chroma-key display screen when it is needed.

6.21 Facing reality

As you will have found by now, it is one thing to have armchair dreams about a program, and quite another to turn them into reality. Among the problems facing all program-makers are the inevitable limitations of budget and facilities. Some of the things you need, may not even be available.

When faced with such problems, it is tempting to think small; to cut back on ambition, and do a simpler version. *Don't!* Do not immediately abandon your ideas. Instead, ask yourself if there is another way of tackling the situation to get virtually the same effect. How can you get round the difficulty?

What you are looking for are *imaginative substitutes*. You are producing *illusions*. However basic the materials really are, there need be nothing crude or trashy about the results in the finished program. There they can appear to be the real thing.

As an introductory example of this way of thinking, let's look at an actual setting that was used convincingly on air. The scene was the banqueting hall of an ancient castle. The king sat on a throne at one end of a long table, eating from golden dishes. That was the illusion.

What of reality? Two small foreground flags on wooden floor stands masked the edges of the shot, so we could not see the rest of the small studio. The 'wooden table' was of painted boards on trestles. The far 'stone wall' was of photographic wallpaper on a flat (black-sprayed slightly to 'age' it). The 'throne' was an old wooden armchair, with a red damask drape thrown over it. The 'gold dishes' were sprayed plastic plates. A 'lancet window' was painted, black on white, and stuck to the 'stone wall'. But nobody could recognize all this in the long shot they saw! Of course the scene would not have stood close shots, but under patchy lighting, we saw it as it was intended to be – the banqueting hall of an ancient castle!

One last word before we explore. Some of these ideas may seem basic, even crude – but they work. Try them for yourself! Often, the only alternative would involve more complicated methods, or expensive equipment. You may never need these particular effects, but they should encourage you to find ways round the 'impossible'. Remember, *it is the result that counts!*

Economic scenic materials:

A spray coating of color can transform the appearance of rope, plastic netting or plastic sheeting for decorative effect.

Paint sprayed through stencils cut in kitchen foil or perforated board, can decorate surfaces quickly and regularly. Similarly, you can hold suitable objects against a background, and spray silhouette outlines (leaves or tools).

Full-size photographic prints stuck to card can produce scenic miracles! In a front-on view, the camera cannot see that they are actually flat, so you can provide a wide range of articles to dress a room, either stuck-on to backgrounds or as free-standing cut-outs. In some cases, even a photo-copied version will suffice. Typical items include: calender, certificates, wall-plate, clock, ornaments on walls and shelves, tools, machinery, equipment, plants, mirrors, book backs on a library shelf, paintings (use standard color reproductions in a photographed 'gold-frame'), view from window (a mosaic of several prints as 'panes of glass' build up the overall view), etc.

6.22 Titling

Your audience's first impressions of your show come from its opening titles! These don't have to be elaborate – even a chalked sign may be just the thing to arrest their interest. But they do need to be brief, clear, and appropriate in style. You can use rub-on letters, titling kits, scrabble, even a finger trace in the sand. Each can be effective when applied imaginatively.

Titling has various purposes:

Opening titles announce the show.
Sub-titles identify people and places.
Credits recognize those appearing in, and contributing to the program.
End titles draw the program to its conclusion.

Titling helps throughout the show: to announce the place or time, *to identify* a plant, *to display* data, *to clarify* how a term is spelt, etc.

Character generators (CG) are a regular graphics tool in video/TV production. Instead of having the camera shoot *title cards*, letters are typed on the character generator's computer-type keyboard can be electronically inserted, direct into the video picture. You can change the shape, size, color and design of the lettering, perhaps making it flash, flip, crawl (sideways), roll (vertically), animate etc. Lettering can be presented as outlines or as solid characters, given a black border (black edge), or a drop shadow around it. Having typed out your titling, you can arrange and store it, ready to be presented on cue at the press of a button.

For many video program makers, the *personal computer* (*PC*) undoubtedly offers the greatest opportunities for titling. It can be used as a character generator as well as for many video effects. Suitable software can provide a wide range of fonts and backgrounds; even allowing quite elaborate treatments to be animated or processed in various ways.

Titling hints

- Always arrange your layout in a 4 × 3 proportions.

- Keep titling well away from the edge of the frame, to avoid edge cut-off.

- Simple, bold typefaces are best. Avoid thin-lined, elaborate lettering.

- Lettering smaller than about 1/10 screen height can be hard to read.

- Don't fill the screen with too much information at a time. It is often better to use a series of brief frames, or to use a *crawl*. (Continuous information moving vertically into the frame, and passing out at the top.)

- Leave a space between title lines of around 1/2 to 2/3 the height of capital letters.

- When smaller lettering is given a black-edged outline, it may become hard to read. The holes in "Bs", "Os", "As", "Rs", fill in.

- Lettering should generally contrast strongly with its background. (Usually much lighter).

- Strongly saturated colors can be distracting, dazzling or cause unattractive effects, particularly against contrasting color backgrounds. (e.g. strong red lettering appears fuzzy.)

- Check the lettering does not merge with any pictorial background. Outlining often makes lettering easier to read.

- Check whether the titling is clearly readable in a monochrome picture. Different colors can reproduce the same shade of gray!

- If you set up titling or graphics in front of a camera (e.g. title cards), make sure that lettering appears level and centered!

Chapter 7

The basics of videotape recording

An outline of the principles

7.1 Various designs

Although videotape recorders use very sophisticated technology, they are designed for simple straightforward operation; as home videotape recorders demonstrate daily.

There are now around 15 different incompatible videotape recording formats. They are all methods of recording picture (video) and sound (audio) simultaneously on magnetic tape. Video recording equipment ranges from broadcast quality formats to compact lightweight systems suitable for general use. Thanks to ingenious technical developments, even low-cost video equipment is capable of remarkably high picture and sound quality.

7.2 Incompatibility

Although you do need to worry about design specifics, it is as well to realize that there are important differences between formats. Tapes can only be recorded and reproduced on identical equipment standards.

Design features can vary considerably between video recorders. For instance, most record a composite video signal which incorporates both color and luminance (brightness) information. In professional camcorders, the component colors are recorded separately from the black-and-white signal.

There can be further complication. For example:

- While a *S-VHS* machine will record/reproduce either a *S-VHS* or a *VHS* tape, a *S-VHS* tape will only replay on a *S-VHS* machine.
- A VHS-C cassette (which is a compact version of the normal VHS tape housing) needs an adapter to allow it to play on a standard VHS machine.
- There are variations in recording tape speeds. If you have for example, recorded a VHS tape at half speed, the replay VCR will need an identical speed selection.
- Some designs of video recorder provide only a medium quality mono sound, while others include very high-quality stereo audio.

Table 7.1 Summarizing current videotape recording formats

The 8 mm series
- *Video 8*. The smallest, most compact systems, using 8 mm wide videotape. Results are comparable with VHS. Tapes are replayed either direct from the camera to the TV set/monitor, or with a separate 8 mm playback unit.
- *HI-8*. An enhanced 8 mm development using metal tape, resolving about 430 vertical lines.

The VHS series
- *VHS*. The commonest consumer (domestic) format, using ½ in. wide tape. Also available in compact form (VHS-C). Resolution is around 250 vertical lines.
- *S-VHS (Super VHS)*. A development of the VHS system, providing superior sound and picture, using high grade tape. Also available in compact form (Super VHS-C). Resolution is over 400 vertical lines.

The U-matic series
- *Standard or low band U-matic*. This ¾ in. format was originally intended for non-broadcast industrial and closed-circuit applications, and is still widely used. It can resolve around 240 vertical lines (similar to the VHS system).
- *High band U-matic*. An upgraded improved high-band (BVU) version, used for mobile/news-gathering video work. Not compatible with low band U-matic.
- A *high band SP* (*Superior Performance*) version using a different type of cassette with improved tape, has a resolution of around 330 lines. A system widely used for news gathering and location work, as well as in-house corporate production units.

The Beta series
- From the original *Betamax* domestic VCR design, a series of VCRs were developed, including *Beta-SP, Beta-ED* (*Extended deinition*), *Beta Hi-Fi* and *Super Beta*.

Professional videotape systems

In addition to the above, professional formats include:

- Betacam, Hawkeye, Recam, Quartercam, M-II, DX systems, which are ½, and ¼ in. systems, based on superior high speed versions of the Betamax and VHS methods.
- 1 in. Type 'B' and 'C' standards.
- Digital VTR systems (D.1., D.2., D.3.).

Although there are so many video recorder formats, in practice, most of us use only one system, and few problems arise.

7.3 Recording principles

Virtually all videotape recorders use a similar basic method of recording – a 'helical scanning' system. Fundamentally, it works this way:

- The *recording tape* itself, is a thin plastic ribbon (8 mm, ¼ in. ½ in. ¾ in. wide) coated with a layer of tiny magnetic particles. Because these are dispersed at random, the tape is magnetically neutral at that stage.
- The *video recording head* behaves as an electromagnet. Fluctuating currents corresponding to the video, pass through the coil in the head, and produce a varying magnetic field.
- As the tape passes a fine slit in the recording head, it becomes magnetized according to the strength of the video signal at each instant.
- The result is a tape with a continuous magnetic pattern corresponding to the original signal fluctuations.

- When you reproduce the magnetized tape, it passes a *replay head*. The varying magnetic strengths of the recorded track induce tiny currents in the replay head, which are recovered as a video signal.
- Because we are recording such rapid fluctuations (high frequencies), the tape needs to move at a fast rate, to accommodate the fine magnetic pattern. (Otherwise the magnetic changes would be too cramped together and lost.)
- We could run the tape through the system at a very high speed, in order to spread out the pattern (e.g. 200 in. per second). But then a tape spool of a reasonable size would only last a few minutes.
- Instead, the VCR designer uses a trick, and spins the video head(s) themselves against the slow moving tape. Their combined speeds creates a fast *effective* recording rate, allowing high quality video to be recorded.
- This technique is known as helical scanning.

7.4 Helical scanning

This is a simple yet ingenious idea. The magnetic tape is pulled through the video recorder at a constant speed. In its path is a spinning drum, and the tape presses against this at an oblique angle. Just protruding from the surface of this drum, are tiny video recording heads. These scan across the tape, recording a regular series of long parallel slanting tracks.

When you 'pause' the VCR, to hold a *freeze frame*, the tape stops moving, but the tape drum continues spinning, continually re-scanning the same track.

Figure 7.1 Typical helical scanning system
As the videotape passes a full-width erase head, it is magnetically neutralized (wiped).
The tape then wraps round a drum in a slanting path. Record/replay heads fitted to the drum assembly, press against the tape at an acute angle as it slides past.
The tape then passes over a unit containing heads which record/replay an *audio* edge-track, and also *control track pulses* (to stabilize tape speed).

Figure 7.2 Typical helical scan tape tracks
Various systems have different track layouts. This U-Matic format shows the video tracks, with a control track at its top edge, and two audio edge tracks along the lower edge.
Running parallel with them is a time-code track (address track).

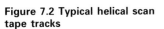

7.5 Cue pulses

Running along one edge of the tape, is the all-important *control track*. This is recorded during taping, and provides regular reference *cue pulses* (rather like a clock ticking), which accurately synchronize the tape movement and the scanning rate. On replay, these pulses ensure that the video heads re-scan the recorded tracks accurately, and so ensure color fidelity.

If you record a sequence on videotape, then stop, the control pulses cease at that point on the tape. When you next start to record, the pulses begin again. So at the moment on the tape where you stopped and re-started recording, the control-track pulses have been interrupted. When you replay the tape, this means that the synchronizing system is upset at that point, producing an unacceptable 'dirty cut' between shots.

Some videorecorders overcome this embarrassing situation by *back-spacing* a few seconds, every time you start to play or record. But as you will see, this can prove a hazard to beware of when *assemble editing*. You can accidentally lose the end of the previous scene! So check out how your particular equipment behaves.

7.6 Tape formats

You will find videotape used in three formats:

● In the familiar *VCR* (*video cassette recorder*), all the videotape is wound onto two spools (supply and take-up), totally enclosed within a plastic *cassette*. The equipment automatically self-laces the tape through the system, so you do not need to handle it in any way.
● For short duration sequences – e.g. commercials or news inserts – tape is often housed in a *cart* (*cartridge*). This is a plastic container with an endless loop of tape wound onto a single reel. Broadcast organizations use carts stacked in *carousels*, which allow items to be played automatically in a prearranged sequence.
● In an *open reel/reel-to-reel VTR* (*videotape recorder*), the tape is stored on a single reel. It is laced through the recorder by hand, and wound onto an empty spool. You have to be careful not to damage or contaminate the tape, or it will spoil the recording.

7.7 Audio on videotape

Audio is recorded on videotape in two ways:

● On a narrow track along the edge of the tape (*linear track*) as in the VHS and U-Matic systems. Sound quality is satisfactory for most purposes.
● By a special 'two-layer' method ('depth multiplex'), in which the picture (video) is recorded *over* the FM stereo sound signals, on the *same tape track* (using different head azimuths). This hi-fi technique is used in certain high-quality VCR audio systems, including Video 8, S-VHS, and Hi-Fi VHS.

Some VCRs have considerable audio flexibility. On S-VHS and Hi-Fi VHS systems you can make stereo audio recordings on both the linear and the multiplex soundtracks at the same time. It is even possible to record *different* audio on these two sets of soundtracks simultaneously. In Hi-8 systems, audio is recorded on a multiplex audio track only.

Although multiplexed audio has great advantages, for it provides near-CD quality sounds, it does have drawbacks when editing. Because it is inextricably tied in with the video track, you cannot 'lift off' and 're-play' ('lay back') the sound, as you can with the standard edge-track.

Where there are two sets of audio edge-tracks, one is often used as a *cue track*, to record a *timecode* signal.

7.8 Standards conversion

If you have a tape recorded in another country, there are problems you should know about. A VCR designed for e.g. the NTSC system, will only record and replay with that standard. It cannot replay a tape recorded on a different transmission system (e.g. PAL); even where both video recorders have the same format e.g. VHS. There is equipment that *can* reproduce different standards (perhaps in monochrome only), but it may require a multi-standard TV receiver/monitor to display the picture.

Table 7.2 Videotaping hints

Before loading a cassette:	• Check that its safety/protection tag has not been removed. If it has, cover the hole with adhesive tape. (On U-Matic, replace red protective button.) Otherwise you will not be able to record on the tape.
	• Check its label.
	• Check that the tape is *clean* (i.e. free to be used). If there is a previous program on the tape (now unwanted, and to be erased) note the fact. (It may save confusion during editing.)
	• Check that the tape is not slack; especially if it has been stopped/started and re-run several times. Perhaps the takeup spool needs turning clockwise slightly to improve tape tension; but do not over-tighten.
	• Check *humidity* (*dew*) warning indicator.
While recording	• Record at standard speed rather than half speed whenever possible. (Easier editing, and better sound quality.)
	• Keep a lookout for elapsed time, the amount of tape left, the state of the battery.
After recording	• Reset the tape counter whenever you change the tape.
	• Review the end of the take, to check that the recording is satisfactory – i.e. no head-clog.
	• If necessary, remind yourself of the end of the shot just recorded, in order to ensure good continuity and shot matching with the next take.
	• Consider whether you want to record further material on the tape now loaded. During editing, a great deal of time can be lost, shuttling to and fro, picking out required takes from a long tape.
	• When you take out the cassette, remove the protection tag (or pop out protect button).
	• Keep a log of all shots, with details of action, and indicator readings (or time code). If the take is faulty, note what is wrong.
	• After extensive recording, use a wet tape-head cleaner cassette. Some VCRs have a built-in head cleaner, but it pays to clean the entire tape path.

Chapter 8

Editing

Through editing, the material that you have shot is blended together to form a convincing, persuasive presentation.

8.1 The need to edit

The simplest method of shooting a scene is to use one video camera, and to record the action continuously from start to finish. These are occasions when you can do exactly this, and produce a satisfactory result. You do not *have* to edit the tape. It can be replayed straight away.

But even if you do zoom in and out at times to vary the shot, a long 'take' of this kind can become tedious to watch, particularly if it is from one viewpoint. Of course, if you are shooting a particularly fascinating subject, or the action is very exciting, you may get away with it; but don't rely on that! There will invariably be dull periods, and the lack of visual variety soon palls.

To hold the attention on the small screen, and build enthusiastic interest, we usually need to change the shot size, the viewpoint, and even the locale, quite frequently.

If you were shooting an event such as a marathon race, you would not expect to record every minute of the occasion. It would be impossible for the camera to be everywhere, seeing everything. Instead you select the highlights, such as preparations for the race, the start, difficult moments, the winning tape, talking to the contestants, etc. In other words, you excerpt from the action, and join the sections together to form a continuous presentation (continuity editing).

You shoot events in the order that is most convenient or practicable, then join these takes together so that they appear consecutive. The eventual 'running order' may be very different from the order in which you shot them (the 'shooting order').

- Sometimes you will shoot action through from start to finish – e.g. watching someone blowing a glass vase.
- You may deliberately shoot only sections of the total action, omitting unwanted action.

- You may have the action repeated, so that you can shoot it from various positions.
- You may shoot all the action at one location before going on to the next, although the story line may intercut between them.
- You may shoot a series of *similar* subjects which have reached different stages – e.g. shots of various new-born foals, yearlings, colts, ageing horses edited together to imply the life-cycle of a *particular* horse.

As we shall see, for most productions, editing has a much more subtle role to play than a simple 'jointing process'. The way in which a program is edited will have a considerable influence on your audience's reactions to what they see and hear.

8.2 Editing opportunities

You can edit a video program in one of two ways. You can edit it as you shoot ('edit in camera'), taking care to record each shot in order, until you have built up your complete program. The result could be a finished tape.

Alternatively you can take as many shots as you wish, in any order, and sort them out later at an editing session, where the selected takes are re-recorded onto a new master tape. We'll talk about these techniques in more detail later.

The kind of editing you do will depend very much on your facilities. So the first thing you need to know at this stage is:

- How do you make edits, with the particular equipment available to you? Some systems are simple to operate, but limited in what they can do. Other facilities are elaborate, but extremely flexible.
- Can you only make cuts between the shots you join together, or can you introduce mixes/dissolves, wipes, and other transitions?

If you know what opportunities you have, you can shoot the program accordingly.

On the other hand, it would be very unwise to record a series of shots in a random order, errors and all, assuming that you can sort this out during editing, only to find that this is the version you are stuck with! Yet this could be the situation if you are 'editing in camera'.

8.3 The principles of editing

When you are editing a program, you have two major considerations.

On the one hand, you are concerned with organizing the material you have shot, into a coherent, flowing development. These are the *mechanics* of editing.

On the other hand, every choice you make, must directly affect how your audience responds to what they are seeing. You are influencing their interpretations, as you select and interrelate pictures. There are the *aesthetics* of editing.

8.4 Organization

Editing provides you with ways of correcting and improving the finished product:

- You can remove or shorten sequences that are uninteresting, irrelevant or repetitious.
- You can correct errors, by omitting faulty sections, and inserting 'retakes'.

- You can extract just the sections you need for your program.
- You can adjust the overall duration.

There is nothing inherently dishonest or deceitful about such editing, provided you do not distort or falsify the spirit of the occasion.

8.5 Editing begins

Editing begins with sorting through the available material, and:

1. Selecting the required shots.
2. Deciding on the order and duration of each shot.
3. Deciding on the cutting point (when one shot is to end, and the next to begin).
4. Deciding on the type of transition between shots.
5. Creating good continuity.

Let's look at these points in more detail.

8.6 Selecting required sections

It is normal practice to shoot much more than you finally expect to use. In *film-making*, professionals often have quite a high 'shooting ratio'; only one tenth or one twentieth of the total material shot is used in the final edited version! That is partly because they cannot check results while shooting, and partly to give more choice during editing.

When you replay what you have recorded, you will find that you have:

- good shots that you will use,
- shots that cannot be used due to defects or errors of various sorts ('no-good takes'),
- repeated shots (retakes to achieve the best version),
- redundant shots (too similar to others to use),
- JIC shots (that you took 'just-in-case' they would be useful as cutaways or insert shots/pickups during editing),
- shots that didn't work for some reason.

So the first stage of editing is to sort out what is available to use and what is to be junked, and form a list. If you kept a log while you were shooting, giving details of the shots, this will help considerably. Otherwise, you will have to play back the tape, and make notes to guide the editing.

You can identify the individual shot:

- visually ('the one where he gets into the car'),
- by shooting a 'slate' (clapper-board) before each shot, containing the shot number and details (or an inverted board, at the end of shots),
- by electronically inserted data printed in the picture at the start of a shot (a facility in some video cameras),
- By *timecode*; a special continuous time-signal throughout the tape, showing the precise moment of recording.

Once you know which shots you are going to use, the next step is to decide on the order in which you want to present them.

8.7 The order of shots

To edit successfully, you need to imagine yourself in the position of your audience. They are seeing a succession of shots, one after another, for the first time. As each shot appears, they have to interpret it and relate it to previous shots, progressively building up ideas about what they are seeing.

In most cases, you will show the shots in chronological order. If the shots jump to and fro in time or place, the result can be extremely confusing. (Even the familiar idea of 'flashbacks' only works as long as the audience understands what is going on.)

When you cut a series of brief shots together, the fast pace of the program will be exciting, urgent and confusing. A slow cutting rhythm using shots of longer duration, is more gentle, restful, thoughtful, sad, etc.

8.8 Cutting points

The *moment* you choose for a cut can affect how smoothly one shot leads to another. If the first shows someone walking up to a door to open it, and the second shot as a close-up of him grasping the handle, you usually have to make sure that there is:

- no missing time (his arm hasn't moved yet . . . but his hand is on the handle in the close-up),
- no duplicated time (his hand takes hold of the handle in the first shot . . . then reaches out and grasps it again in the close-up),
- no over-extended time (his hand takes the handle in the first shot, and holds it . . . and is still seen holding it waiting to turn it, in the second shot).

There are various opinions as to whether the cut should occur before a movement, after a movement or during it. The smoothness can vary with the situation. But here we are talking about the finer points of the editing art.

There are occasions when we deliberately 'lose time' by omitting part of the action. For instance, someone gets out of a car, and a moment later we see him coming into a room. We have not watched him through all the irrelevant action of going into the house and climbing the stairs. This technique of *filmic time* (*cinematic time*) tightens up the pace of the production, and leaves out potentially boring bits when audience interest could wane. Provided the audience knows what to expect, and understands what is going on, this ploy is an effective way of getting on with the story without wasting time.

Similarly you can 'extend time' to create a dramatic impact. We see someone light the fuse of a stick of dynamite . . . cut to people in the next room . . . cut to the villain's expression . . . cut to the street outside . . . cut to him looking around . . . cut to the fuse . . . and so on, building up tension in a much longer time than it would really have taken for the fuse to burn down and explode the dynamite.

Again, you can introduce *filmic space*. We see a person getting into an aircraft . . . and cut to others at that moment at his destination, preparing to welcome him.

8.9 Transitions

In Figure 8.1. you can see the regular methods of changing from one shot to another.

The *cut* is the commonest, general-purpose transition, and can be made simply and directly, either during shooting ('editing in camera') or afterwards during editing.

Many video cameras have a lens iris (aperture), that can be fully closed. If you start to shoot with the lens closed right down, than open it up until you reach the aperture needed for correct exposure, the picture will *fade up* from a black screen to full intensity ('fade in'). Similarly, by closing

Figure 8.1 Transitions

The cut (straight cut, flat cut). An instantaneous switch from one shot to another. A powerful dynamic transition that is easiest to make.

Picture 1

Picture 2

The mix (dissolve). An effect produced by fading out one picture while fading in another. A quiet, restful transition. A quick mix tends to imply that the action in the two scenes is happening at the same time. A slow mix suggests passing of time, or moving to a different place. Mixes are generally comparative. If a mix is stopped halfway, the result is a *superimposition.*

Picture 1

Superimposition
Picture 1 + Picture 2

Picture 2

Fade out. A gradual reduction in the strength of the picture, by stopping down (manually or motorized iris), or by fading out a video source. A slow fade suggests the peaceful end of action. A fast fade is rather like a 'gentle cut', used to conclude a scene.

A *fade-in* is the opposite process. A slow fade-in suggests the forming of an idea, while a fast fade-in introduces action without the shock of simply cutting from a blank screen to a full picture.

All picture tones progressively darken

the iris while shooting you can fade the picture from full down to a black screen ('fade out'; 'fade down'). Some cameras have an *auto-fade* button.

If you are using a *switcher* to control cameras you produce a fade by operating a fader control (rather as you would adjust the gain control/volume control on audio equipment).

A *mix* or a *superimposition* will normally need two video sources, and a switcher (vision mixer) to fade between them.

A *wipe* pattern is produced by a *special effects generator* (SEG). This can be either a separate unit or incorporated in a switcher.

8.10 Good continuity

If we see a series of shots that are supposed to show the same action from different viewpoints, we do not expect to see any radical changes in the appearance of things in the respective pictures. In other words, we expect *continuity*.

If a glass is full in one shot and empty in the next, we can accept that, if something has happened between the two shots. But if someone in a storm scene appears wet in all the long shots, but dry in the close-ups, something is wrong! If they are standing smiling, with an arm on a chair in one shot, but with a hand in a pocket and unsmiling when seen from another angle in the next shot, the sudden change during the cut can be very obvious. The sun may be shining in one shot and not in the next. There may be aircraft noises in one but silence in the next. Somebody may be wearing a blue suit in one shot and a gray one in the next.

These are all very obvious – but they happen. In fact they are liable to happen whenever action, that is to appear continuous in the edited program, stops and restarts.

There is an opportunity for the continuity to be upset when you:

● stop shooting, move the camera to another position, and then continue,
● repeat part of an action (a retake); it may be slightly different the second time, so cannot edit unobtrusively with the original sequence,
● shoot action over a period of time, e.g. part of it one day, and the rest on the next,
● alter how you are going to shoot a scene, after part of it is already taped.

The only way to achieve good continuity is to pay attention to detail. Sometimes a continuity error will be much more obvious on the screen than it was during shooting. It is so easy to overlook differences when you are concentrating on the action, and the hundred and one other things that arise during production. If there are any doubts, there is a lot be said for replaying the videotape to check back on previous shots of the scene, before continuing shooting.

8.11 Physical editing

When you are editing a film, you cut out the parts you want, splice them together in the chosen order, and so build up the finished version. If you want to include mixes, fades, wipes, etc., you put appropriate wax marks on the print, and these transitions are carried out by the film laboratories as they print the final version.

Video editing is a very different process. First of all, you do not *cut* your videotape if you are wise. Although it is physically possible to cut and splice the magnetic videotape, just as one edits audio tape, the result can be disastrous. Not only is it liable to damage the VCR's tiny delicate heads, but the join will replay as a major picture interruption (a wipe, with picture break-up, etc.). Physical editing was feasible on earlier types of VTR (quad), but should be avoided on today's helical-scan VCRs.

8.12 Editing during shooting

Most lightweight video cameras have a switch that enables you to remotely start and stop the VCR, so that you can 'edit in camera'. This simply means that you tape the first shot, stop the VCR, set up the second shot, and then continue taping; and so progressively *assemble* your program.

Some VCRs provide a method in which you watch a replay of your previous shot, and switch at the appropriate moment, using an 'edit' or 'mode-change' button, from *replay* to the *record* mode.

In another method, you play up to the cue point, and press the *pause* button on the VCR. This stops the tape moving, but continues to replay a still picture as the heads go on scanning the tape width. While the tape is temporarily paused, you switch the VCR to *record*, then release the pause button. The VCR begins recording the new shot without a disruption on the tape.

Most modern VCR systems produce a clean noiseless cut between two shots, on replaying the tape. (Unfortunately, some show momentary picture defects during 'in camera' cuts, due to sync problems.)

So where are the snags?

1. Well, you have to record the program in its final 'running order'; and that may not be convenient, or even practicable. Although you can *insert* a new item within the existing recording (wiping out that section of the original), you cannot do this with great accuracy.

2. 'Tight' accurately placed cutting is not really practicable, when 'editing in camera'. You need to make sure that you have sufficient material at the finish of each shot, and the beginning of the next, to avoid clipping the start or end of action during editing.

You need to make allowances too, for the fact that, unlike an audio recorder, the VCR does not start to replay or record immediately you press the appropriate switch. There is a momentary pause before the picture and sound appear. This delay is deliberate, to allow the machine to stabilize. It happens this way.

When we start a VCR, it takes a moment for its tape to get up to full speed, and its synchronizing system to settle down to produce stable pictures ('lock up').

So, many VCRs include a special *back-space editing* arrangement. Every time you press the play or record button, the machine starts by *rewinding* itself just a little (e.g. 5 s) before then running forward. Thanks to this brief back-track, the machine gives itself sufficient time for the system to stabilize, before it actually begins to replay or record. Picture and sound appear 'clean' and without slurs or disturbances of any kind.

That is fine, but if your last shot ended at a crucial moment (as the villain fires the gun), there is a chance that it will be chopped off, when the tape rewinds itself a little on starting the second recording. You will not know if you have lost the end of the previous action during the restart until you replay the sequence to check the edit. So make sure there is sufficient room at the end of each shot to accommodate this situation.

3. Probably the main disadvantage of 'editing during shooting' is that there is little leeway for mistakes. If you misjudge, previous shots can be spoiled. You need to re-record an unsuccessful shots straight away, and that involves running the tape back to the edit point ready for the retake, and checking each shot after recording it, to make sure that it is satisfactory.

A different method of editing is possible, when you have two or more cameras. The cameras are cabled to a switcher, where editing is carried out 'on the hoof' during the production, intercutting, mixing and wiping between shots at the required moments. The output of the switcher can be taped continuously, from opening to closing, as a 'live on tape' recording.

Alternatively, you can use a stop-start recording approach. If there are any faults during the production, recording stops, the tape is rewound to the end of the last good shot, and the recording and action are re-cued. This way, it is not necessary to carry out post-production editing, to correct and rearrange the recorded videotape.

The great benefit of all 'editing during shooting' approaches to production, is that you finish up with a *first generation* recording. The picture quality represents the best the system can provide. And as a bonus, the videotape can be ready at the end of the shooting session.

8.13 Editing after shooting

The regular method of videotape editing is a *dubbing* or re-recording process. You select the section you want on the original recording, and as you replay it, record a copy onto a new videotape.

Clearly, you can dub off parts of the original tape in any order, ignoring shots you don't want, even repeating bits if you wish. The original tape can be played at normal speed, in fast or slow motion, or you can hold a frame (pause, freeze frame), maybe even run the tape backwards. Using a switcher, you can intercut and mix the outputs of two or more VCRs, insert material from a live camera (e.g. titles, graphics) and introduce various video effects.

Such a process clearly has enormous flexibility, although it also has its drawbacks.

8.14 Generations

Whenever we dub, with current VCR systems, the quality of the copy can never be as good as the original recording. If you are using state-of-the-art professional VTRs (e.g. Type-B, Type-C), the differences may be slight. But when a picture recorded on a domestic VCR is dubbed onto a similar machine, the quality losses are noticeable. At worst, video noise is more pronounced, detail is less clear, color tends to bleed or smear, there may be horizontal streaks across parts of the picture, edges of subjects appear ragged and color errors arise.

Copy this copy, and sound quality worsens, color disappears, and eventually both picture and sound break up completely.

The higher the quality of the system you are using, the less the deterioration during dubbing. There are more generations before losses become unacceptable. Thus tapes made with Super VHS for example, will survive editing and copying better than tapes made on the standard VHS system.

When you edit by dubbing, the composite copy that results is a *second generation* version. If you make a straight copy of this final videotape, perhaps for distribution, this is a *third generation* version. So it will unavoidably have lost some of the quality of the original *first generation* recording.

Because the progressive deterioration at each dubbing is cumulative, we cannot disregard it if we want a high-grade end-product. Any multiple dubbing you do, to produce special video effects, can result in copies that are third generation or so. If you include any 'library shots' in your program (i.e. material recorded for another production), which may themselves be third generation, the final version seen in a distribution copy could be fifth generation or more!

How far all this matters depends on the quality of the original. If it is really excellent, or ironically, if it is so poor that a little more noise will not make much difference, then the third generation version can be quite acceptable. Much depends on the system used, and on the purpose of the program. If it is important to show detail in print, fine texture or subtle tonal difference, then results may not be acceptable in a multi-generation copy. If it is a news scoop of a once-only event, standards become flexible.

8.15 Electronic splicing

Some types of VCRs give you the option of recording in two different modes.

The first is the *assemble* (assembly) mode. When you use this system, it not only records picture and sound, but also records *new reference pulses* on the control track of the tape at the same time.

The second is the *insert* mode. Here, you record new video and audio, but the VCR leaves the *old control track* that is already on the tape, untouched.

The original idea was that one should use the 'assemble' mode when adding new shots *on to the end* of an existing recording. The 'insert' mode on the other hand, enabled you to slot some new material *into* an existing recording (e.g. replace a faulty shot) without interrupting the existing control track pulses, for that would cause picture disturbance on the cuts.

However, the disadvantage of the 'assemble' mode is that whenever you stop and re-start recording, the system begins to record a new set of pulses on the tape. So with certain recorders (e.g. U-matic) there could be a momentary hiccup in the recorded pulses at the editing point on replay, enough to cause a brief picture disturbance perhaps (frame roll or tearing).

When you are using such VCRs to assemble a tape shot-by-shot, you can use a simple technical trick to ensure maximum stability at each re-start. Take the videotape before the actual editing session, and record it throughout (without picture or audio) using the *assemble* mode. This will prepare the tape by laying down a continuous uninterrupted *control track* throughout. Rewind the tape.

Then for the editing session, switch the recording VCR to the *insert* mode and use this prepared tape to record the master program. (The video will be recorded without affecting the control track pulses already on the prepared tape.) As you record each shot in turn, to build up the program, the VCR will use these pre-recorded uninterrupted control pulses throughout as a reference, and all transitions will be 'clean' on replay.

In a more complex editing set-up, where you are using various pieces of video equipment interlinked (e.g. several VCRs, an SEG, etc.) there is always the danger that the video system's sync pulses might be disturbed at some time or other and upset picture stability on the master recording. To prevent this, a *time base corrector unit* (TBC), may be needed, which corrects any sync errors in the video signal before recording, and ensures absolutely accurate synchronization.

8.16 The editing process

Although it is simple enough to play one tape and make a copy on another, the mechanics can be tricky, and somewhat laborious, when you are aiming at any sort of precision. If your pictures show unrelated general shots of countryside, factory and city streets, and you are going to edit them together and put a commentary over the result, cutting points are not at all critical, so there are no difficulties. But if you have a series of brief shots containing tight action, that have to be intercut precisely, the dubbing operation can be very demanding.

Let us go through the basic mechanics of editing, so that we can see the potential problems.

Figure 8.2 Methods of videotape editing

Assemble mode. This method can be used to add a further scene to an existing recording (A), or to replace a faulty scene at its end (B). But because the VTR lays down a fresh set of synchronizing cue pulses on the control track, whenever it records in this mode, its pulse pattern is disturbed at each join.

Insert mode. In this mode, the original control track pulses are not erased and re-recorded, so there is no pulse disturbance at joins when recording new material. New scenes can be inserted within an existing recording, or added to its end, if an uninterrupted control track has been prepared beforehand.

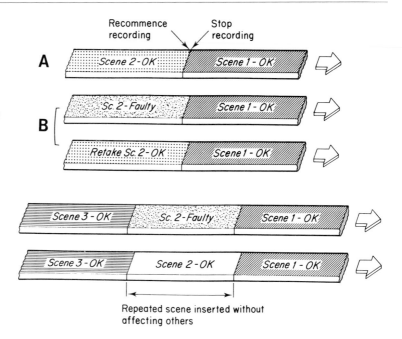

1. First you have to select and locate the shot you want. Whereabouts is it, on which tape? (section 8.6). You then run that tape up to the 'in-cue' point, and check how much you are going to copy. You now have in and out cues, and a duration. You know exactly when to stop the replay.
2. You load 'blank' videotape on the recording VCR, ready to make the copy.
3. To make the dubbing, you need to switch both machines on, so that they come up to speed, to *replay* and *record* simultaneously. (But remember, there is run-up period before a machine stabilizes, and this varies between machines.)
4. At the appropriate moment (the 'out-cue'), stop *record* and *replay* simultaneously.
5. If the next shot you want to copy is on the same source-tape, you must run it backwards or forwards to find the *exact cue-in point*. (Again, you will need to know the duration, and out-cue.) If the shot is on a different tape, you have to replace the cassette on the replay machine, and run it through to the new in-cue point.

There are several different ways of locating the 'in' and 'out' cue points on the master tape (the source tape), as you run through it:

- A digital counter on the machine, showing how much tape has run through the system since it was reset to zero.
- A digital display that shows the lapsed time (in frames, seconds, minutes and hours) derived from counting the tape's control track pulses.
- Timecode, which accompanies the original recording, as a direct reference time showing exactly when each shot was taken (frames, seconds, minutes and hours).

A 'picture-search' facility helps one to reach the required cue-point, by fast winding to near the point, then using slow motion to get to the nearest frame. This sounds like a lot of work. And if you do it entirely manually, it certainly can be, especially if you make a mistake, misjudge or have to copy sections from several different tapes.

As VCRs have become even more sophisticated, tracking down the wanted material on a tape has become increasingly easier. Many of the tape access methods you will meet, are remotely controlled:

Manual

- *Search/shuttle*: allows the tape to be played forwards or backwards at variable speeds (briefly or continuously), from very slow to very high.
- *Jog-frame*: provides precision frame-by-frame searching forwards or backwards.

Automatic

- *Cue marks*. You can insert a 'bookmark' cue-marker during recording or playback, which will then automatically stop/start the tape at that point.
- *Time search*. This will run the tape to stop at (or play from) a particular time (dial) setting; either from the beginning of the tape, or from the current tape position.
- *Blank search*. This will search for a cued blank in the sound track.
- *Index search*: Automatically places index codes at the beginning of each new recording (take). These can be located by remote control.

8.17 Off-line and on-line editing

You can organize your editing selection in two ways:

Off-line editing. The best method is to play through tapes long before the actual editing session, selecting the takes you want to use, and making a list of your various editing decisions (in/out points, order of shots, transitions), perhaps preparing tapes in readiness.

On-line editing. Alternatively, you can leave your selection until the actual editing period. But that can be very time-consuming – and if you are paying for facilities, can be a very costly process!

8.18 Edit controllers

Thanks to ingenious devices called *edit controllers*, a lot of this work can be automated.

The edit controller is a computerized switching panel. This 'magic box' remotely controls the VTR equipment, selecting and controlling the replay, rewind, and record mechanics. Designs range from simple editing aids to very sophisticated computerized equipment.

Edit controllers serve as 'intelligent interfaces', for they activate the right functions in the right order at the right moment. In doing this, they calculate and time all the machine processes, such as the run-up times, and synchronize the switching. You have to indicate what you want selected, and they do the rest – well much of it!

With this system, you play through the source tape and the recorded copy, to select the *in* and *out* edit points; and decide on the types of transitions needed (cut, mix, wipe). You then make a *rehearse edit*. This just plays the tapes, making a switch at the edit point, to show you on the screen, what that edit will look like. If the trial results are OK, the system will make the edit for real. You then check the final result.

Some systems will also provide *split-edits*, in which you can treat the recorded audio separately from the video. A *synchronizer unit* allows you to 'lift off' the original sound from the VT recording, add effects, commentary, music, and then 'lay it back' exactly in sync with the pictures. You may also be able to mix between two audio tracks on the same tape.

Where you are using a VCR with a multiplexed 'hi-fi' track (*Hi-Fi 8, S-VHS*, or *Hi-Fi VHS*) which is layered with the video track, the sound cannot be substituted in this way. Then you can only *audio dub* while copying.

More comprehensive editing systems give you an *edit decision list* display (perhaps with a printout), identifying the shots you have selected, their positions, timings, etc. This list is not only a valuable reference, but when confirmed, will rewind tapes to selected points, and automatically compile the dubbing to match (*auto-assemble*).

The 'edit decision list' may even remotely control a switcher (for transitions), an audio recorder (audio inserts), a character generator, a computer, etc. (for titling, graphics inserts, special effects).

The accuracy of the editing points will depend on the system. Where a *time code reader* generates, reads and edits the tape using SMPTE time code, accuracy can be ±1 frame, with no tape slippage errors. Other methods may be more approximate; e.g. ±2–3 frames.

In a typical basic professional two-machine edit system, two 'edit recorders' are used, with an 'edit controller' and two picture monitors. For economy, you can use a standard 'replay-only' or 'record-replay' type VCR to reproduce the tape, instead of using an edit recorder for that purpose.

Running tapes to and fro to their edit point can be very time consuming; particularly if one shot is near the end of the videotape, and the next near its beginning. That's why it is often better to use a series of short tapes. Then of course, you have to keep changing the cassettes!

8.19 Post-production editing

As you saw in Chapter 5, the program audio is usually a composite, made up of:

- the direct pick-up sound recorded during shooting (e.g. dialogue),
- any sound effects (background or synchronized spot effects),
- music,
- 'voice-over' commentary, announcements, etc.

Now is the time to combine and correct the program sound, and relate it to the picture.

It is worth remembering at this stage that either the pictures or the audio may be given *priority* during the dubbing process.

If you are for example, making a complete record of a speech, the dialogue has priority. Although the camera will concentrate on the speaker, a single unchanging shot would become visually boring, even with judicious changes in shot-size. So you will probably include 'cutaway shots' of his audience, special guests, reactions, and so on. But the dialogue is continuous and unbroken – whatever picture editing you decide to do.

Where a speech is to be edited because it is too long for the allocated program time, or you are selecting the most important passages, the dialogue will be edited, and commentary or intercut shots of the audience interposed to disguise parts of the speech that are missing.

You may have a scene in which two people are supposed to be speaking to each other, although they were actually shot separately. For instance, all the shots of a boy stranded on a cliff would be taken at the same time (with dialogue). All the shots and comments of his rescuer at the top of the cliff would be shot at another time. During editing, the shots with their respective speech, would be intercut to give a continuous interchange.

There are times when the pictures have priority, and the sound has to be closely related to what we are seeing. You may have to adjust its start, its synchronism, its duration and its emphasis to match the pictures.

8.20 Good editing techniques

Editing, like so many of the crafts we have been examining in earlier pages, is an unobtrusive skill. If it is done well, your audience does not notice it, but is absorbed in its *effect*.

During an exciting scene, for example, when the duration of shots is made shorter and shorter as the tension grows, the audience is only conscious of growing agitation, and fast-moving action.

There are certain established principles in the way one edits, and although like all 'rules' you may occasionally disregard them, they have been born of experience. Here are a few of the most common:

● Do not cut between shots that are very similar or even matching (e.g. frontal close-up of person A to frontal close-up of person B.)

● Avoid cutting between shots of extremely different size of the same subject (e.g. big close-up to long shot).

● Cutting through an angle, to similarly sized shots of a subject (e.g. frontal to side view) produces unattractive jumps.

● If two subjects are going in the same direction (chasing, following), have them both going across the screen in the same direction. If their screen directions are opposite, this will suggest meeting or parting. (This arises if you intercut between camera positions on either side of the action's direction.)

● Generally avoid cutting between static and fast-moving pictures, except for a specific purpose.

● Take care in cutting *in* from a blank screen to full picture strength, or cutting *out* to a blank screen except for a deliberate shock effect.

Figure 8.3 Intercutting
Tension can be increased by quicker cutting. Here an increasing cutting rate is combined with closer and closer shots.

Figure 8.4 Matching cuts

When pictures are intercut, take care to avoid the following distracting effects.

Part 1 *People*

A Mismatched camera height.

B Changes in headroom.

C Size jumps. Avoid cutting between shots of only slightly different size (e.g. a–b, b–c, c–d). The subject suddenly appears to shrink or grow! Aim at size changes of at least 4:3 or 3:4 (a–c, b–d).

D Transformations occur if identical size shots of two different subjects are intercut.

E Cutting over a wide angle, to a similar size shot, is distracting.

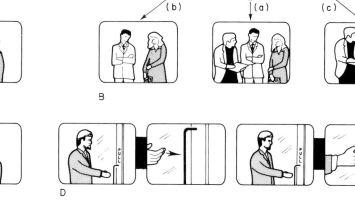

Part 2 *Jump cuts*

A If you have the same subject in two adjacent shots, it may jump across the screen on the cut.

B This can happen in group shots too (in shots (b) and (c)).

C Cutting between similar shots of the subject from slightly different viewpoints, can create a 'twist' on the cut.

D If continuity is not matched when shooting discontinuously, parts of the action may be missed or repeated.

1   2   3   4   5

Figure 8.5 Point of view
The camera can change from a bystander's objective viewpoint, to the performer's own subjective viewpoint. 1. We are simply following the man. 2. Here we become aware of what is happening around him. 3. We look at the scene with him. 4. A reaction shot as he greets the child 'through his eyes'.

● If you have to break the continuity of action (deliberately or unavoidably), introduce a cutaway shot. But try to ensure that this relates meaningfully to the main action. During a boxing bout, a cutaway to an excited spectator helps the tension. A cutaway to some garbage, or a bored attendant (just because you happen to have the unused shot!) would be meaningless, although it can be used as a comment on the main action.

● If someone walks out of shot (apparently exiting), don't re-discover them nearby in the next shot, taken from another angle.

● Avoid intercutting shots that make a person or object jump from one side of the screen to the other, on the cut.

● Intercut shots where a person is facing (or moving) left, then seen on the cut facing (or moving) right, are seldom acceptable, expect to suggest confusion perhaps. 'Reverse cuts' arise if you alter your camera viewpoint during the action, and cross from one side of their route to the other ('crossing the line').

When you have the opportunity, do *all* these things deliberately! You will see how strange, how ambiguous, or how disturbing the effects can be, and you are less likely to do them again, except by accident!

Chapter 9

People

Your entire program could rest on how well people perform in front of the camera. How do you help them to give their best?

9.1 Talent

Although the broad term 'talent' is widely used to refer to those appearing in front of the camera, we must always remember how very varied this talent really is. It covers a remarkable spread of experience and temperaments; from the professional actor working to a script and playing a part, to the impromptu, unrehearsed interview with a passer-by in the street.

When you invite someone to appear in front of the camera, that is only the *beginning* of the story. Their performance can have a considerable influence on your program's success. So you will need to help them, to make their contribution as effective as they are able. Their particular role may be a major one, or it may be slight, but the impression they make on your audience can decide whether that part of your program wins or fails. The television camera is a great debunker. Under its scrutiny, brashness, pomposity and false bonhomie are weighed and found wanting; while sympathy goes out to those who are shy and ill at ease.

For all practical purposes, we can divide talent into the *professional performers*, who are used to appearing in front of the camera, and the *inexperienced*, for whom your program is likely to be a new, strange, exciting yet worrying event.

Professional performers usually work to a prepared format. Some, like an actor in a play, will learn their lines, their moves and the mechanics of the production. Others work from an abbreviated cue sheet near the camera, or a running text projected onto the screen of a prompter. Some will extemporize from guide notes, others will read from a printed script.

The best professionals can be relied on to repeat, during the actual taping, the dialogue, the moves, the pace and the timing that they gave in rehearsal. One knows what they are going to say, and that they can modify the delivery of their piece to suit the occasion, showing enthusiasm, vigor, calm detachment, patience or reverence. They can take guidance and instructions, and follow this through without being confused. They can improvise when things go wrong, and remain calm and collected if the unexpected happens.

Any program-maker using talent not used to working to a camera, has to make certain allowances, and take precautions that are not necessary where professional performers are involved.

How well inexperienced people fit into their roles in your program will depend to quite an extent on you. Do not expect them to have the self-discipline and efficiency of the professional. There is, after all, a scary novelty about finding yourself faced with an impersonal camera, a microphone pointing to pick up your slightest remark, unfamiliar people grouped around, the powerful lighting and sundry disruptions. The occasion can become very unreal to inexperienced talent.

9.2 Inexperienced talent

Many a person who appears to be a 'natural performer' in the finished program is really the product of a very understanding, yet wily director. Typical ways of handling inexperienced talent include:

● Careful planning, so that not much is required of the talent. You put them at ease by the way you make them welcome; by letting them know what you want them to do; making them feel that their contribution is an important and interesting part of your program; and assuring them that if anything goes wrong, there is nothing to worry about, for it can be taped again.
● Letting them do it their way, and editing the result.
● Letting them reminisce, for example, then selecting the most interesting or the most relevant parts.
● Keeping the tension down, by shooting when they do not know you are doing so.
● Interviewing them in a situation that is natural to them (e.g. their workshop) rather than in a formal studio setting.
● Wherever possible, avoid showing the talent just standing, waiting. They will feel more at ease (particularly in their own surroundings), if they have something to do; e.g. a cook might be cutting up some vegetables before speaking.
● Giving them a few instructions; e.g. telling them when, where or how to hold the items to the camera.
● Using plenty of cutaway shots, so that the picture is not concentrating on them all the time. As far as possible, we look at what they are talking about instead, together perhaps with intercut shots of the host smiling and nodding ('nod shots').

Figure 9.1 Guiding the talent
The experienced performer can help the inexperienced guest in many ways:
1. Putting them at ease.
2. Keeping an eye on the monitor shot.
3. Keeping the table clear of unwanted items.
4. Placing items on a pre-arranged mark.
5. Having the next item ready.
6. Positioning items to suit the camera.
7. Avoiding shadowing the item, or lens flares or reflections.
8. Aware of the running time.

It may be a wise plan to tape the rehearsal, and if possible, to run through the material several times, recording everything, so that you can select and combine the best parts of each version.

If sections do not join neatly for editing, the interviewer can record a question or a statement later, that will bridge what would otherwise be disjointed material. With care, this can be done quite ethically, even although it was not part of the original interview.

9.3 The presenter

Many of the problems of handling inexperienced talent can be reduced, if they are supported in the program by someone who is used to production routine.

This person, who serves as the host or presenter, will probably meet them beforehand, help them to feel at ease, introduce them to the camera, and gently guide them through the production. By interjecting such phrases as: 'Earlier, you were telling me about . . .' or 'I wonder if we could look at . . .' or 'Isn't the construction of this piece interesting . . .', they can move the program smoothly from one section to the next. Especially when you are shooting intermittently, or out of order – both very confusing to the novice – the guiding hand can be very welcome.

The host can help the guest with the mechanics of the situation. Instead of the nervous guest grasping something unreliably, partly hiding it and catching the light, or wobbling about in a very close shot, the host might tactfully do it for him, by taking it to admire, then holding it quite still to camera at exactly the right angle, while looking in a nearby monitor to check the shot.

9.4 When there are problems

There are those sad occasions when the talent you have invited simply does not come up to expectations. They are so wooden, or so hesitant and nervous, that they do little justice to themselves. Or they over compensate, and become loud and verbose. There is often little opportunity to actually replace them, if you do not discover the problem until camera rehearsal.

It is a cruel solution, to see how bad someone is during rehearsal, then to say: 'I'm sorry, but there isn't time for your item after all. The program is too long'. It is far better to tape him, hoping either that he will be better next time or that part at least of his contribution can be used. It has been known for a director to record the item, then quietly junk it during editing.

But leaving aside these drastic methods (which can leave you with no material), it may be better to simplify or to shorten their contribution. Include lots of cutaways (e.g. close-ups of details on items being shown) that you can use to cover edits later. If necessary, you can take these after the main taping with the guest is over.

Another approach is to have the host present the items in the program, continually referring to the guest. For example, pick up an item, hold it to camera, and remind the guest of the information he gave about it before or during rehearsal. At worst, he has to do little more than say: 'Yes' and 'No'!

As a last resort, if the combination is mainly a demonstration, you might keep most of the pictures of the items being demonstrated (e.g. showing steps in a cookery demonstration), and lay a commentary track over them, explaining what is going on, based on the original recording. In fact, if you see from rehearsals that there is little profit in taking shots of the guest speaking to the host, you might deliberately restrict shots to showing what he is doing, omitting shots of the speaker in anticipation of final voice-over treatment.

9.5 The camera's viewpoint

Because talent is expert at a particular subject, this does not mean that they can present it convincingly to the camera. Ironically, a presenter working from a prompter script may appear more authentic; even though the words were written for him by someone else.

How you can shoot action is influenced not only by the nature of the subject, but by the talent involved.

You may need to *sneak* shots as unobtrusively as possible, so that you do not intrude on the situation, and to avoid people playing up to the camera. If for instance, you are shooting children at play, or at work in a classroom, you are likely to get a far more accurate account of what really happens if they do not know you are there (unlikely!), or do not know that you are shooting them at that moment. Some program-makers contend, hopefully, that people simply ignore the lights and the microphone, and behave perfectly naturally after a while. But this is very challengeable.

The camera can behave rather like a bystander who moves around to get to a good viewpoint of whatever is going on. This happens in street interviews. At best, one hopes that someone who is being interviewed, will be preoccupied with the questioner, and barely notice the camera and microphone, although the curiosity of bystanders, particularly children, seldom lets them forget the artificiality of the occasion.

Inexperienced talent is seldom able to *speak to camera* completely naturally, without a certain amount of hesitation or over-playing, especially if they have to remember to cover particular points in order, and take various precautions as they go through their piece.

Even when someone is at ease speaking directly to camera, they may not *work to the camera* successfully. An inexperienced person holds something up so that *they* can see it, whereas what you really want is for them to handle it so that the *camera* can see the details clearly — and that can feel quite unnatural at times. They may need to hold the item awkwardly, to avoid fingers obscuring parts of it or casting shadows. They have to ensure that reflections do not prevent surface features being seen. And over-shoulder shots, looking at things from their viewpoint, are seldom the solution.

And here we come to the real decisions you will often have to make when working with people who are unused to the camera. Are you going to let them do things in their own way, and take what happens, hoping that they will do it more or less right? Are you hoping that something interesting will turn up while you are shooting? Or are you going to give them advice and instructions about what you want to see, and guide them until you get just that?

In practice, of course, the situation largely depends on the people involved, and on the amount of time (and patience) you have. Some people improve with practice, while others feel that they are failing and get worse. Some people gain confidence with rehearsal, others wilt. Some leave things out during repeats, others put more in. Some lose their naturalness, and begin to 'perform'. Some find it easier, others become more confused.

Figure 9.2 Bringing the scene to life
Empty shots. Without people, the scene looks empty, and desolate. With people, the scene becomes lively and interesting.

Foreground interest. The shot looks bleak, open, and uninviting. (You may want this effect.)
But use a foreground tree to provide an upper border, and the picture looks more complete and attractive.

9.6 People passing by

From people as performers, let's turn to the importance of people as incidental passers-by in many kinds of scenes.

Supposing you are making a program about a town, describing its character and its special features and showing details of its buildings. If you shoot early in the morning before people are about, you have a better opportunity to get clear uncluttered views. But do they really convey its typical atmosphere?

On the other hand, if you wait until the town has come to life, and you have to shoot in the hustle and bustle of passing traffic, it may be difficult to get the shots you want, although the place now has exactly the right feel to it. A reminder than, that there may be advantages, in shooting various aspects to your subject at different times, according to the light, the weather, the passing crowd, and so on.

And finally, do not overlook how important people are in giving life to a scene. Rather than pan along an empty sidewalk, it is more interesting to follow someone who is passing. (Although there is the possibility that your audience may now wonder who this is, speculating on them instead of the real subject.)

A shot looking along an empty bridge, is all too likely to bore your audience within a few seconds. But have someone walk across that same bridge, and the scene immediately becomes more interesting. So you can hold the shot much longer, while a commentary tells us about its history. Whether you will have to provide your own 'passer-by', or wait for someone appropriate to come along, is another matter.

Chapter 10

Organizing your production

A lot of this is obvious; so obvious, that many program-makers overlook these essentials in their initial enthusiasm – and their product is less effective!

10.1 Art conceals craft

Watching a show on TV, our thoughts are normally centered on the program material: the story-line, the message, the argument. We become interested in what people are saying, what they are doing, what they look like, where they are, and so on. Unless we start to get bored, or the mechanics become obtrusive, we are unlikely to concern ourselves with how the production is actually *made*.

We 'believe' what we see. We respond to techniques, but remain unaware of them unless they happen to distract us. We even accept the drama of the hero dying of thirst in the desert, without wondering why the director, camera and sound crew do not help him!

All this is fine, but when you set out to make programs for yourself, you will soon realize the gulf between 'watching and enjoying' from the audience, and 'creating the illusion' by the way you use the equipment.

10.2 How techniques develop

You cannot just point a camera at a scene and expect it to convey all the information and atmosphere that the on-the-spot cameraman is experiencing. A camera is inherently selective. It can only show certain limited aspects of a situation at any time. If, for instance, you provide a really wide shot of the entire field at a ball-game, your audience will have an excellent view of the movement patterns of teamwork – but they will be unable to see for themselves who individuals are, or to watch exactly how they are playing the ball. A close shot can give details, even show how a player is reacting to a foul – but prevents the audience from seeing the overall action at that time.

10.3 The problem of familiarity

There is an important difference between the way a *director* looks at his program, and how his *audience* reacts. And that is not surprising when you stop and think about it. For the director, the subject is *completely familiar*; he knows what he is trying to say; he knows the location. His audience on the other hand, are *continually finding out* what the program is about. They have not seen any of the shots before. They probably do not know the location. For them, it is a *fresh impression*. They are interpreting each shot as they see it, often having only a brief period to respond to whatever catches their attention.

A member of the audience, only sees as much of a situation as the camera reveals. He can be quite unaware of things that are even a short distance outside the lens' field of view, unless they happen to move into shot, or the camera viewpoint changes, or they make a noise that he is able to construe.

Because the director becomes so familiar with his subject, he may feel that it only needs a very brief shot. Something can seem so obvious to him that he does not include it at all! But for the viewer, the omission can be quite disconcerting.

Show a big close-up of odd detail without revealing the complete subject from which it comes, and it can leave the audience very puzzled. But the director knows, it obviously comes from that article over there!

You meet the opposite situation too, when a director holds a shot for some time, so that his audience can assimilate all the information in it, when in fact, they have lost interest in it, and their minds have wandered onto other things!

10.4 The problem of quality

When shooting pictures for pleasure, you can be philosophical if the odd shot happens to be slightly defocused, or lop-sided, or cuts off part of the subject. It is a pity, but it doesn't really matter too much. You can still enjoy the results.

But when you are making a program for other people, any defects of this kind are quite unacceptable. They will give a production the stamp of carelessness, amateurishness and incompetence, so that it loses its appeal and its authority. Faulty camerawork and poor techniques will not only distract your audience, but can turn even a serious well thought-out production into a complete farce!

10.5 Elaboration

How you can tackle any program will be directly influenced by your resources (equipment, finance, team-help, their experience, etc.), time, conditions, standards, intended market, and so on. There is no *correct* way to handle any subject, but there are usually a number of *bad* methods.

Suppose you want to discuss the problems of growing a particular crop. You could make an impressive program using special computer graphics, electronic titles, an expert walking through the crops speaking of problems, aerial views of the fields, time-lapse demonstrations, and so on. This would be an extremely expensive, time-consuming treatment requiring many resources.

Alternatively, you could use a very simple, yet equally informative approach. The camera could explore a typical field, and show the program title finger-traced in the earth. It could look at typical crop features, with close-ups of specimens. A commentary could provide an explanatory 'voice-over' to pictures. If any additional sounds are required, they could be the natural ones of wind, birdsong, tractors, or whatever, recorded as wild-track at the site.

Elaboration does not necessarily result in greater audience appeal. Sometimes it distracts them from the real subject itself, and draws their attention to the clever techniques instead. It is a great temptation to do it *differently*, not because it is better, but because the idea looks fresh and will attract attention. Is a weather forecaster any more informative because he stands out in the rain beneath an umbrella, rather than beside a map in the studio? Some stations have though so. Or is it an amusing gimmick to hold the audience's attention? Does it do that, or does it *divert* their attention instead?

10.6 Communication can be elusive!

There are no absolute 'rules' when creating a program, but there are quite a lot of well-established guiding principles. These have been discovered through experience. Occasionally you can deliberately ignore such guides, and create an interesting or unusual effect. But take care how you do so, for the audience response may not turn out as you hoped.

The human mind is great as seeing *relationships*, even when there aren't any! We all spend our time *interpreting* the world about us, frequently seeing meanings or significance where there is none.

In an experimental film made up of a random series of close-up stills from magazines covers, the disjointed fragments of buildings, foliage and objects appeared on the scene as patches of color, progressive patterns and geometric forms. When this film was run at 24 frames a second and accompanied by any music, from Bach to Brubeck, the result was interpreted by the audience as an exciting animation sequence, with the visual theme changing to the beat of the music. Yet in reality there was no theme, no editing (for the film was as shot in the camera, frame by frame). It was all in the minds of the audience!

This example reminds us how frail the process of communication really is. The audience will at times accept and interpret visual/audio garbage, for they assume that it has a valid purpose, even if they cannot themselves understand what this is. We shall discuss this more fully later, with *visual padding* (in section 11.8).

At other times although we select images and sound carefully, we find that the audience's attention has been taken by some odd irrelevant distraction in the background. They were reading the book titles on a shelf, and not listening to what was being said.

10.7 Begin at the end

Whether your program is a video 'family album', or a lecture on nuclear physics, the essential first step in program making is to think out *who* the program is for, and its chief *purpose*.

Your intended audience should determine your program's coverage and style. It is self-evident that the sort of program you would make for a group of specialist experts would be very different from one made for young children.

The conditions under which your audience is going to watch your program are important too. Most video programs are not made to be broadcast. They are to be viewed in classrooms, offices, factories, community halls, for home study, and so on. So the wise director tries to anticipate these conditions, for they can considerably affect the way he presents his program:

- How and where is your audience going to see your program? Will it be a seated group in a darkened classroom, watching a series of mid-sized monitors?
- Perhaps it is to be seen at an open-air meeting in a rural village, on a single monochrome receiver.
- Or it could be for close study by a student at a carrel.

If your program is intended to be seen in daylight, it is as well to avoid dark or low-key scenes. The pictures displayed on many receivers/monitors in daylight leave a lot to be desired. Tonal gradation is coarse, lighter tones block-off, smaller lettering bleeds and may be indecipherable, color is often either paled out or overemphasized. All this is frequently due to incorrect adjustment, as the users try to get the brightest possible picture.

Sound quality too is often poor, due to overload distortion. So keep the sound track simple. Loud background music is liable to distort, while quiet music may not be audible. Reducing the bass can improve the sound's intelligibility. (Listen to the sound quality of drums, thunder and an organ played over a small loudspeaker in the open air, and you will soon get the idea!)

You may need to anticipate the problems for an audience watching a distant picture monitor. Long shots have correspondingly little impact. Closer shots are essential. Small lettering means nothing on a small distant screen. To improve the visibility of titles, charts, maps, etc., keep details basic, and limit the information. White lettering on a black background is clearest, and you should be very cautious about using colored lettering on a colored background. (Try red on blue, or green on yellow, to see how bad the wrong choice can be!)

If your audience is watching on a monochrome monitor, you cannot use color to identify items, or directly demonstrate an effect that relies on color, such as a chemical change. They can only see tonal differences. When faced with this situation, make sure that you have an explanatory commentary, such as: 'You see how this light green solution is beginning to turn dark red . . .'. Do not assume that your audience can interpret things for themselves in these circumstances.

Here are a number of reminder questions that can guide you to anticipate your audience's problems:

- Does your program rely on their previously established knowledge? How much do they know about the subject already?
- Does your program relate to others (e.g. in a series)?
- Is your audience going to see the program singly, or in a group?
- Are they watching it once only, from the beginning, or as a continuous repeat replay?
- Can they see the program as often as they want, and stop and replay sections (carrel viewing)?
- Is your program to be watched straight through, or will it be stopped after sections, for discussion?
- Is your program a step-by-step demonstration, in which you show a process which they carry out, or compare your version with theirs?
- Will there be any accompanying paperwork (e.g. map, graphs or statistics) to which your audience can refer? (You cannot expect them to hold detailed data in their heads, as they follow the program's argument.)
- Where possible, try to relate your program to the world of your particular audience. Is it likely to appear strangely foreign, abstract, too academic, too parochial, etc?
- Will there be other competing, noisy attractions as they watch, e.g. at an exhibition?

- Will your program soon be out of date? (Does this matter?)
- Is the program for a very formal occasion, or will a certain amount of careful humor sweeten the pill?

10.8 Develop a system

Great ideas are not enough. Ideas have to be worked out in realistic, practical terms. They have to be expressed as pictures and sound. In the end, you have to decide what the camera is going to shoot, and what your audience is going to hear. Where do you start?

Broadly speaking, you can approach program-making in two quite different ways:

- the *empirical* method, in which instinct and opportunity are your guides.
- the *planned* method, which organizes and builds up a program, in carefully arranged steps.

10.9 The empirical approach

Directors following the empirical approach get an idea, then look around for subjects and situations that relate to it. After shooting likely material, they later create a program from whatever they have found. Their inspiration springs from the opportunities that have arisen.

Let's suppose you are going to make a program about 'Safety at Sea'. Using the empirical approach, you might go along to a marina, and develop a production based on the stories you hear there. Or you could discuss the idea with coast-guards or life-guards, and find yourself following another train of thought. Again, visiting some commercial docks, you might discover material there of an entirely different kind.

After accumulating a collection of interesting sequences (atmospheric shots, wild track, interviews, etc.)., you check through these, and get them into a meaningful order. Having done so, you then prepare a program that fits this material, probably writing a commentary as a 'voice-over' to match the edited pictures.

At *best*, this approach is fresh, uninhibited, improvises, makes use of the unexpected, avoids rigid discipline, and is very adaptable. Shots are interestingly varied. The audience is kept alert, watching and interpreting the changing scene.

At *worst*, the result of such shot-hunting is a haphazard ragbag, with little cohesion or sense of purpose. Because the approach is unsystematic, gaps and overlaps abound. Good coherent editing may be difficult. Opportunities may have been missed. The director often relies heavily on a commentary-over (perhaps with music) to try to provide any sort of relationship and continuity between the pictures.

10.10 The planned approach

This method of production, tackles the problem quite differently, although the results on the screen may be similar.

Here the director works out in advance, the exact form he wants the program to take, and organizes accordingly.

Fundamentally, you can either

- Begin with the environment or setting, and decide on how you can position cameras to get effective shots,

or you can

- Envision certain shots or effects you want to see, and create a setting that will provide those results.

A lot will depend too, on whether you are:

- *Interpreting an existing script* (as in drama). This will involve analysing the script; examining the story-line and the main action in each scene, and visualizing individual shots.

or

- *Building up a treatment framework.* Considering how you are going to present a particular program subject (as in Section 10.18), and working out the kinds of shots you want.

At *best*, the planned approach is a method in which a team can be coordinated to give their best. There is a sense of systematic purpose throughout the project. Problems are largely ironed out before they develop. Production is sensibly related to what is feasible. The program can have a smooth-flowing, carefully thought-out, persuasive style.

At *worst*, the production becomes bogged down in organization. The program is stodgy and routine, and lacks any spark of originality. Opportunities are ignored because they were not part of the original scheme, and would modify it. The result may even be hack work.

In practice, of course, the experienced program-maker uses a combination of the 'planned' and the 'empirical' approaches. He starts off with a plan of campaign, and takes extra opportunities as they offer themselves.

10.11 Storyboards

As you run through each scene in your mind, you can capture these imaginings, and turn them into practical program making, by preparing a *storyboard* as you go.

The storyboard is simply a series of rough sketches, that help you to visualize and to organize your camera treatment. It shows how you hope to arrange the *key shots* for each scene or action sequence.

You will find it a valuable aid, whether you are going to shoot action:

- Continuously, from start to finish.
- In sections or scenes; i.e. one complete action sequence at a time.
- Or as a series of separate shots or 'action segments', each showing a part of the sequence.

To begin, draw a grid of 40 mm by 30 mm frames. Now start to imagine your way through the first scene, roughly sketching the composition for each shot in turn. You don't have to be able to draw well to produce a successful storyboard. Even the crudest scribbles can help you to marshal your thoughts, and show other people what you are aiming at. If the action is complicated, you might need a couple of frames to show how a shot develops. In our example, the whole scene is summarized in just five frames.

Let's look at a very simply story line, to see how the storyboard provides you with imaginative opportunities.

The child has been sent to buy her first postage stamp.

There are dozens of ways to shoot this brief sequence.

You could simply follow her all the way from her home, watching as she crosses the road, enters the post office, goes up to the counter...

The result would be totally boring!

1

2

3

4

5

Figure 10.1 Analyzing action
When edited together, a sequence looks obvious and natural. But even a simple scene showing a child buying a stamp needs to be thought through. Note how shots 1 and 3 are taken on one side of the counter, and shots 2,4,5 on the other.

Let's think again. We know from the previous scene, where she is going and why. All we really want to register, are her reactions as she buys the stamp. So let's cut out all the superfluous footage, and concentrate on that moment.

1. *The child arrives at the counter, and looks up at the clerk.*
2. *Hesitatingly, she asks for the stamp.*
3. *She opens her fingers, to release the money she has been clutching so carefully all the way from home.*
4. *The clerk smiles and takes the money.*
5. *A close shot of the clerk tearing the stamp from a sheet.*

You now have a sequence of shots, far more interesting than a continuous 'follow-shot'. It stimulates the imagination. It guides the audience's thought processes. It has a greater overall impact.

However, if this type of treatment is carried out badly, the effect can look very disjointed, contrived, posed, 'bitty', or mannered. It is essential that your treatment matches the style and theme of the subject.

You could have built up the whole sequence with dramatic camera angles, strong music and effects. But would it have been *appropriate*? If the audience knows that a bomb is ticking away in a parcel beneath the counter... it might have been. It is all too easy to over-dramatize, or 'pretty-up' a situation (e.g. star filters producing multi-ray patterns around highlights, diffusion filters for misty effects). Resist the temptation, and keep them for the right occasion!

This breakdown has not only helped you to visualize the picture treatment. You begin to think about how one shot is going to lead into the next. You start to face practicalities. You see for example that shots 1 and 3 are taken from the front of the counter, and shots 2, 4 and 5 need to be taken from behind it. Obviously, the most logical approach is to shoot the sequence *out of order*. Your storyboard becomes a shooting plan.

To practice 'storyboarding', videotape a broadcast motion picture off-air, and check through it carefully, making a sketch of each key shot. This way, you will soon get into the habit of thinking in picture sequences, rather than in isolated shots.

10.12 Why plan?

Some people find the idea of planning very inhibiting. They want to get on with the job. For them, planning, somehow turns the thrill of the unexpected into an organized commitment.

But many situations *must* be planned and worked out in advance. You will need for instance, to get permission to shoot on private premises, to make appointments to interview people, to arrange admissions, etc. You might occasionally have success if you arrive unannounced, but do not assume this. Other material turns up quite unexpectedly, or is quite impromptu, and you need to make the most of any opportunity. After all, you can always reject the result during editing, if it proves unsuitable.

10.13 Thinking it out

Most programs go through three main stages:

1. *Pre-production.* The preliminaries, preparation and organization beforehand.
2. *Production.* Rehearsals and shooting.
3. *Post-production.* Editing, additional treatment and duplication.

The amount of work entailed at each stage will be influenced by the nature of your subject. One that involves a series of straightforward 'personality' interviews must be a lot easier to organize than one on Arctic exploration, or an historical drama. But in the end, a great deal depends on how you decide to approach the subject.

Working to the highest standards, you can provide extremely stimulating programs using simple methods. Treatment does not have to be elaborate to make its point. If someone in the desert picks up his water bottle, finds it empty, and the camera shows a patch of damp sand where it rested, the shot has told us a great deal without any need for elaboration. A single look or a gesture can often have a far stronger impact than lengthy dialogue purporting to show how two people feel about each other.

It is important to realize right from the beginning, that it is largely in your own hands how difficult and complex a production becomes. Some ideas seem simple enough, but can be difficult or impossible to carry out.

Others look very difficult or impracticable, but are easily achieved on the screen.

For example:
'Let's zoom in to an extreme close-up'. (Impossible because the minimum lens angle only provides a chest-shot at this distance.)
'Make her vanish!' (Simple. Keep the camera still, have her exit and edit out the walk.)

10.14 Start with an idea

It is very unlikely that you will suddenly decide, out of the blue, to make a video program on a particular subject, such as 'building a wall'. Something has triggered the idea. Perhaps you realized that it could help a class you are teaching. Or a local store has asked you to make it to aid sales to the home handyman. Here is the starting point.

You know the *subject* to be covered (in principle at least), what the program is to be *used* for, and *who* the program is for.

The next question might reasonably be: '*How long* is it to run?'. There is no point in settling down to a two-hour epic, if the client wants a two-minute repeat-cycle demonstration.

Consider how your audience is going to relate to your program. If it is one of a series, you obviously do not want to go over the same ground again unless it requires revision, or they may not see the other video.

10.15 Coverage

What do you want to cover in the available time? Or perhaps we should say, how much is it *reasonable* to cover in that time. If you have too many topics, it will not be possible to do justice to any of them. If you have too few, the program can seem slow, labored and padded out.

There is nothing to be gained by packing the program full of high-speed facts, for although they may sound impressive, your audience is unlikely to remember more than a fraction of them. Unlike the printed page, the viewer cannot refer back to check an item, unless the tape can be stopped and rewound when necessary, or is frequently repeated.

In most cases, it is a good general principle to structure a program, so that it has:

● An *introduction*, indicating what the program is to be about, also perhaps, its aim or who it is for.

- The *development*, i.e. the body of the program.
- A *conclusion*, summing up, perhaps reminding the audience of the main points, possibly referring them on to a further program in a series.

10.16 Building an outline

Now you can start to prepare the program outline. This begins with a series of *headings* showing the main themes you are going to discuss.

In the case of our 'building a wall' program, these might cover topics such as tools needed, materials, foundation, making mortar, method of laying bricks and pointing.

You now have to get a rough idea of how much program time you can devote to each section. Some will be brief, others relatively lengthy. You will no doubt emphasize some, and skip over others, to suit the purpose of the program.

The next stage is to take each of these topic headings, and note down the various aspects you want to cover there, as a series of *sub-headings*. Under 'tools', for instance, you would list those you need to demonstrate.

Now you have a structure for the program, and can begin to see the form it is likely to take.

10.17 Broad treatment

Next in your planning process, you will be deciding how you are going to approach each of the sub-headings in your outline. Remember, you

Figure 10.2 From ideas to finished shots
A reminder of the stages that a program has to go through, from the original idea, to the end product.

are still thinking things through. At this stage, you might decide to alter an idea, develop it, shorten it, or even drop it altogether.

It is a question and answer process. Let's imagine the situation:

> *What is the topic, and what is its purpose?*
> It is discussing 'animal hibernation in winter'.
> *How will you approach it?*
> It would be nice to show a bear preparing its den for hibernation, and settling down . . . show the hard winter weather with the animal asleep . . . and later, waking up in the spring and foraging. All with a commentary over.
> *A good idea, but where are the pictures coming from?*
> *Do you have any?*
> *Are you using a film library's services?*
> *Do they have that sort of material?*
> We could not afford that. It has to be a cheaper method. Perhaps we should forget it.
> *You could have an illustrated discussion, or a commentary, over still photographs and drawings (graphics, artwork).*
> That could be boring; like a slide show.
> *Not necessarily, for you can explore the still pictures with your camera, giving them a certain amount of movement. The secret is to keep the shots very brief, and to add sound effects and perhaps music. Supposing for instance, you had a still of a bear standing on its hind legs. Shooting its upper half, you turn the picture quickly, and create the impression that it has lurched forward. Pan towards a head, and it pushes into the frame. A series of intercut shots can look highly dramatic . . . if that's the effect you want. Anyway you could include some video of bears.*
> Where would we get these various pictures of the bear?
> *Stills could come from books (with permission). And you could shoot video in a zoo, or a museum.*

. . . and so it goes on.

Note how each decision leads to another development. If you decide on the zoo, you then have to follow up how, when and where you are going to get these shots. If you prefer to use the museum specimen, does it have to be lit? Are there glass reflection problems? Can you get the viewpoint needed?

You may not be able to decide at this point, but will have to do some *research*, to see how feasible that particular idea is.

10.18 Finding out

There are, in fact, several stages during the creation of a program when you will probably need more information before you can go on to the next step.

Your 'research' might amount to nothing more than hearing that Uncle David has a friend who has a stuffed bear that he would lend you for your program. You discover extra opportunities and problems as you search. They could even alter the way you eventually decide to treat the subject. You might encounter an enthusiast who can supply you with enough material to fill a dozen programs on the subject, or you might have to scout around for crumbs here and there.

As you work through the production process, you will find various areas in which you want information, or have to make special arrangements. In Checklist 10.1, you will find a very general indication of the sorts of things you might need to enquire into, although these can vary considerably with the nature of the production.

Checklist 10.1 Typical research information

Lists can be very daunting, but here are reminders of typical areas you may need to look into, in the course of planning your production.

The idea

The exploratory process:
- Finding sources of information on the subject (people, books, publications).
- Arranging to consult these.
- Accumulating data.
- Selecting matter that is relevant to your idea.
- Who is your program for?
- What is the purpose of the program?
- Does it have to relate to existing program? (level; standards?)
- How long is it to run?
- Coordinating ideas into an outline, with headings, subheadings.
- Considering the program development, forming a rough script, or shooting script.

Practicality

Let's think about your ideas in practical terms:
- What will you actually want to see and hear at each point in the program?
- Where will you shoot the action?
- What sort of things do you expect to need for each sequence (e.g. items, furnishings)?
- How do you think of arranging the scene? (Action in broad outline.)
- Do you want any particular effects?
- Are other people involved (e.g. demonstrator, actor)? Do you know suitable people?

The mechanics

What you need to shoot the program:
- Are you using a single camera? Consider the ways you will shoot the action (shot breakdown; sound or mute, editing).
- If you are using more than one camera, consider the equipment needed for the treatment you anticipate (including post-production work).
- Do you need to make, hire or buy any production items (e.g. graphics, furniture)?

Feasibility

Check what is really involved:
- Are the ideas and treatment you are developing, reasonable ones for your resources?
- Is there another way of achieving similar results more easily, more cheaply, more quickly, with less labor?
- Can you really get the items you need?
- Will you be able to get to the location?
- Is there sufficient time (to do research; carry out schedule, etc.)?
Costs:
- What is your budget?
- You may need to research possible costs for a sequence, before including it in your production.
- Can you get advance payments for expenses?
- Do you have to pay in advance for services, purchases?
Assistance:
- Will you need assistance, manpower, expert aid or advice, extra transport, etc., to do the job?
- What talent is involved? (amateur, professional, casual?)
- Do you need professional services? (to make items, service, prepare graphics, etc.)
Facilities:
- Are your available facilities sufficient for the shooting anticipated, and post-production work?
- Will you need to augment them?
- Will you need to borrow, hire, buy, adapt?
Problems:
- Try to anticipate any major problems such as whether a sequence can still be shot if the weather deteriorates.

- Is there any obvious danger factor (e.g. shooting a cliff-climb)?
- Will the situation you need for the program be available at the time you are shooting (e.g. snow in summer)?

Time:
- Will there be sufficient time to shoot the sequence?
- Prepare for eventualities. Instead of taking a couple of hours to shoot, it might take two days with an overnight stay, if things go wrong (high wind, rain, noise, etc.).

Administration

Various business arrangements and agreements:
- Permission to shoot, passes, permits, fees, etc.
- Copyright clearances, if you are using music, copying photographs, etc.
- Insurance may be necessary, to cover losses, breakages, injury, etc.
- There may be union agreements, and so *ad infinitum*.

Hiring

You might need to consider:
- Contractual arrangements for hiring performers,
- Operators, equipment, transport, scenery,
- Properties, costumes, services (e.g. editing suite, tape duplication), etc., etc.

Organizing

Another broad area, including such things as:
- Arranging transport, accommodation, food, storage.
- Return of borrowed/hired items.
- As you build up the program, you draw up a shooting diary, that helps you to avoid overlapped appointments, or wasted periods.

Remote survey (the 'recce')

The preliminary survey of the site of a location:
- Checking out the local conditions, anticipating any problems.
- Local organization.
- See Checklist 10.2 for details.

10.19 Remote surveys (the 'recce')

Fundamentally, there are two sorts of conditions under which you will be shooting: at *base*, and away *on location*.

Your *base* is wherever you are normally centered, and shoot indoor work. It may be a studio, classroom, hall or a room. The sort of material you are likely to shoot at base includes 'formal' interviews, announcements to camera, table-top work, graphics, titles, etc., and perhaps demonstrations, musical items and talks.

You use your base all the time, so you know exactly what facilities are available (e.g. equipment, supplies and scenery), where things are, the amount of room free, and so on. If you need to supplement what is there, you can easily do so.

A *location*, on the other hand, is anywhere away from your center. It may just be outside the building, or way out in the country. It could be in any sort of vehicle, down a mine, or in someone's home. 'Location' is a good broad catch-all term.

The main thing about shooting away from base is to find out what you are in for beforehand. You could simply arrive hopefully, and not have a single problem. But it is a lot better to be prepared!

The preliminary visit to any location (remote survey; site survey; location survey; 'recce'/reconnaissance) is an essential bit of program preparation. In practice, it can become anything from a quick look around, to a detailed survey of the site. What you find there may (probably will) influence the production treatment you have in mind.

In Checklist 10.2, you will find typical items you may need to check out, in preparation for your shooting schedule.

Checklist 10.2 The remote survey ('recce')

How much detail you need about a location site, varies with the nature of your production. Information that may seem trivial at the time, can prove valuable later in guiding others.

Location sites can be interiors, under-cover exteriors or open-air sites. Each has its own problems.

Useful 'tools' for the visit
Note-pads, pens, maps (route, local), compass, measure, photo-camera (Polaroid), video camera/VCR for site check, light meter, stopwatch, flashlight, small audio recorder with mike, string, gaffer tape, protective clothing, radio intercom.

Sketches
- Prepare rough maps of route to site (include distance, travel time).
- Show position of location.
- Rough layout of site (e.g. room plan).
- Anticipated camera viewpoints.

Local conditions
- Contact local people for information and advice on the site, local conditions, etc. Their guidance can be invaluable.
- Are there any known local problems relative to the tide, wind, animals, low-flying aircraft?
- Is there easy access to site? At any time, or at certain times only?
- Any traffic problems? Do the public have access to site? Are crowds likely during shooting?
- On the shooting date, will it be market day, early closing, carnival, parade, etc.?
- Any obvious problems in shooting there? Dangerous? Protective clothing needed? OK if raining?

Selected viewpoints
- Check around location for best/most appropriate viewpoints.
- Are these what you want? Are they optimum positions? Is the required range of shots possible from them?
- Are the positions easy to reach, and safe to use? (Any precautions needed, e.g. rope, scaffolding?)
- Will the camera mounting be safe there? (stable, unlikely to move or fall?)
- Any obstructions? Any obvious distractions (e.g. large signs, reflections)?
- Are the viewpoints spread around? Easy access between them (e.g. top and bottom of a cliff)?

Other people on site
- Is anyone else using or working on site during scheduled shooting (e.g. people walking through, working, sightseeing)?
- Are people using equipment on or near site during shooting (e.g. machinery, lorries, excavators, fairground, tree felling, airfield)?

Aid needed
- Do you need assistance from site custodian, electrician, engineer, security?
- Local transport needed (e.g. truck, horses, boatman)?
- Are local police required (crowds), or fire services needed on call?
- Local addresses and phone numbers for police, fire, hospital, doctor, hotel, restaurant?
- Ensure anyone assisting you knows necessary details of when/where you are shooting.
- Are you shooting an event arranged by others (e.g. parade, ceremony, display)? If so, get their guidance about shot selection, times, durations, routes, etc. Will there be any rehearsals you could attend?

Permission needed
- Is site access restricted? Do you need to get permission (or keys) to enter site? From whom?
- Any parking problems? (Where to park?)
- Any payments, fees, gratuities involved? Any insurance needed (against damage or injury)?

Intrusions	• Do you need to take care in which direction you are shooting (distractions, anachronisms)? • Is the public likely to get into shot or prove an embarrassment (as passers-by or spectators, chatter, litter)? • Any animals wandering nearby (e.g. cattle, sheep, horses)? • Will you be creating hazards for other people (e.g. cables, equipment)? • Are there any possibilities of interference from high-power radar, strong magnetic fields, heat, medical equipment, etc.?
Lighting	• Will you be shooting in daylight? How will the light change throughout the day? (How will sun direction change? Is tonal contrast OK? Are light levels likely to be OK? Any deep shadows? Are you augmenting daylight with reflectors, or punch lights?) • Will you be shooting in artificial light? (theirs, yours or mixed?) Will they be on at the time you are shooting? • If you are lighting the scene, are appropriate supplies available nearby? • Estimate number of lamps, positions, power needed, supplies, cabling required (and its routing), and safety considerations. • Who is transporting, rigging, cabling, supplying lighting equipment? (local hire?) Does equipment need manning (e.g. following with reflector or spotlight)?
Sound	• Consider method of sound pick up. • Any potential problems with acoustics, sound carrying, strong wind rumble? • Any extraneous sounds (elevators, phones, typewriters, machinery, children, aircraft, seagulls, plowing, etc.)? • Any playback needed (e.g. music for miming in sync with a recorded song)?
Wind and weather	• Alternative positions/locations if weather is bad? (shelter available?)
Continuity	• Do the light or weather conditions for the scenes shot on this site relate to material shot elsewhere (e.g. a studio interior setting)?
Set dressing	• Do any items need to be brought to the site to augment what is there, or alter its appearance (signs, graphics, posters, props, drapes)?
Time	• Consider the time taken for travel, setting up the unit, arranging camera/lights/sound/scenery. • Consider time and effort involved in moving from one camera viewpoint to another. • Consider the difficulty of shots or action, and possible time involved in retakes if they do not work.
Cueing	• Consider methods and problems of cueing action to start (e.g. when someone should enter a room). • Any arrangements needed, for lighting operator to switch lights on cue? • Any radio intercom needed?
Staffing/labor	• Consider manpower requirements; especially if action is spread around a site.
Welfare	• Transport for performers and staff. • Feeding arrangements? • Accommodation needed (where, when, how many)? • Washing and personal comfort? • First aid arrangements?
Security	• Consider arrangements for security (e.g. personal items, equipment, props, etc.).
Travel arrangements	• Personnel, baggage, equipment.

10.20 Developing the contents

To recap, we now have:

- The *main subject* of the program.
- An outline with *headings* of topics to be covered.
- Under each heading, we have *sub-headings* guiding us to the features we are going to discuss.
- Finally, we checked out whether these ideas are viable.

Do not regard this 'weeding out' process as one that stifles the imagination. It is a way of avoiding wasting time and money on profitless effort; a way of keeping one's feet firmly on the ground.

Now you are reaching the stage at which you should be thinking about how you are going to present these ideas.

At one point perhaps, you want someone to show a series of objects and pictures to the camera. How do you do this?

He could have them on his desk, and hold them up to the camera, one at a time. But wouldn't that be boring?

It might be. To some extent, it depends on his manner. If he is condescending, or lectures us, or goes through them mechanically, it certainly would be. But if he shows enthusiasm, and reveals them to us one by one, rather like bran-tub 'goodies', the result could be really interesting, in spite of the simplicity of the presentation.

However, to create visual variety, let's assume that he gets up from the desk and goes over to show us a picture on the wall. It is of a group of polar bears on an ice floe, and below the picture on a side-table is a carved group, and so on.

That's fine for the moment. It is beginning to sound like part of a script. The treatment seems quite *practicable*. A desk and side-table will be easy to get, and there was a picture in the book we looked up the other day . . .

Of course, you might well find that the first idea you have for a sequence is obviously *impracticable*.

Supposing your program includes a scene from a moment in history. It's easy to be ambitious, but the scene only lasts for about a minute. It tells how a raging mob besieges a house, battering at the door, throwing rocks . . . Hardly the sort of thing one can tackle on a low budget! Isn't it out of the question?

Why not approach the scene *indirectly*? What if we watched the terrified expression of the person in the house, the camera getting closer and closer until the screen is filled by a single eye with a falling tear, as the noises of the mob, and the pounding (effects discs) echo louder and louder in his head? A commentary over sets the scene. Whether the result is poignant or corny, is up to you.

10.21 Freedom to plan

In practice, how far can you plan a production, depends on how much control you have of the situation. If you are shooting a public event, your planning may consist of finding out what is going on, deciding on the best visual opportunities, selecting viewpoints, etc. You'll have little or no opportunity to adjust events to suit your productional ideas.

If on the other hand, the situation is entirely under your control, you can arrange matters to suit your particular needs. Having rationalized your ideas, you then have to organize the contributory elements of the production, and explain your ideas to other people who are involved.

Single camera shooting. When you are shooting with a *single camera*, you will usually find yourself in one of two situations:

- *Planning in principle, and shooting as opportunity allows.* For example, you intend taking shots of local wildlife; but what you actually shoot, must depend on what you find when you get there.
- *Detailed analysis and shot planning.* This approach is widely used in film making. Here you examine the action in a scene, and break it down into separate shots. Each shot is rehearsed and recorded independently. Where action is continuous throughout several shots, it is *repeated* for each camera viewpoint.

    Shot 1. Long shot: an actor walks away from camera, towards a wall mirror.
    Shot 2. Mid shot: he repeats the action, approaching the camera located beside the mirror.
    Shot 3. Close shot: he repeats the walk as the camera shoots into the mirror watching his expression as he approaches. . .

When edited together, the action is to appear continuous. So it's essential to keep the continuity of shots in mind throughout.

It is regular practice to record the complete action in long shot, then take close shots separately. These can then be relit for maximum effect. Even when a person is supposedly speaking to someone else, it is quite usual to have them alone, repeating a speech to camera, to allow the camera to be placed in the best position.

Multi-camera shooting. When shooting with two or more cameras, a director tends to think in terms of *effective viewpoints* rather than specific shots. The results may be similar, but the strategy is different, for cameras have to be positioned to catch various aspects of continuous action.

When planning a multi-camera show, the director has to consider various mechanics, including:

- Whether one camera will come into another's shot.
- Whether there is time for cameras to move to various positions.
- The variety of shots possible in different cameras.
- Whether a camera needs to be released to move over to another setting.
- How the sound boom, lighting, etc., relate to the camera's movements.

It all becomes a lot simpler of course, if you record the program as a series of brief sequences (which are edited together afterwards), but that takes much longer.

Writing the script

10.22 The script's purpose

Most of use prefer to avoid unnecessary paperwork. If you are working entirely by yourself, you might possibly get away with a few notes on the back of an envelope. But planning is an essential part of serious production, and the script forms the basis for that plan.

- it helps the director to clarify his ideas, and to develop a project that will work.
- It helps to coordinate the production team.

● It helps them to assess the resources needed.

Although you will meet professional crews on location (at a news event for instance) who appear to be shooting entirely spontaneously, they are invariably working to a pattern that has proved successful in the past.

For certain types of production, such as a drama, the script actually *begins* the production process. The director reads the draft script, which contains general information on characters, locations, stage directions, and all the dialogue. He/she envisions the scenes, assesses possible treatment, while anticipating the script's opportunities and potential problems. At this stage, changes may be made to improve the script, or make it more practicable. Next the director goes on to prepare a camera-treatment.

Another method of scripting begins with an *outline*. Here you decide on the various topics you want to cover, and the amount of time you can allot to each. You then develop a script based on this outline, and decide on the camera treatment for each part in turn.

When preparing a documentary, an extended outline becomes a *shooting script*, showing the location unit details of typical shots required. It may include any on-the-spot dialogue to be delivered to camera. All other dialogue (commentary) is developed later, together with effects and music, to suit the edited program.

10.23 Is a script needed?

The form of script you use, will largely depend on the kind of program you are making. There will be situations, particularly where talent are extemporizing as they speak or perform, when the 'script' simply lists details of the productional group, facilities needed, scheduling, and shows basic camera positions, etc.

An *outline script* will include any prepared dialogue (e.g. opening and closing announcements). Where people are going to improvize, the script may just list the order of topics to be covered. (These may be written on a *cue board/cue sheet* and presented to them as reminders while they are speaking.)

If it is a multi-item program, then a *breakdown sheet/show format/ running order** will prove useful. This lists the program segments (scenes), showing:

● The *topic* (e.g. Guitar solo).
● The amount of *time* allowed for each time – essential in a live multi-contribution show.
● The *names* of talent involved.
● *Facilities* – cameras and audio pickup allocated.
● *Contributory sources* – details of any videotape or film inserts, etc. Where various items are already recorded on tape or film to be inserted into the program, the script will usually show the opening and closing words of each contribution (*in-words, out-words*) and its duration. This assists accurate cueing.

*Often wrongly called a *rundown sheet* – the term for a 'fact sheet' which summarizes information about a product or item for a demonstration program; details of a guest for an interviewer.

Table 10.1 Breakdown sheet/running order/show format

This lists the items or program segments in a show, in the order they are to be shot. It may show durations, who is participating, shot numbers, etc.

Example:

	CARING FOR THE ELDERLY	Total duration 15 min
1	OPENING TITLES & MUSIC	00:10
2	PROGRAM INTRO.	00:30
3	PROBLEMS OF MOBILITY	02:20
4	INJURIES	02:15
5	DIET	02:45
6	DAILY ACTIVITIES	03:40
7	EXERCISES	01:20
8	AIDS & GADGETS	01:15
9	CLOSING LINK	00:25
10	END TITLES	00:10
		15:00

10.24 Basic script formats

Basically, script layout takes two forms:

● a single-column format,
● a two-column format.

Single-column or filmic format. In this arrangement, all video and audio information is contained in a single main column. Before each scene, an explanatory introduction describes the location and the action.

You can make any reminder notes in a wide left-hand margin, including transition symbols (e.g. X=Cut; FU=fade-up; SUPER 2=superimpose Cam.2.), indicate cues, camera instructions, make thumbnail sketches of shots or action, etc.

This type of script is widely used for film production, and single-camera video, where the director works alongside the camera operator. It is perhaps less useful in a multi-camera setup, where the production team is more dispersed, everyone needing to know the director's intentions throughout.

Two-column format. This traditional TV format is extremely flexible and informative. It gives all members of the production team shot-by-shot details of what is going on. They can also add their own particular information (e.g. details of lighting changes) as they need.

Two versions of the script are usually prepared. In the first (*rehearsal script*), the right-hand column only is printed. Subsequently, after detailed planning and pre-studio rehearsals, all production details are added to the left hand column, to form the *camera script*.

SINGLE COLUMN FORMAT

SINGLE CAMERA SHOOTING SCRIPT

FADE IN:

1.   EXT: FRONT OF FARMHOUSE – DAY

     Front door opens. FARMER comes out, walks up to gate.
     Looks left and right along road.

2.   EXT: LONG SHOT OF ROAD OUTSIDE FARM (Looking east) – DAY

     POV shot of FARMER looking along road, waiting for car.

3.   EXT: FARM GATE – DAY

     Waist shot of farmer leaning over gate, looking anxiously.
     He turns to house,
     calling.

        FARMER:
        I can't see him. If he doesn't come soon, I'll be late.

4.   INT: FARMHOUSE KITCHEN – DAY

     Wife is collecting breakfast things. Sound of radio.

        WIFE:
        You're too impatient. There's plenty of time.

5.   EXT: FARM GATE – DAY

     Mid-shot of FARMER, same position. He looks in other direction.
     Sound of distant car approaching. Sudden bang, then silence.

     Etc.

TWO-COLUMN FORMAT

MULTI-CAMERA SHOOTING SCRIPT

SHOT	CAM (Position)	SCENE / ACTION / AUDIO	
CAMS:	1B, 2D, 3A	*SOUND: SMALL BOOM B*	
		SCENE 4. INT. BARN – NIGHT	
15.	*F/U 2 D* *L/S DOORWAY* *Zoom in to WS* *as FARMER enters*	*(FARMER ENTERS, HANGS* *LAMP ON WALL-HOOK* *BESIDE DOOR)* *FARMER: It's getting late.* *How is the poor beast doing?/*	*TAPE 7:WIND* *DISC 5:RAIN*
16.	*1 B O/S SHOT* *SON'S POV*	*SON: I don't think she'll last the night.* *She has a high fever./*	
17.	*3 A LS FARMER* *He comes* *into WS*	*(FARMER WALKS FORWARD TO THE STALL)* *FARMER: I called Willie. He's* *on his way.* *(FARMER KNEELS BESIDE COW)/ DISC 9:THUNDER*	
18.	*2 D CU SON*	*SON: D'you think he'll be able to get* *here?/*	
19.	*1 C CU FARMER*	*FARMER: If the bridge holds.* *But the river's still rising/*	
Etc.			

. . . .

Abbreviations used:

F/U	*Fade up*		*CU*	*Close-up*
O/S	*Over shoulder*		*WS*	*Waist shot*
POV	*Point of view*		*LS*	*Long shot*
___/	*Indicates point to 'cut to next shot'*			

10.25 The full script

When a program is fully scripted, it includes detailed information on all aspects of the production.

- *Scenes*. Most productions are divided into a series of *scenes*. Each covers a *complete continuous action sequence* and is identified with a number and location (e.g. Scene 3 – Office set). A scene can involve anything from an interview, to a dance routine, a song, or a demonstration sequence.
- *Shots*. When the director has decided how he is going to interpret the script, each scene will be sub-divided into a series of *shots*; each showing the action from a particular viewpoint. These shots are numbered consecutively for easy reference, in the order in which they will be screened.

In a live show, you shoot in the scripted order (*running order*). When taping a production, you can shoot in whatever order is most convenient (*shooting order*). You may decide to omit shots ('drop Shot 25'), or to add extra shots (Shots 24A, 24B, etc.). You may record Shot 50 before Shot 1, and edit them into running order later.

- *Dialogue*. The entire prepared dialogue; spoken to camera, or between people. (They may learn it, or read it off prompters of some kind.)
- *Equipment*. The script indicates which camera/microphone is being used for each shot (e.g. *Cam. 2. Fishpole*).
- *Basic camera instructions*. Details of each shot and camera moves (e.g. *Cam. 1 close shot on Joe's hand; dolly out to long shot.*)
- Switcher (*vision mixer*) *instructions* – i.e. cut, mix, superimpose Cam. 2.
- *Contributory sources*. Details of where videotape and film inserts, graphics, remotes, etc., appear in the program.

10.26 The drama script

Although a drama script too follows this arrangement, many organizations prepare the full script in two stages; the *rehearsal script* and the *camera script*.

The rehearsal script. This begins with general information sheets, including a cast/character list. production team details, rehearsal arrangements, etc.

There may be a synopsis of the plot or story line; particularly when scenes are to be shot/recorded out of order.

The rehearsal script includes full details of:

- Location – The setting (e.g. Lounge).
- *Time of day, and weather conditions* – Night, storm.
- *Stage instructions* – The room is candlelit, and the log fire burns brightly.
- *Action* – Basic information on what is going to happen in the scene (i.e. actors' moves, business (Joe lights a cigar.))
- *Dialogue* – Speaker's name (character) followed by their dialogue. All delivered speech, voice over, voice inserts (e.g. phone conversation), commentary, announcements, etc. (Perhaps with comments; e.g. 'sadly', 'sarcastically'.)
- *Cues/effects* – Indicating the moment for a change to take place (e.g. lightning flash, explosion, Joe switches light out).
- *Audio instructions* – Music and effects.
- Information on titling, video effects, other contributory sources, etc.

The camera script. This is built up by adding full details of the production treatment to the left side of the 'rehearsal script', and includes:

● The shot number.
● The camera used for that shot.
● The position of that camera on the set (optional).
● Basic shot details and camera moves (e.g. CU on Joe. Dolly back to LS as he rises).
● Switcher instructions (e.g. cut, slow mix, superimpose Cam 2. etc.).

10.27 Hints on script-writing

There are no short cuts to good script writing, any more than there are to writing short stories, music or painting a picture. You will learn techniques through observation, experience and reading. But there are general guides that are worth bearing in mind as you prepare your script. You will find a useful list on pages 177–178 (Hints on developing the script).

10.28 Be visual

Aim to present your material in visual terms as far as possible. Where you want your audience to concentrate on what they are hearing, try to make the picture less demanding at that point. If for instance, they are listening to a detailed argument, and trying to read a screenful of statistics at the same time, they may well do neither successfully. Your picture can strengthen or emphasize what they are hearing.

Programs vary in the way they distribute audience interest between the sound and the picture. A show may be mainly visual, with comparatively few words to script. Or conversely, it may rely almost entirely on what is being said, while the pictures are little more than an interesting accompaniment. There are even programs in which either the pictures or the sound are virtually unnecessary!

There will be times when you may find it hard to decide on any relevant picture to accompany the all-important sound, and then you may need to resort to a certain amount of improvised 'visual padding'! (See section 11.8.)

10.29 Assimilation rate

Whatever type of program you are preparing, aim to develop it as a smooth-flowing sequence, making one point at a time. Avoid those tempting diversions that keep leading your audience well away from the main theme. As far as possible, try not to hop back and forth between one subject and another. Especially, you should avoid the three-ring circus effect, in which you are trying to cover several different activities simultaneously. Ideally, one sequence should seem to lead naturally on to the next.

There were a number of important points in the previous paragraph, and if you presented ideas at that rate in a video program, there is every chance that your audience would forget most of the information. Unlike them, you can read this at your own pace, stop and re-read whatever you like. They usually cannot. An essential to remember when scripting, is the difference between the rates at which we can take in information in different media.

A lot depends, of course, on how familiar your audience already is with the subject and the terms used. Where details are new to them, and the

Hints on developing the script

Effective *script writing* comes from:

- Carefully assessing your audience.
- Appropriate techniques and style.
- A treatment of appropriate length.
- A treatment suitable for the budget and facilities available.

Different kinds of script need different approaches; but they all have common ground. Although we cannot hope to detail techniques and processes, here are some guiding principles, and questions you will need to ask yourself.

Ask yourself

Who is the program for?
- Age group? (e.g. Children, college classes, mature students.)
- A specialist audience? (e.g. Salesman, teachers, hobbyists.)
- Where is it to be shown? (e.g. Classroom, home, public place.)
- Is it for private study (carrel) or mass audience?
- Display screen use? (e.g. Museum display, marketing, exhibition.)

What is the purpose of this program?
- Entertainment, information, instruction?

Is the program one of a series?
- Does it relate to or follow on other programs?
- Do you need to remind viewers of past information?
- Does the script style need to be similar?

Does your audience already know?
- Are they familiar with the subject?
  Do they understand the terms used?
  Is the information complicated?
  Do you need to recap previous information?
- Would a brief outline or introduction help (or remind) them?

How long is the program?
- Is it brief? (Having to make an immediate impact.)
- Is it long enough to develop arguments or explanations, for a range of topics?

What is the program's emphasis?
- On *display and visual effect* (e.g. visual flim-flam),
- On *techniques* (e.g. training program),
- On *data* (e.g. economics),
- On *personalities* (e.g. interview),
- On *persuasion* (e.g. advertising spot).

How much detail is required in the script?
- Is the script to be complete, with dialogue and action?
  (Actual visual treatment depends on the Director.)
- Is the script a basis for improvization (e.g. by a guide or lecturer)?
- Is it an ideas-sheet, giving an outline for treatment?

Is the script to be written before or after shooting?
- Is it to guide shooting treatment?
- It is commentary for an edited picture sequence?

Are you writing dialogue?
- Is it for actors to read, or inexperienced performers?
  (For the latter, keep it brief, in short 'bites' to be read from a prompter, or spoken in their own words.)
- Is it to be naturalistic or 'character dialogue'?

Is the subject a visual one?
- If the subjects are abstract, or no longer exist, how will you illustrate them?

Have you considered the script's requirements?
- It only takes a few words on the page to suggest a situation, but to reproduce it in pictures and sound may require considerable time, expense, and effort (e.g. a battle scene). It may have to rely on available stock library film.

Does the subject involve research?
- The script may depend on what researchers discover while investigating the subject.

Where will your picture come from?
- Will the subjects be brought to the studio? (This allows maximum control over the program treatment and presentation.)
  Or will cameras be going on location to the subjects – e.g. shooting in museums, etc.? Script opportunities may depend on what is available when you are shooting.

Remember

Be visual
- Sometimes pictures alone can convey the information, and no commentary or accompanying sound.
- The way a commentary is written (and spoken) can influence how the audience interprets a picture (and vice versa).
- Pictures can distract. People may concentrate on looking instead of listening!
- Avoid 'talking heads' wherever possible. Show the subject being talked about, rather than the person who is speaking.
- The script can only *indicate* visual treatment. It will seldom be specific about shot details, unless that is essential to the plot or situation. Directors have their own ideas!

Avoid over-loading
- Keep it simple. Don't be long-winded, or use complicated sentences. Keep to the point. When a subject is difficult, an accompanying diagram, chart, or graph may help to make the information easier to understand.
- Do not give too much information at a time.
- Do not attempt to pack too much information into the program. It is better to do justice to a few topics, than to cover many inadequately.

Develop a flow of ideas
- Deal with one subject at a time. Generally avoid intercutting between different topics, flashbacks, flashforwards.
- If the screen has text to be read, either have an unseen voice read the same information, or leave the viewer time to read it.
- Do not have quite different information on the screen and in the commentary (distracting, confusing).
- Aim to have one subject or sequence lead naturally into the next.
- Where there are a number of separate different topics, consider how they are to be related; e.g. speaker walks from one display to another; a decorative transition.

Pace
- Vary the pace of the program. Avoid a fast pace, when imparting facts. It conveys an overall impression, but facts do not sink in. A slow pace can be boring or restful, depending on the occasion.
- Remember, that your audience cannot refer back. If they miss a point, they may fail to understand the next – or even lose interest.

Style
- Use an appropriate writing style. Generally aim at an informal, relaxed style – avoiding slangy colloquialisms.
- There is a world of difference between the style of the printed page, and the way people normally speak. Read from a prompter, it produces unnatural, stilted effect.
- Be very careful about introducing humour in the script!

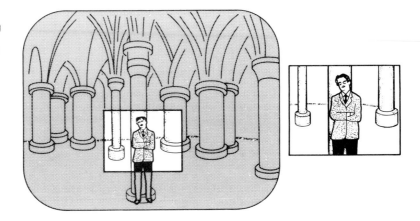

Figure 10.3 Over-familiarity
The director knows how interesting the location is . . . but does he reveal it to his audience? Or is it a 'pillar-through-the-head' to them?

information is complicated, it is better to linger rather than leap ahead. Ironically, something that can seem difficult and involved at the first viewing, can appear slow and obvious a few viewings later. That is why it is so hard for program-makers to estimate the effect of material on those who are going to be seeing it for the first time. They have themselves become so familiar with it, that they know it by heart.

Simplify! The more complex the subject you are dealing with, the easier each stage should be. If the density of information, or the rate at which you deliver it is too high, it will confuse, bewilder or just encourage your audience to switch off – mentally, if not actually.

10.30 Relative pace

You will soon find as you build up a sequence of pictures, and an accompanying soundtracks, that both the picture and the sound track have their own natural pace. It may be slow and leisurely, medium-paced, fast or brief. If you are fortunate, the pace of the picture and the sound will be roughly the same. However, there will be occasions when you find that you do not have enough picture to fit the sound sequence, or you do not have enough soundtrack to put behind the amount of action in the picture.

Often, when a commentary has explained a point (perhaps taking 5 secs.), the picture is still showing the action (perhaps 20 secs.). We need to let the picture complete, before taking the commentary on to the next point. In the script therefore, a little dialogue may go a long way, as a series of interjections, rather than a continual flow of verbiage.

The reverse can happen too, where the action in the picture is brief, e.g. a locomotive passes through the shot in a few seconds, quicker than it takes us to talk about it. So we need more picture of the subject, from another viewpoint perhaps, to support the dialogue.

Even when picture and sound are more or less keeping the same pace, do not habitually cut to a new shot immediately the action in a picture is finished. Sometimes it is better to continue the picture briefly, in order to allow time for the audience to absorb the facts, rather than press on with fast cutting and a quickfire commentary.

It is all too easy to overload the soundtrack. Without pauses in a commentary, it can become an endless outpouring. Moreover, if you have a detailed script that fits in with every moment of the picture, and the commentator happens to slow down at all, the words can get out of step with the key shots they are related to. Then you have the choice of cutting parts of the commentary, or building out the picture (e.g. with cutaway shots) to enable picture and sound to be brought into line.

10.31 Style

The worst type of script for video, film or radio, is the sort that has been written in a formal literary style, as if for a newspaper article or an essay, where the words, phrases and sentence construction are those of the printed page.

When you read this sort of script aloud, it tends to sound like an official statement or a pronouncement, rather than the fluent everyday speech we are really aiming at. Not, of course, that we want a script that is so colloquial that it includes all those hesitations and slangy half-thoughts one tends to use, but certainly one that avoids complex sentence construction.

It takes some experience to be able to read any script fluently, with the natural expression that brings it alive. But if the script itself is written in a stilted, fussy style, it is unlikely to improve with hearing. Try to present your material as if you are talking to the individual in your audience, rather than proclaiming on a stage, or addressing a public meeting. Probably the best way to achieve this, until you are more used to the style needed, is to prepare it by chatting to an audio recorder, as if you were explaining the subject to a friend opposite. And talk in the present tense rather than the past, for it is more vital.

The way you deliver information can influence how interesting it seems to be. The mind boggles at: 'The retainer lever actuates the integrated contour follower'. But we immediately understand: 'Here you can see, as we pull this lever, the lock opens'.

If your audience has to pause to work out what you mean, they will not be listening closely to what you are saying. You can often help them by anticipating the problems; with a passing explanation, or a subtitle (especially useful for names), or a suitable diagram.

10.32 Copyright and contracts

Whenever you want to make use of material prepared and created by other people – a piece of music, a sound recording, video tape, film, a picture in a book, a print, a photograph, etc. – you are liable to pay a fee to the *copyright holders*, or an appropriate organization operating on their behalf, for copyright clearance.

The copyright law is complex and varies between different countries, but it protects the originators from having their work copied without permission. So you cannot for example, prepare a video program with music dubbed from a commercial recording, with inserts from TV programs, magazine photographs, advertisements, and so on, without the permission of the respective copyright owners, and appropriate fees. These fees will depend on the purpose and use of your program. (There are exceptions when the program is only to be seen within the home, or is restricted to permitted study use.) In most cases, you can trace the copyright obligations through the source of the material you want to use (e.g. the publisher of a book or photograph).

Agreements take various forms. They may be restricted or limited. You may have a license, and/or pay a fee for use. For music and sound effects, you may pay a royalty per use ('needle time'), buy the rights to use an item or a package ('buy-out method').

Organizations concerned with performance rights for music (copyright clearance for use of recorded music, or to perform music) include The Harry Fox Agency (New York), ASCAP (American Society of Composers, Authors and Publishers), SESAC (Society of European Stage Authors and Composers), BMI (Broadcast Music, Inc.) the MCPS (Mechanical Copyright Protection Society Ltd., London), the Performing Rights Society (PRS).

When clearing copyright for music, both the record company and the music publishers may be involved.

Music in *public domain* (e.g. old traditional songs) will not itself be subject to copyright, but any arrangement or performance will.

Whenever you hire talent (e.g. actors, professional talent) or use services (e.g. scaffold construction) contractual agreements arise. Union agreements may also be involved. So, before committing yourself in any way, find out exactly what is entailed both financially and legally.

Apart from general shots, whenever you want to shoot in the street, it is wise to let the local police know in advance. You may cause an obstruction, or contravene local by-laws. Strictly speaking too, if you are shooting people, you must get their permission in writing (with their name and address) on a *release form*. Terminology varies, depending on the purpose for which you are shooting the scene, and the nature of their contribution; but the release form is couched in legal terms generally authorizing you to use their performance – free or for a fee.

Chapter 11

Production techniques

Watch broadcast programs carefully, and you will see the whole gamut of techniques: dull routines, imaginative interpretations and pretentious flim-flam.

The production team

Production groups vary in size, according to the organization and the complexity of the production. Titles and responsibilities differ. In some groups there are strict demarcations, in smaller units work is shared. Here are typical key positions.

Producer

Usually responsible for overall business organization, budget. May originate and write the production. (In smaller units the producer will often direct the production too.)

Director

Responsible for interpreting and staging the production. Advises, instructs and coordinates the production team. Chooses, hires and directs talent. Guides and cues performance; either directly or through the *Floor Manager*. Instructs cameras, switcher, sound specialists, etc. Supervises post-production editing.

Director's assistant

Production Assistant (*PA*), *Assistant* or *Associate Director*. Exact function varies. Takes director's notes (*re.* changes, retakes, performance, etc.), checks timings, gives routine cues (e.g. countdown for film insert), warns of camera moves and upcoming action, etc., while the director guides performance and cameras. Also general liaison between the director and crew.

Floor Manager

The director's representative and contact in the studio. Cues talent. Checks and directs floor crew. Responsible for general studio organization, safety, discipline, etc.

Switcher

Production switcher (vision mixer) operator. Job done by the director, a specialist operator, or the *Technical Director*.

Crew Chief
Technical Director. Supervises technical facilities and operations crew. May operate switcher. May instruct operational crew during production.

Cameras
Camera operators/cameramen responsible for all camera operations on a production. (Larger crews are led by a senior supervisory cameraman.)

Lighting
Lighting director designs, arranges, and controls all lighting treatment. Supervises *electrician(s)* who rig and set lighting equipment.

Audio
Audio engineer or specialist operator responsible for the sound balance, and technical/artistic quality of program sound. Supervises personnel operating microphones and all audio equipment.

Video control
Picture-quality control (adjusting video equipment) carried out by a specialist operator, or a *video engineer* (*shader*).

Make-up
Artist who designs and applies all make-up treatment.

Set design
Specialist designer who conceives, designs, and organizes the entire scenic treatment for a production. (Perhaps including graphics). Supervises scenic crew in erecting and dressing settings.

Videotape
Engineers/operators recording and replaying videotape machines. Videotape editing may be done by a specialist editor.

Video engineer
Technicians responsible for the maintenance and adjustment of all electronic equipment (cameras, sound).

Floor crew
(*Stagehands, grips*) Operatives who set up and dress settings; operate cue cards, prompting devices, etc.; may assist in moving equipment, etc.

Single- and multi-camera production

11.1 Opportunities and styles

There are radical difference between shooting with a *single camera*, and using a *multi-camera* set-up. Each method has its advantages and limitations.

If you are shooting continuous action with a *single camera*, and want to change your camera's viewpoint, you have two choices. You can move to the new position while still shooting (move 'on shot'), or miss some of the action between set-ups. A *multi-camera* group simply switches from one camera to another to alter the viewpoint – a clear advantage when you are shooting a series of events going on at the same time, or spread over a wide area.

Table 11.1 Prepare to record

- Check details of the next shot.
- Mark clapper board with scene No. and shot No.
- 'Is everyone ready?'
- 'Quiet please!'
- Start VCR and audio recorders.
- Show clapper board (5 s).
- 'Action!' (Cue; action begins).
- End of action. 'Cut!' (Action stops, talent wait)
- Stop recording.
- Check recording (end only, or 'spot check')
- Note final frames for continuity, log shot details (identification, duration), label tape.

either

- 'TAKE IS OK. LET'S GO ON TO SHOT 5'.

or

- 'WE NEED TO RETAKE THAT SHOT BECAUSE . . .'.
- Set up for next shot.

On the other hand, a single-camera video unit is independent, compact, and can go anywhere. There are none of the problems that can arise in coordinating a group of cameras. The director can be right there on the spot beside the cameraman, seeing opportunities, and explaining exactly what he/she wants. (The program-maker may operate his own camera!) The director of a multi-camera production is remote from his cameras, watching a series of picture monitors, and issuing instructions over an intercom. He has to contact talent through his floor manager.

In a multi-camera production most of the inter-shot transitions are made on a switcher. Editing techniques are rudimentary. (On a live show there are no opportunities to correct or improve.) However, you do have the great advantage that you can continuously monitor and compare shots. And you do not have the continuity problems, that can develop when shooting with a single camera.

The major benefit when shooting with a single camera, is that you are doing one thing at a time. You are concentrating on the picture and its immediate sound for a *specific shot*. You are not having to worry about intercutting, music, sound effects, video effects, etc., as in most multi-camera productions. They are added at a later stage. You can often adjust the camera position, composition, lighting and sound to suit each particular shot; unlike multi-camera treatment, where these may be a compromise. This all takes time of course, and tapes from a single camera invariably need extensive post-production work (editing, sound treatment, etc.). A multi-camera crew may rehearse and record a show, to produce the finished article in just a few hours.

11.2 What is the aim?

Some directors (and cameramen) imagine that they are using their cameras to show their audience 'things as they are'. They are not. The medium is inherently *selective*.

Even if you simply point your camera at the scene, and leave the rest to your audience, you have, whatever your intentions, made a selective choice on their behalf. *They* have not chosen to look at that particular aspect of the scene; *you* have. How much they see is determined by the type of shot you have shown them, and your camera's viewpoint. They cannot see the rest of the scene.

In fact, a skilled director uses the camera and the mike to give his audience the *impression of reality*. Through the images he presents, he creates an illusion.

Program-making is a *persuasive* art – persuading your audience to look and to listen; persuading them to do something in a particular way; persuading them to buy something, whether it is an idea or a product.

You want not only to arouse their interest, but to sustain it. You want to direct their attention to certain features of your subject, and would prefer that their minds did not wander to others.

You achieve all this by the shots you select, and the way you edit them together; by the way you use sound. Persuasion is not a matter of high budget and elaborate facilities, but of imagination.

You can even take a dull unpromising subject, such as an *empty box*, and influence how your audience feels about it!

Imagine you are sitting in darkness, when up on the screen comes a shot containing nothing more than a flatly lit wooden box in light gray surroundings. How do you think your audience would react?

Intercom instructions

In a multi-camera production, the director gives instructions to the studio crew through their headsets (cameras, sound, etc.). This *intercom* (*talkback*) cannot be overheard by microphones or performers.

Opening shots please	Cameras to provide initial shots in the show (or scene).
Ready 2	Stand-by cue for Cam. 2.
Give me a single (two shot)	Just have person(s) indicated in the shot.
Tighten your shot	Slightly closer shot (slight zoom in).
Go wider	Slightly more distant (slight zoom out).
Lose the hands	Compose shot to omit the hands.
Cut at the hands	Compose shot to just include the hands.
Kill the flowers	Remove them (unwanted, obtrusive).
Lose focus on Joe	Let Joe become defocused.
Stand-by for a rise (or sit)	Talent is about to stand (sit).
Hold the boy	Keep subject in shot as he moves.
Let him go	Allow subject to move out of shot.
Lose him	Recompose or tighten shot to exclude him.
Clear on 2	Cam. 2 can move to next position.
Stand him by	Alert him, ready for a cue.
Cue action/cue Joe	Give hand signal to Joe to begin action.
Hold it	Stop action/performance (to correct error).
Freeze there	Stop movement; hold it quite still (e.g. to check a position).
Back to the top/take it from the top	Begin again at start of scene; repeat the rehearsal.
Pick it up from 20	Recommence rehearsal (or shooting) from Shot 20.
Would they just walk it?	Ask actors to move through their action, without dialogue or performance.
Clear 2's shot	Something/someone is obscuring Cam. 2's shot.
Tighten them up	Move the people closer together.
Give him a mark	Make a floor mark (chalk) to show him a location point.
He should work to 2	He should face Cam. 2.
Stretch him	Tell him to go more slowly (i.e. there is time to spare).
Tell him to pad/keep talking	Tell him to improvize until next item is ready. (Hand signal: thumb and extended fingers touch and part.)
Give him a minute	He has a minute left (hand signal).
Give him a wind/wind him up	Signal him to finish.
Kill him/cut him	He is to stop immediately.
Give him a clear/clear him	We have left him. He is free to move away.

Also general camera guidance such as 'pan left', 'dolly back', 'zoom in'.

On seeing the shot, most us would *assume* that the picture is supposed to have some sort of meaning or purpose. So we start by wondering what it is all about. "What are we supposed to be looking at? Does the box have some significance that we've missed? Is someone coming on in a minute to explain?"

You have your audience's attention for a moment or two, for they are trying to understand what is going on. If there is a word stenciled on the box, they will probably read that, and then try to puzzle out what it means. They will look and listen, and finally get bored. But all that has probably only taken a few *seconds*!

You cannot rely on the *subject* alone, to hold your audience's interest. How you present it, is all important.

Let us imagine ourselves again in darkness, but now on the screen appears . . . a box, half-lit from behind . . . only part is visible . . . the rest falls away into a silhouette. A low rhythmical beat steadily fills our ears . . . The camera creeps slowly along the floor . . . creeps forward . . . very very slowly . . . pausing . . . then moving onward . . . stopping abruptly . . . then moving on again . . . Slow chords from an organ grow louder . . . and louder . . .

How is your audience going to react to *that*? If you have done it well, they are on the edges of their seats, anxious to find out what is in the box! The same box!

All right, so you cannot use such dramatic techniques in all programs! But it does show how persuasive the medium can be. It shows us how even such a simple situation, with an empty box, can be influenced by techniques.

But it is a reminder too, that the production treatment needs to be *appropriate*. It needs to create an ambience, an atmosphere, that is suitable for the occasion. Whether your program is to have show-biz glitter, or the business-like neutrality of a newscaster's reports, the enthusiastic participation of a kid's show, or the reverential air of a remembrance ceremony, its style of presentation should suit the occasion.

11.3 The camera's role

The camera is an 'eye'; but whose eye? It can be that of an onlooker, watching the action from the best possible position at each moment. This is its *objective* role.

Or you can use your camera in a *subjective* way. Moving around within the scene, the camera represents your own eyes, as you move through a crowd, or push aside undergrowth. The effect can be quite dramatic, especially if people within the scene seem to speak to you directly, through the camera's lens.

11.4 The camera as an observer

This is the way the camera is used in many types of program. It shows us the scene from *various viewpoints*, and we begin to feel a sense of space, as we build up a mental image of a situation – although the camera is only showing us a small section of the scene in each shot. The camera becomes an observer, moving close to see detail, and standing far back to take in the wider view.

We might, for example, watch two people sitting talking. As one speaks, we see a close shot of him. A moment later, the camera switches to show us the other person listening. From time to time, we see them together.

There is nothing *imaginative* about this treatment; but then, it is not intended to work on the audience's emotions. It is intended to show us clearly what is going on, who is there, where they are, what they are doing. It intermixes closer shots of the detail we want to see at a particular moment (people's expressions) with wider shots giving us a more general view of the situation. In fact, to treat a conversation in front of the camera in any other way, by dramatizing its presentation, would normally be quite inappropriate.

11.5 The persuasive camera

If, on the other hand, you are shooting a pop group, shots may be as bizarre and varied as you can make them. You are aiming to excite and to shock, to create great visual variety. There is no room for subtlety. Picture impact, strange effects and rapid changes in viewpoint thrust the music at your audience.

Between this brash display, and the subtle play on the emotions we met earlier (section 11.2), there is a world of difference. Yet they all demonstrate how you can influence your audience through the way you choose and compose your shots, move the camera, and then edit those shots together.

The high viewpoint looking down on the subject with an air of detachment; the low viewpoint that gives the subject exaggerated importance; the increasing tension as the camera dollies in, and which falls as we move away from the subject, are all typical of the ways in which the camera can affect your audience's responses to what they are seeing.

11.6 Beginning and ending

Part of a program's impact lies in the way it is packaged, how it is introduced, and how you bring it to its end.

At its start, your main aim is to grab the audience's attention, to arouse their interest and to hold it. You can do this in various ways: by shocking them, by intriguing them, by making them feel welcome, by impressing them, and so on.

One of the dreariest ways of introducing any program, is to provide a series of titles in dead silence, giving the name of the program, followed by lists of those appearing in it and those responsible for the production.

Music and attractive graphics can set the scene: jaunty happy music and quirky titles for a comedy; severe regal music and formal titling for a solemn occasion.

Today, titling does not pose too many problems, for apart from 'casual titling' that is finger-drawn in sand, or formed from children's blocks, or chalked on a wall, you can achieve excellent results with rub-on transfer sheets, or even home-computer generated lettering.

At the end of a program, you want your audience to be left with a feeling of completeness: that the program is now concluded; not that the show has petered out, or that someone has forgotten to put on the last reel!

You can achieve this partly by the inflexions in a commentator's voice during his concluding words, or by the way a musical background winds up. Generally speaking, it is poor practice to fade out in the middle of a musical passage, or as it is just beginning a new sequence, or to use music that has no apparent conclusion.

Again, you can end your program in several ways:

- gradually winding down to a quiet conclusion,
- with a climax; with a logical ending to a statement,
- with an open question, for the audience to answer,
- with a summary of earlier facts.

And finally of course . . .**THE END**. . . leaves your audience in no doubt.

11.7 Production methods

Most types of program follow paths that have been trodden in the past. For instance, there is no sparkling new way of interviewing someone; pretty well all feasible methods have been tried at some time or other. But that does not make such programs any less interesting. It does mean though, that you can benefit from what others have discovered.

There are no infallible, all-purpose formulae. But there certainly are approaches that experience has shown to suit particular subjects. In the following sections, you will find hints and reminders that could help you when shooting various regular forms of program.

11.8 There is nothing there!

We become so accustomed to seeing pictures accompanying any subject under the sun, that we can overlook one fundamental paradox. For many situations there is, strictly speaking, *no subject to shoot!* There are no pictures!

You will meet this problem on various occasions:

- Abstract subjects have no direct visuals (philosophical, social, spiritual concepts).
- General non-specific subjects (transport, weather, humanity).
- Imaginary events (fantasy, literature, mythology).
- Historical events – where no authentic illustrations exist.
- Forthcoming events – where the event has not yet happened.
- Where shooting is not possible – prohibited, or the subject is inaccessible.
- Where shooting is impracticable – dangerous, or you cannot get the optimum shots.
- Events now over, that were not photographed at the time.
- Events where the appropriate visuals would prove too costly – would involve travel, or have copyright problems.

So how do you cope with such situations? The least interesting method is to show someone standing outside a building, where the camera was not allowed in to watch a meeting, telling the audience what they would have seen if they had been there.

Newscasts frequently use this approach, for the event has come to an end. The bank robbery, the explosion or the fire are now over, and we can only look at the results.

Another method is to show photo-stills, or artwork of the people or places involved, with explanatory commentary over. And this could be the solution if you were discussing history such as the discovery of America or the burning of Rome. There might be some museum relics available to show, to enliven interest, but they are usually only peripheral to the main subject.

Sometimes you can show substitutes; not a picture of the actual bear that escaped from the circus, but one like it. You cannot show pictures of next month's parade, but you may be able to use shots of last year's fun and frolics.

At times, you may not be able to illustrate the subject directly. Instead, you will have to use visuals that are closely associated with it. For instance, if you do not have photographs or drawings of a composer, you might be able to show shots of his native country (e.g. by exploring projected slides with the camera). At a pinch, you could even zoom in to his birthplace, on a map. Otherwise, you could use atmospheric effects to accompany his music, such as pictures of sunlight rippling on water, wind in trees, waves breaking on the shore, reflections, children at play, or any other associated image that will serve as a visual accompaniment.

'Visual padding' of this kind (sometimes called 'wallpaper shots') is widely used in broadcast programs, in the form of general views of town and countryside, shots of traffic or people moving around.

These shots can:

● serve to fill out scenes that may running short during a commentary,
● be used as cutaways,
● be used wherever we do not have suitable visual material for one reason or another.

11.9 Shooting objects

Figure 11.1 Shooting objects
Here are a few 'obvious' points to remember, when presenting an object. But count how often you see them overlooked on air!
1. Avoid clutter.
2. Try to have contrasting background tones.
3. Multi shadows can confuse and distract.
4. Avoid confusing or distracting backgrounds.
5. Do not cut off parts of the object, unless you are showing detail.
6. See that handling does not obscure important detail.
7. Avoid shadowing the object (demonstrator or camera).
8. Do not show an unfamiliar viewpoint, unless you want puzzle pictures.

If you simply put something down in front of the camera and shoot it, results are often disappointing compared with those you can achieve with a little extra care. So here are a few reminders on how you can give such shots that added quality.

One successful method of arranging background material is to form a continuous crease-free plane from a hanging sheet of seamless paper, draped onto a table-top.

Whether you are shooting a vase of flowers, a sculpted form or a piece of jewelry, try to ensure that it has a suitable background. Plain contrasting tones are best (light against dark, or dark against light), or a contrasting pale colored background (e.g. fawn, light blue or pale green).

Dazzling white backgrounds make the subject itself look darker than normal, and exaggerate the brilliance of its colors. They can overwhelm the subject.

Black backgrounds too need to be used with care, for although they can throw the subject into prominent relief, they may emphasize color, and dark areas around the edges of the subject can vanish into the

1. Avoid clutter

2. Have contrasting background tones

3. Multi-shadows can confuse

4. Avoid confusing or distracting background

5. Do not cut off parts of subjects

6. Handling can obscure

7. Avoid shadowing the subject

8. Don't show an unfamiliar view of subject

surroundings. If you increase backlight to prevent this, it can produce an inappropriate glittering halo of light around the subject.

It is not always practicable to increase the illumination of large areas (e.g. a cyc) as it would involve more lamps or extra power. If a background appears too dim, consider reducing the subject/foreground lighting a little and opening up the lens. If the background is too bright, increase the subject lighting and stop down a little.

Strong background colors (e.g. red, yellow, or bright green) are not only very distracting, but they will modify the apparent colors of your subject.

If the subject you are showing is *flat* (e.g. a framed picture), shoot it from a straight-on viewpoint, and tilt the frame down a little to avoid light reflections, camera reflections or a shadow.

If a demonstrator has to put the item in position for the camera, it is often a good idea to have an unobtrusive position-mark on a table, to guide where it should be placed. A nearby monitor can show the camera's shot, to ensure that there are no reflections.

Solid objects are best lit with 'three-point lighting' (key; fill; backlight), or a side light to left and right with some frontal fill-light.

Close shots with a wide-angle lens, will create considerable distortion.

If the depth of field is too limited in a 'detail shot', you probably need to use a smaller *f*-stop; but this requires higher light levels. Instead of trying to increase the *overall* light level, take a separate close-up shot of the item afterwards, under stronger *localized* lighting, and insert this. Otherwise you will have to take a longer shot.

Rather than move the camera in an arc round the object (a difficult move to carry out smoothly), you may find it better to place the object on a turntable (manual or motor driven), which is slowly turned to see it from all directions.

A camera looking down on to an object on a table may not show it particularly successfully. Try putting the object on a small box or block on the table, to raise it, so that the camera can get a better straight-on shot. (Directors sometimes use this idea for seated people, placing their chairs on a raised platform or rostrum, so that the camera has a level viewpoint.)

Try to show objects *individually*, either by displaying them one at a time, or excluding others nearby with a tightly framed shot. If objects are in a group, you may be able to use localized lighting to select an individual item. Otherwise you may have to rely on differential focusing (i.e. a carefully focused zone) to give you a sharp image of your subject while blurring others. At worst, you can use a pointer to concentrate the viewer's attention on a particular object (see section 6.15).

Shooting people

11.10 A single person

Yes, it *is* possible to shoot a single person badly, so let us go over the basics and see how.

When anyone is speaking straight to the camera, you will not normally want anything larger than a close-up, framed to just below the neck-tie knot. Think twice before using really close shots of a person, because

Figure 11.2 Shooting a single person

Be prepared! A. When someone is sitting, be ready to follow him if he stands ('rises'), or you will cut his head off! B. Similarly, be ready for him to sit, if he is standing. Both situations are a reminder that you cannot lock-off the panning head during action.

(a)

(b)

Be prepared for him to move

Space restrictions. As shots get tighter (closer), the amount of action they can enclose becomes less. Demonstrators often need to know how much room they have available to work in.

your audience is more likely to start inspecting than listening. They become more aware of the trim of a mustache, a facial defect or teeth. A screen-filling full-face shot is out of place in most everyday productions, although it can be dramatically powerful when used at the right moment.

Unless it is quite unavoidable, do not take close shots of people on a narrow-angle lens (e.g. 10° or less), particularly if their head is angled to the camera, for the flattening 'cardboarding' effect can be most unattractive.

A waist shot (mid shot) will still show a person's expressions clearly, while allowing them a certain amount of movement. If they move around in a tighter shot though, they are likely to move out of the frame.

The more a person wriggles around in a chair, leaning, settling back or waving arms, the wider the shot you will need. You could cut off the gestures deliberately and let them fall outside the frame, but the resulting shot will look very cramped.

When someone walks around, you will usually find that a waist shot is the closest you can use comfortably, although a full-length shot gives a better impression of the surroundings.

A sustained shot of someone speaking to the camera soon becomes boring, and you can improve the picture by gradually tightening the shot to increase interest, or slowly widening it, to relax the audience's concentration. But don't overdo camera movement on a static person, or the effect becomes fidgety.

You can create visual variety, by *cutting* to different sized shots, but avoid either very slight size-changes or extreme changes. They are distracting. If you make a cut at the end of a thought sequence, preferably at the end of a sentence, it will not disrupt the flow.

You can help to 'motivate the cut' by having the speaker turn at an agreed moment, to be shot from another direction; although this can look mannered if it is done too deliberately. Position cuts of this sort can be useful too, when the speaker has made a mistake and re-started from the break, or cannot remember more than a few sentences at a time. In these circumstances, the cut will hide the intermittent shooting, and result in a smoothly flowing narrative.

Instead of continually showing shots of *a person talking*, try wherever possible to show what they are talking *about*. This not only makes the program more interesting to watch, but it becomes more informative, for it gives the viewer time to examine the subject itself, rather than just hear about it.

If the program is intended to concentrate on the *personality* of the speaker, then use plenty of portraiture shots. But if it is really intended to be showing us how to do something, or how something works, that should decide the sort of shots you mainly use – not continual shots of the cook, but shots showing us the cooking process.

A warning here! Although you can change the size and angle of the speaker's shot while screening a picture of what he is talking about, take great care if you cut to a shot of him in *another location*. Your audience will be stopped in their tracks, if a person they last saw in a lounge suit in an office, appears in the next shot on board ship in Bermuda shorts, without some sort of explanation.

11.11 Conventional arrangements

Generally speaking, you will find that shots showing people talking, fall into 'formal', 'informal', or 'grouped' arrangements.

Formal arrangements are the normal format you meet in studio interviews, newscasts, public affairs programs, games shows and similar situations, where people are grouped around (all sitting or standing) in a regular layout.

Informal arrangements include people sitting in their own home, standing in the street, walking, driving or speaking while working. Informal approaches also include *wildtrack interviews*, in which we see pictures of someone busily occupied (sawing wood for instance), and hear them in a non-synchronous audio wild-track of an interview made separately. The audience accepts this convention, without wondering how the talent is speaking without moving his lips!

Arranged groups are mostly found in drama productions, where people are deliberately positioned to form compositional patterns, that direct the eye, and influence our response to the action.

11.12 Effective shots

When you are shooting groups of people (anything from two upwards), your shots should always answer the basic questions: Who is there? Where are they? What do they have to say?

We want to see reactions, and to hear replies. Shots of people just sitting listening quietly without expression have limited value. So effective shooting is a matter of appropriate selection of the right person at the right time.

A regular productional approach is to begin with a group shot showing everyone present ... cut to the chairperson ... then cut to close-ups of individuals as they speak ... with intercut reaction shots. Shots of part of the group are often included, e.g. a person with their partner. But if a shot includes more than three people, details of their expressions may be lost.

Figure 11.3 Following movement

Part 1 *Uneven framing.* 1. Varying framing during movement looks crude and clumsy. 2. As you pan with a moving subject, try to keep it steady in the frame, just behind picture center. The amount of offset increases with the subject's speed.

Part 2 *Direction and effective speed.*
A. Someone moving across the screen quickly passes out of shot.
B. Diagonal moves are more interesting (and take longer).
C. Moves towards (or away from) the camera are sustained longest. But they may take too long (distant walk on a narrow-angle lens).

Figure 11.4 Improving viewpoints

Part 1 *Widely spaced moves.* If two people are some distance apart, you can cut between them , pan between them (A), or shoot the action from a more oblique viewpoint (B).

Intercutting does not interrelate them effectively. Panning from position A can create greater tension, but may cover irrelevant background. The shot from position B can appear more dynamic.

Part 2 *Masking.* When one performer obscures another ('masks them'), move the camera sideways slightly to correct the shot.

For most purposes, frontal shots (with the person facing the camera), or ¾-frontal shots (looking 45° to either side), are the most effective. In a profile shot (side view), which is the least familiar view of most people, the camera seems to be *scrutinizing* the guest, and the effect is not particularly attractive, although admittedly, it can be dramatic in a strong aggressive interview.

You can use a back view (or ¾-back) of an interviewer, or a member of a group, to form a foreground silhouette on one side of the picture. But take care in case they lean into the frame and mask other people in the shot.

11.13 Under questioning

If you are shooting a craftsman at work while someone talks to him, it is quite natural for the camera to look closely at what he is doing, rather than study his expression throughout.

But some directors even watch what people are *doing*, in formal interviews, and include 'fidget shots' of drumming fingers, hands fiddling with jewelry, straightening a tie, and so on. Although such shots may seem to reveal the guest's unconscious reactions, more often they just distract the audience from what is being said.

If someone is being questioned closely during an interview, you might use a tighter shot than normal. And should the situation become particularly heated, you could even move closer and closer to the 'guest' during questioning. But these are not techniques to be used lightly during a normal, cool, polite interview. In any case, there's always the risk that once you have reached the closest shot, anything after it is an anticlimax!

11.14 Interviews

If you are shooting two people in a continuous interview or discussion with a single camera, treatment is inevitably restricted to some extent. But with a little foresight, your audience will not even realize that you had any problems!

There are two ways of approaching the interview:

● In the first, the camera moves around, changing its viewpoint.
● In the second, the camera remains with the guest throughout.

Interviews are best shot in one continuous take. You could open with an establishing long shot, showing the participants and where they are. Gradually move in to a close shot of the interviewer as he speaks . . . and as he turns to his guest . . . pan slightly and widen the shot to include them both again. You can then tighten the shot, to a single close-up of the guest.

Using a different approach, you could begin with a waist shot of the interviewer . . . slowly pull out (zoom or dolly) to include the guest in a two-shot . . . then gradually pan over and move in at the same time to concentrate on the guest, and exclude the interviewer. As the interview ends, you can simultaneously pull out and pan over to a two-shot . . . finally tightening on the interviewer for his closing words. If the interview is quite long, you can vary the guest's shot from time to time by very gradually zooming in and out. Much depends on how interesting, and how animated, the guest proves to be.

Location interviews are often 'one-take' opportunities, in which the camera concentrates on the guest (zooming to vary the shot size). The interviewer, who is unseen, stands near the camera to ask the questions (out of shot, off camera).

Figure 11.5 Formal interviews
In a formal interview, there are relatively few effective shots.

Afterwards, the interviewer speaks directly to camera, to tape an introduction to the guest. If his original questions were not picked up by the guest's mike (i.e. he was 'off-mike'), the interviewer goes on to ask all the questions again, but this time to camera. If these were prearranged questions, he refers to his notes. If they were spontaneous during the interview, they can be checked from the audio recording of the interview.

Many interviews and discussions simply involve straightforward once-through taping. But results can be disappointing. Then it is advisable to do it again, and select the better version, or use parts of each take. Another approach to interviewing is to tape a much longer session than you really need, and extract the highlights to suit the required program length.

This last method overcomes the frustration of finding that the session was just becoming interesting at the point where it was wound up. It copes with guests who take some time to settle down, or who wander from the point, or have more to say than there is time for. To provide continuity, and a smooth visual flow in the edited program, questions from the interviewer can be recorded later, to provide cutaways, which edited in at appropriate points to introduce each topic.

11.15 Editing continuous interviews

A regular method of handling interviews with a single camera, is to concentrate the camera on the guest throughout. The interviewer remains out of shot. This treatment is simple, and least likely to distract the guest. But it does leave you with one very long take!

The result is usually a sequence that is far too long for your program slot. It needs 'tightening'. You want to use the most important and interesting passages, discarding any unwanted or irrelevant overmatter.

If you just cut out the parts you require, and join them together, there will be a distracting *jump cut* at the start of each new section, with sudden changes in positions, expressions, and shot sizes. Directors have tried disguising these cuts, with fast mixes or wipes, but the result is seldom satisfactory.

The answer to this dilemma, is to take a series of *nod shots* at the end of the interview, and to edit them into the main sequence.

The *nod shot* is a familiar feature in all broadcast interviews. It is simply a *silent* reaction shot of the interviewer looking 'with interest', or 'reacting' with occasional head-nods, smiles or concern. The director may also ask the guest to oblige with similar nod shots, to give variety to the editing.

During editing, you use the original interview shot with its soundtrack, and introduce the nod shots wherever necessary, without interrupting the sound.

To be convincing, it is important that the person in the nod shot doesn't speak. If you are taking an over-shoulder shot, make sure that the mouth of the person with their back to the camera cannot be seen moving. Too often they chat to their companion while the nod shot is being taken, with the result that after editing, their mouth movements do not match the sound being heard!

11.16 Shooting groups

Shooting a group effectively with a single camera is a challenge, but still quite practicable. You use the mobile techniques we have just discussed for the interview.

If you possibly can, avoid *hosepiping*, in which the camera continually pans across from one person to another. It looks pretty clumsy, particularly if people are sitting some distance apart, and the camera is panning over meaningless background. If you are shooting with one camera, it is usually better to zoom out, to include the new speaker in a wide shot, then perhaps, zoom in on him.

Figure 11.6 Shooting groups

1. *Isolating sections.* You can break a static group into a series of smaller individual shots. Using a single camera, this involves repositioning the camera (or repeated action). With multi-camera shooting, you intercut between viewpoints.

2. *Reforming grouping.* You can introduce 'natural moves' to form new groupings. Here C sits, B turns to him, A turns and exits. The shot tightens on BC. The action has created a series of groupings, and moved attention between the performers.

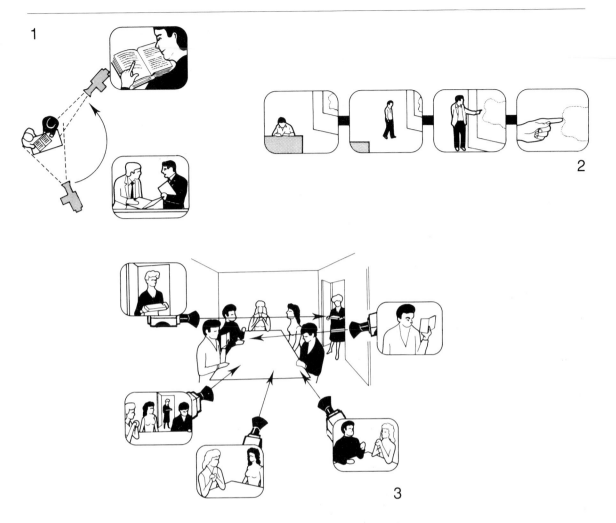

Figure 11.7 The camera explores

Part 1 *The inquisitive camera.* Although the action itself is static, the camera moves round to examine the subject more closely.

Part 2 *The camera follows.* As the speaker gets up and moves to the map, the camera follows, and goes in to the detail he is pointing at.

Part 3 *The developing (development) shot.* The camera moves around within the scene 'motivated' by the turn of a head, by somebody moving, by the newcomer's entrance . . . so that in the end, the audience has seen the situation from many interesting angles, in a continuous shot, without the interruptions of a series of cuts.

The exception is when something really dramatic happens (e.g. someone suddenly stands and shouts in opposition). Then you would pan over very rapidly to show the interrupter. However, the disadvantage of a *whip pan* (zip pan, blur pan) of this kind is that, although it makes a strong visual impact, it is liable to end up with a defocused or badly framed picture that has to be corrected on air.

However, if instead of a whip pan, you had quickly zoomed out from a close-up to a group shot, then immediately zoomed in to a close shot of the interrupter, the out-in maneuver would have looked extremely awkward.

When shooting a group in which people speak at random, avoid the temptation to continually arc round and move to new positions, particularly when someone out of shot suddenly starts talking. It is usually less obtrusive to zoom out, and include them in a wide shot.

The trick is to make any camera moves appear as natural as possible. Supposing you were covering a street interview. You might begin with a mid-shot of the interviewer speaking to camera, introducing someone. Then as he turns towards them saying: 'Tell me Mr Able, what were the first signs . . . ', the camera arcs round on the turn, to shoot Mr Able for the rest of the sequence.

As a general principle, if you can use movement to 'motivate a pan' (i.e. follow something or someone moving past), the result will look much more natural and unobtrusive than simply panning over 'the empty air'.

If you are using two or more cameras to shoot a group, you can pre-arrange various shots between them. For example, *Camera 1* can take a cover shot (wide shot) of the entire action, and shots of the interviewer or host. *Camera 2* can take opening title cards, and shots of the guest.

Where there are more guests, you can introduce various permutations of singles, pairs, sub-groups and group shots, always being ready to come back to a cover shot if somebody speaks unexpectedly, when you are in a close single shot on the other camera.

There is, in fact, an important difference between shooting a group who are going to speak in an agreed order, and a group where members speak whenever they wish. In the first case, cameras and microphones can follow along systematically. Where people speak at random, they will be off-mike until the sound man has been able to locate them and direct his mike. The cameraman, who has been concentrating on a shot, now has to look around, turn, re-frame and refocus on the new speaker, before the shot can be used. Again, zooming out to a wide shot may save the situation. If you have a group of people, it is often an advantage to have in the front row those you know are going to speak.

During shooting, it is best to check that shots are reasonably compatible so that there are no wild jumps in size, or variations in headroom (the space from the top of the head to the upper frame), or changes in camera height. Eye-lines too (i.e. where people appear to be looking) ought to be sufficiently related to suggest that people are talking to each other. If you are not careful when intercutting between various camera positions round a group, they can appear to be looking off camera or at the wrong person.

11.17 Car interviews

Interviews in cars are quite common, although if the driver is unused to a close camera, has to consider his replies, and has to drive at the same time, it can be somewhat unnerving for the inexperienced!

A steady camera is essential, whether the operator is located beside the driver (seated or crouched down) or shooting over the front seats. It can even be clamped to the outside of the car, looking in.

To give the shots variety, or to provide cutaways, you can cheat by re-shooting the driver alone or with the interviewer (and no camera in the car!) from another vehicle traveling alongside, or slightly ahead.

Some directors create cutaways shots by showing the passing scene through the car windows, shots in a driving mirror, shots showing a gear change, and so on. But unless these pictures are directly related to the interview (e.g. discussing road safety, the route or driving techniques), they are simply a distraction.

11.18 Walking interviews

Walking interviews do at least get away from the regular seated situation, but don't underestimate their problems. If you just clip personal mikes to the interviewer and guest, or use a communal hand mike, you will have trailing wires – which can be handled perhaps by a sound-man walking alongside but out of shot.

Interviewing techniques

Interviews range from casual *vox pop* street encounters, to friendly chats and hard probing interviews.

- Why are you interviewing the person? Is he a *personality* in town? Has he *done* something unusual? Has he *seen* something unusual? Is he an expert *explaining* something? Is he an expert giving an *opinion*? Whatever the reason, this will form the basis of your questions, and influence how you approach the interview.

- There are circumstances where instead of interviewing people on camera, it is more convenient, or easier, to visit them, and audio record the interview. Their information can then be quoted by a commentator or reporter, or form part of a script.

- Preliminary research on the person always pays off, whether this takes the form of reading their book, biography or newspaper clippings, or asking around.

- Get to know the guest before the taping session if possible (hospitality), to put him at ease, to guide him on the form of the interview and to prime him on the mechanics, for example, 'Don't bother about the camera . . . If anything goes wrong we can start again . . . I suggest that we just chat as we walk along the path . . .'.

- Avoid going over the whole interview with him beforehand, for the taped version will lose its freshness. The talent is likely to leave out information during the repeat, or forget sections, thinking that he has already covered those points. If that happens, you can always prompt him with: 'Earlier, you were telling me . . .'.

- Are there any personal items (e.g. mementos or family album photos) that the guest will want to show during the recording? (You may shoot details later, as cutaway or insert shots.)

- It may be helpful to agree beforehand, whereabouts in the interview you are going to introduce any personal items, maps or photographs.

- Some directors diplomatically ask the guest what they anticipate wearing at the interview, to avoid picture problems with extreme tones (such as white or black velvet), close checks or stripes, vibrant colors or shine (plastic), or noise from personal ornaments. Others dodge the issue, and accept the results.

- Before a taping session, check that chairs are comfortable enough, but will not allow people to swivel around, or lounge back to frustrate good shots. Check the shots with stand-ins, or if necessary with the interviewer and guest, and mark floor positions of chairs (tape or chalk). Similarly note floor positions of cameras.

- If there is a picture monitor nearby, angle it so that the guest cannot see it. Certainly avoid letting him see himself; it could make him nervous (or vain).

- Before taping, have a *voice test* (level test), in which the interviewer and the guest both speak for a few seconds at normal volume, so that the audio channel gain can be adjusted, and prevent 'over or under moding'. Do not use interview questions for this purpose, but ask him about his journey, or a similar neutral subject.

- Develop a fact sheet or background card, noting the points you want to bring up, based on research and conversation. (Don't prepare detailed, written-out questions, which you then read at the guest!)

- Do not have a script yourself, or let the guest work from a script or prompter. Results are so forced and artificial.

For the interviewer, an introduction to the guest may be read from a prompter, as can any statistics or data referred to.

- It is best if questions *appear* to develop from the guest's answers, moving back to prepared topics when possible. Do not simply work through a tick-off list of questions. Quick brief surreptitious glances at your notes are better than your appearing to ignore replies while you read them.

There are regular do's and dont's for interviewers:

- Be punctual for the interview and the preliminary checks: i.e. fitting intercom earpiece, checking voice levels, checking any prompter, shot check (hair, tie, clothing OK?).

- Check which camera is opening the interview. If its tally light goes out, the director has switched to another camera. Simply look down momentarily, then look towards the camera showing the lit tally light.

- Take cues over intercom or from the FM, without any outward sign, and follow them immediately.

- Restrict your hand and arm gestures. If you are going to get up from a chair (rise) or sit, begin the move slowly to enable the camera to follow you smoothly.

- Try to maintain eye contact with your guest as much as possible. It helps them to feel 'involved' rather than interrogated.

Ask specific questions, not general ones. And keep to the point of the interview. If for example, you are talking to a witness to a fire, his opinions about the neighborhood may be relevant or a sidetrack.

Avoid questions which can be answered 'Yes' or 'No'.

Avoid questions with obvious answers, or unrelated questions, or futile questions; e.g. 'Do you think your product is a good one?'

Do use questions beginning: 'Where? When? Why? How? Who? Which? What?

Use invitations such as: 'Tell me about . . .'; 'Let's talk about . . .'; 'Do you remember, you were telling me about . . .'.

- Ask one question at a time, and wait for replies. Some interviewers get their best responses by simply waiting. The talent feels uneasy at the silence, and says something (often revealing) to break it, so giving the opportunity for further questions.

- Never interrupt interesting replies, for the sake of asking prepared questions. And never ignore answers. Even if you only reply: 'I see', or nod, this avoids a feeling of interrogation.

- Do not say too much. (Some interviewers do most of the speaking!)

Use a polite, friendly style, not solemn or over-reacting. Smiles help as long as they appear genuine.

- Persuade guests not to wear dark glasses. They can prevent you from seeing expressions. (You can always point out that the camera exaggerates the sinister effect.)

- If guests smoke continuously, you may find on editing the program, that shots appear with and without cigarettes, of varying lengths.

The visual discontinuity can be very obvious.

A less inhibiting method might be to use a shotgun/rifle mike near the camera for sound pickup, provided its operator has a clear view of the action (i.e. no intervening trees, walls or foliage).

Of course, if you have the facilities, you can provide each speaker with a clip-on mike and miniature transmitter, and pick up their speech at a distance (using two separate receivers and antennas). But there is always the hazard of varying reception difficulties.

Try to arrange a walking interview so that you do not pick up a lot of extraneous noise, such as the crunch of pebbles or gravel underfoot, foliage, wind, traffic or machinery.

If you have real sound pick-up problems, one way out is to shoot a great deal of the action so that the mouth movements are not obvious in the picture (e.g. long shots, rear views), and then lay the speech which has been taped separately (non-sync) over the pictures during editing.

Occasionally, what looks like a 'walking interview' is actually a studio interview, with pictures of the people walking, taken on a carefully angled camera.

During a walking interview, the cameraman has the option of:

● walking backwards (guided by an assistant's hand on a shoulder),
● sitting on a wheeled mounting of some kind, and being pulled in front of the action (in a hospital corridor, it could be a wheelchair),
● locating the camera at an uninterrupted vantage point, and panning with the action,
● walking behind the people, taking a three-quarter back or a rear view.

None of these methods is conducive to steady camerawork for any length of time, especially if the camera is hand or shoulder supported, and the ground is uneven.

The best solution is usually to break up the walk into a series of sections; perhaps letting the speakers walk out of frame at the end of a section. Remember though, if they exit frame left, they must enter the next shot from frame right, so that they appear to be walking in the same direction. Alternatively, you can intercut with a head-on view of them, coming towards the camera.

To avoid any walk becoming unduly long, the speakers can pause at intervals, and still talking, lean on a fence, or sit on a log or stand and look at the landscape, or some other natural activity.

Shooting demonstrations

11.19 Typical demonstrations

A very wide range of video programs can be described as 'demonstrations'. They may involve as little as a single piece of paper (e.g. to show us origami techniques) or illustrate in elaborate detail the intricacies of an industrial process.

General interest programs give a lay audience broad information about a subject, and are usually designed to provide persuasive entertainment, from public relations exercises to propaganda. So you meet this kind of program under such titles as: 'How Maps Are Made', 'Safety in the Home', 'The Beauty of Glass', etc.

Instructional demonstrations, on the other hand, are usually intended to guide the audience *specifically*, and are made for particular markets, such

Figure 11.8 Repositioning

Equal distances. If you have a series of things at equal distances from the camera, they can be covered by panning a static camera.

Different sized subjects. When you have subjects of various sizes, put the biggest in the background, and have the demonstrator work towards the smallest, near the camera. This method requires least floor space, and little camera movement.

Moving with the demonstrator. Here the camera zooms out from a close shot, and arcs round to a new viewpoint as the demonstrator walks to the next subject. This dynamic method of presentation requires skilled camerawork (changing focus, smooth arcing and accurate positioning).

as educational, professional, specialist trades, etc. There are several regular types of instructional programs:

- *How it's made*: showing construction, layout, design features, etc.
- *How it works*: showing technology involved, mechanics, scientific principles, etc.
- *How to prepare/build/construct/assemble, etc.*
- *Maintenance procedures*: showing methods of servicing, trouble-shooting, repairs, etc.
- *Operation*: showing how a system or device is used; operational techniques, applications, etc.
- *Organization*: outlining procedures, administrative methods, etc.
- *Sales*: demonstrating product appeal, marketing, etc.

Comparative demonstration: showing how a subject has evolved, been developed, the varieties available, etc.

Longer demonstration programs are usually made up from a number of separate sub-programs. For example:

● a presenter speaking to camera, outlining the subject's history, principles, etc.,
● a bench demonstration showing construction, design, assembly, etc.,
● a field demonstration, showing equipment in action on the farm, building site, factory, etc.

11.20 Approaches to demonstrations

There are some subjects that you cannot really demonstrate effectively in a video program. Instead, you have to rely on *verbal descriptions* of processes, e.g. perfume making. Other subjects may be only partly successful, due to the *limitations* of the system e.g. a demonstration of sound quality.

Arguably, the weakest method of demonstrating anything in a video program is an illustrated talk, showing still photographs, diagrams, maps, etc. However good these may be, the video screen is a place for *action* and you can only introduce very limited movement into such static subjects.

A cookery demonstration, on the other hand, can be extremely effective, for it is full of visual movement and change, a process that develops as we watch – even although the audience cannot smell or taste whether it is as successful as it looks!

The most powerful form of demonstration is where someone speaks to us *directly* through the camera, pointing out each feature of the subject in turn.

The 'documentary format', in which the demonstrator is heard as a 'voice over', making observations on the pictures, is less personal. But it can be more authoritative; especially if the speaker's visual presence is not particularly impressive on camera for any reason. But the documentary approach is very 'greedy for visuals'. Whereas in the 'direct approach' you can always take shots of the demonstrator speaking to camera, with the 'documentary' method the camera is continually looking at the subject and its surroundings – which may not have enough interest to sustain audience attention.

11.21 Thinking it through

On the face of it, one might assume that any demonstration merely involves showing the item to the camera, and pointing out its features. Some very boring programs get made this way! The secrets of really successful demonstrations are *planning, preparation* and rehearsal, even for the most familiar subject. In fact, the more familiar it is, the more difficult it can be to make the program interesting, and hold the audience's attention. Too easily, they can assume that they 'know all about that', and daydream instead, looking without seeing and hearing without listening.

A good demonstration program is designed to suit its audience. If it is pitched at too high a level, the uninitiated become bewildered and embarrassed at not being able to grasp the facts. They become confused. They lose their self-confidence. While sorting out what *has been said*, they lose the thread of what *is being said!*

A successful program encourages curiosity and intrigues, leaving the audience with a sense of satisfaction and fulfilment. 'What do you think will happen now?' is much more involving, than: 'When we do this ... that happens'.

In the panels on pages 205–208, you will find a basic rundown of the points you may need to consider, when preparing a video program of a demonstration. As always, much of it is common sense.

11.22 The problem of time

Demonstrations can take anything from a split second to years to complete. So you often need to stretch or condense time in various ways, to suit the occasion:

- Shoot everything from start to finish. This ensures that your audience misses none of the action, and gets an accurate idea of how long everything takes. Clearly a good approach for relatively brief demonstrations, but quite unsuitable when showing how to paint a portrait or build a house.
- Instead, you can record the action continuously, then edit out the time-consuming, repetitive or boring parts. This can produce a shorter, better-paced program, and ensures that your audience concentrates on the important stages.
- You can arrange the demonstrations in prepared sections. For instance, when showing how to bake a cake, you may first display the ingredients, begin the method of mixing, then place the prepared mixture in an oven (or not, if one is not available). You can then remove (or show) an already cooked cake, and begin to decorate it, finally showing a fully decorated cake.

Not only does this method save a great deal of program time, but it ensures that the results turn out right at each stage! However, it can inadvertently omit points that may puzzle the viewer; e.g. he may not know how to tell when the food is fully cooked.

- Where a demonstration takes a long time to develop (e.g. a plant growing), the simplest plan is to shoot short sequences at strategic moments (hours, days or weeks apart) and show one after the other. Even photo-stills may be enough for this purpose.

The alternative is an automatic timer that takes a brief shot at regular intervals. When the tape is played back at normal speed, time is compressed, and these *time lapse* sequences show the process highly speeded up. A plant can grow from seed, flower and die in a minute or two. But of course, this method does tie up a camera (and VCR) in its rigidly held position for some time.

- Extremely brief events (showing a bullet breaking glass, or showing how a hummingbird flies) have to be captured with a special high-speed cine camera, or flash still photography.

Sometimes a demonstration program has to be made to a prescribed length, e.g. to fit a scheduled time-slot. You can achieve this by deliberately including material that is interesting but can be trimmed or omitted where necessary. These 'cushions' ('buffers') may be complete mini-items, or just introductory/concluding action, such as gathering the components for the demonstration together, tidying the bench and so on.

If your video program is to be used as part of a live presentation, e.g. in a classroom lecture where a teacher will also be speaking and answering questions, you can design it to be extremely flexible. You can arrange the program as a series of pre-timed self-contained sections, so that the teacher can use just as much as is needed for a particular lesson, without the students feeling that they are being prevented from seeing the entire program.

Preparing a demonstration

The following outline checklist shows the kinds of facts you may need to consider when preparing a video program of a demonstration.

What is the demonstration's purpose?

Is it to show:

- how an item is made?
- how to prepare/build/construct/assemble, etc?
- how it works?
- how to use it?
- how to maintain it?
- development of a process?

Who is it for?

Is it for the general public, for specialist groups or a local group?
At what level is it required: basic, intermediate or advanced?
Is any particular background, qualification, language or group-experience necessary for the audience?

What is the program format?

Is it a single program, or one in a series?
Does it relate to other programs (e.g. continue their discussion or use information explained in those programs)?
Do you need to recap, or remind audience of parts of earlier programs?
Does the program have to cover specified topics?
Is a duration specified for the program?

Research

Do you need to research the subject itself, or find appropriate authorities who can provide information?
Who are they? Are they available as information sources, consultants or performers? (Fees?)
Where is the subject of the program available? (Where do they make it, grow it, use it, etc?)
Will you need to go to them to shoot the product or the demonstration? (Factory, laboratory, zoo, museum, research center, etc.)
If you are borrowing/hiring items, consider such aspects as availability, time, transport, weight, dimensions, supplies, precautions, insurance, when and how item is to be returned, etc.
Would staff, demonstrator, keeper or guard come with item?

Subject potentials

Does the subject provide inherently interesting visual material?
Can it be prepared in such a way as to appear interesting?
How can you display the particular features or qualities of the subject?
How long does the action of the demonstration take:

- very brief (e.g. firing a gun)?
- a long time to demonstrate completely (e.g. building a house)?
- continuous operation (e.g. a water pump)?

What is the size/scale of the demonstration:

- microscopic?
- small (e.g. a wristwatch)?
- huge (can only shoot it in sections)?
- contained on a table or bench?

Are any precautions necessary during the demonstration? (Fire, flood, fumes, sparks, explosions, brittle, delicate.)

Are any animals being used? (Care, feeding, security.)
Are there problems of over-heating specimens under lights?
Is any special lighting or sound pick-up required (e.g. ultraviolet light to demonstrate rock-fossils)?

Supplementary items/equipment

Is any artwork required (e.g. drawings, photographs, or animated graphics)?
Are any prepared diagrams, graphs or flow-charts needed?
Are any models or analogues needed (e.g. geometric forms or chemical elements models)?
Are any scale replicas, etc., needed (e.g. ship model)?
Are any drawing materials needed (e.g. flip-chart, magnetic board or chalkboard)?
Is any apparatus or equipment needed (e.g. chemical, electrical, tools, etc.)?

Organization

Who will supply/provide/make the above? (Consider available time, transport, costs, fragility, function checks, storage, return, etc.)
Are any electrical supplies needed for apparatus? (Check voltage, consumption, phase, etc.)
Are gas, water or steam needed? Is water drainage needed? (A bucket, siphon, pump, etc.)
Who will operate or show the equipment? (The supplier, a helper or you.)
Who will install, repair or adjust it?
Does it need priming (e.g. chemicals)?
Does it make a mess (e.g. squirt water, foam, etc.)? Is any protective clothing needed (e.g. goggles, gloves, overall)? Should the floor be protected?
Are there any problems in demonstrating at the proposed place (fire risk, noise, wind, weather, etc.)?
Will the item/apparatus need to be assembled at the demonstration site? Is it connected up? It is temperamental?
Does the subject/item need special care?
Are any people needed as part of the demonstration (e.g. as a mock patient)?
Does the process use expendable material (e.g. a supply of paper or chemicals)?

Liabilities

Consider the involvements, relative to: budget, time available, space available, manpower, hazards, insurance, transport and facilities.

Alternatives

Consider alternatives that may be: easier, cheaper, quicker, more reliable, more readily available, simpler, less hazardous, etc.

Organizing a demonstration

The nature of the subject

The kind of subject you are demonstrating, and the features you want to bring out, will influence how you use your camera . . . where it concentrates . . . how close the shots are . . . how varied they are. What are these features?

- Is there *action* to watch (e.g. parts moving)?
- Are we watching an *effect*?
- Are we watching *an operator* assembling or forming something (e.g. at a lathe, knitting, planting)?
- Are the items simply *there*, to be explored by the cameras (e.g. works of art)?
- Is it a *continuous* process, or a 'once-only' process? Does it need time to recover?

Does each demonstration need a fresh set-up (e.g. new ingredients)?

- Are there any *hazards* that restrict the shot you can use? Can the camera see the action clearly or will, for example, machine guards need to be removed? Should transparent guards be made (e.g. safety glass sheet) to protect the camera?

Presenting the subject effectively

Is the subject best seen from certain angles?
If a process is complex, would a diagram help to emphasize, explain, show features, show what to look out for, or show the stage a process has reached? (Are superimposed subtitles needed?)
Would it help to intercut between the subject and a diagram. Or should you use a superimposition, or a split screen?
Wherever possible, have things prepared beforehand (*viz.* cut up, weighed), so that the demonstration is primarily an assembly process. (For example, in making a bookshelf, saw and drill the wood and fit it up, then dis-assemble ready for demonstration.)
Check that equipment/exhibits/models really do work, before the rehearsal period.

Rehearsal

Remember, there are several methods of demonstrating a subject:

- Demonstrator performs and explains to the camera.
- Demonstrator performs and explains to a student.
- Demonstrator works and explains to an experienced performer, representing the audience (who asks questions about processes, terms, etc.).
- Demonstrator works and explains, aided by an experienced performer (who gives cues, positions items for close-ups, watches timing, hands in articles and removes items after use).
- Demonstrator performs while an expert explains what is going on.
- Demonstrator performs, with a written commentary over.
- Demonstrator performs, with his own recorded commentary over.
- Experienced performer works, to an expert's instructions.

Preferably watch a preliminary non-camera rehearsal, so that you can decide on the best viewpoints and shots. You can also guide the demonstrator on how they can show their work best on camera. Give any advice where necessary about handling items (e.g. avoiding light reflections), showing them to camera, position marks, etc., but keep these points to a minimum.
Try to keep items isolated, so that the camera can shoot one at a time.
Preferably have the items/ingredients/specimens at hand, ready to use, in the order in which you are going to demonstrate them, and move progressively, from one item to the next, rather than hop back and forth between them.

Avoid having a lot of items cluttering the demonstration area (e.g. items you've finished with, others to be used later or some there just for the effect). Aim to clear things away as you go through the demonstration. (Have side benches, shelves under the working surface, or an assistant clearing items.) Do not let items accumulate until a recording break, then clear the working area. Otherwise after editing, the clutter will magically disappear on the cut!

Rather than zoom in to detail frequently, edit in insert shots of detail, taken afterwards. But make sure the audience realizes where the detail is located on the subject.

If necessary, have a cue sheet near the camera, to remind the demonstrator of the agreed order of items, but *not* a fully scripted prompter.

Where material is used during a demonstration (paper, ingredients, etc.), have extra at hand for rehearsals and retakes. Have standby spares for items likely to break and abort the experiment.

If parts of a live demonstration are likely to fail, be ready to use:

● a taped section of an earlier successful recording (e.g. rehearsal),
● specimens of a good/correct result (e.g. a cake that *has* risen properly!),
● a photography of the desired effect,
● a substitute item,
● an explanation of what went wrong, and what the audience *should* have seen.

At the end of a rehearsal, or a take, make sure that equipment is checked over and ready to go, for the next taping – e.g. rewound, reconnected, cleaned off, broken parts replaced, refilled, fresh paper inserted or whatever.

At the end of the demonstration, consider whether any retakes, cutaways or insert shots are needed, before concluding.

Finally, gather demonstration items together and store for dispatch.

Chapter 12

Visual effects

We use an 'effect' to create an illusion. . . which may appear so natural, that the audience accepts it as *real*!

12.1 Using effects

Say 'visual effects', and most people think of impressive spectacle, of lumbering monsters and crumbling cities, raging fires and similar catastrophies. But many everyday 'effects' are quite unobtrusive. They may be decorative or naturalistic, but we use them for entirely *practical* reasons; because they are convenient, safe, save money, and are reliable.

In this chapter, we shall look at various methods and mechanisms. Most are quite cheap and simple to apply. Some need extra facilities, but most just require experiment and patience. They will all extend your opportunities.

12.2 Using filters

There are several types of filter that you can attach to the front of the camera lens in a *filter holder* to modify the image:

- *Neutral density (ND) filter.* A transparent gray-tinted material, that cuts down light without changing its color quality. Available in densities ranging from 10% to 1% transmission. Used in strong sunlight to prevent overexposure, or to allow you to use large lens apertures. Also used over light sources or windows to reduce the light intensity.
- *Sky filter.* A graduated neutral density filter, reducing the brightness of the upper part of the picture (sky), while remaining clear below.
- *Diffusion disk.* Overall image diffusion ranging from slight softening, to dense mist and fog effects (*fog filter*). A piece of net, nylons or gauze has a similar effect.
- *Soft spot.* A filter with a clear center, and a progressively diffused surround.
- *Star filter.* Creates a series of radiating light rays around a localized light source (candle, headlight, specular reflection).
- *Polarizing filter.* A filter eliminating reflections and glare from smooth shiny surfaces, such as windows, glassware, water.
- *Multi-facet filter.* Create multiple images; either around a central subject, or across the frame.

Part 1

Part 2

Figure 12.1 Deliberately distorting space

Part 1 *Distorting people.* Although you will seldom take big close-ups on a very wide or narrow lens angle, unless you want grotesque distortion, it is easy to forget that even natural body moves (A) can become distorted on wider lens angles (B and C).

Part 2 *Compressing and expanding space.* Wider lens angles appear to emphasize distance (A), while narrow lenses compress it (C).

Part 3 *Fisheye lenses.* Ultra-wide-angle 'fisheye' lenses appear to distort and curve space in a dramatic fashion.

Part 3

12.3 Distorted images

Shoot via a plastic mirror (slightly bent or warped), kitchen foil sheet, through a clear tumbler or bottle, or through decorative glass.

Place a piece of clear plastic or glass over the camera lens, and lightly grease or oil the areas you want to distort. You can leave the center untouched to obtain a normal image surrounded by distortion.

Shooting through a tube of kitchen foil, the central image is surrounded by an attractive whorl reflection. A tube of mirror tiles can produce a kaleidoscopic effect.

Foreground matte

Figure 12.2 Foreground matte
The foreground photograph or
drawing has a carefully positioned
hole, through which a distant subject
is visible.

12.4 Mattes

Mattes or masks are simple to make, but can be extremely effective. You
can use them in several ways:

Lens matte. Shooting through a piece of card or a stencil attached to the
lens, you can imitate the view through a telescope, binoculars, or a
keyhole.

Foreground matte (camera matte, gobo). Place a photograph in the
foreground, and cut away an area to show the studio action (e.g. a
doorway), and if you have matched the scale, tones, and colors well, you
have a convincing composite shot. Similarly, you can provide a ceiling for
a setting, or matte out unwanted parts of the shot. To be successful, the
shot must have considerable depth of field.

When you do not want to damage a photograph or painting, you can
reflect it in an angled mirror-plastic sheet in front of the camera, with a
cutaway area for the studio action (similar to the 'Pepper's ghost' setup;
see section 12.8).

12.5 Superimpositions

When you *mix* or *dissolve* between two sources on a switcher (vision
mixer), you gradually fade up one picture, while fading out the other. A
superimposition stops part way through the mix, holding both pictures at
about equal strength.

The result of this 'super' is a 'double exposure' effect. The lighter tones
on one shot stand out against the darker tones of the other. They will
appear *transparent* where the other shot has details, and 'solid' against a
plain black area. If there are similar tones in both shots, they will simply
merge.

12.6 Wipe patterns (See Figure 12.3 on page 212.)

Using a *special effects generator*, you can produce an electronic *wipe*,
which blocks out part of one picture, and replaces it with the corresponding part of another shot, to form a composite image.

The simplest wipes use simple geometrical shapes with sharp ('hard-
edged') or diffused ('soft-edged') borders. The divided areas can be
moved around the screen, and enlarged/contracted in various ways.

In the 'split screen', the left half of one shot is combined with the right
half of another's (traditionally used to show both ends of a telephone
conversation).

You can use the wipe as a moving *transition*, and progressively wipe-out
the picture on the screen as you wipe-in another. Or you can produce a
stationary *insert* matte; e.g. someone at a window in the studio, fitted into
a photograph of a house.

12.7 Reflections (See Figure 12.4 on page 212.)

Water ripple. The usual method involves shining a spotlight onto pieces
of mirror, in a dish of water. (Metal plates, mirror tiles or kitchen foil
can substitute for mirror.)

Thin metalized plastic sheeting (e.g. survival blanket) resting on the floor
can reflect light, which appears to ripple when the sheet is disturbed.

Kitchen foil can be cut out into a shape (flying bird, heart or missile),
and stuck to card. Light from a spotlight will reflect in this shape and can

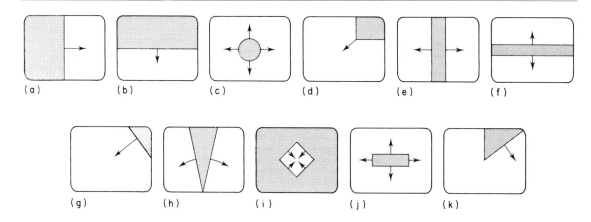

Figure 12.3 Wipes

Common wipe patterns. A. horizontal wipe/line-split; B. downwards vertical wipe; C. iris/circle wipe (out or in, expanding or contracting); D. corner wipe – top right (when static, this provides a corner insert); E. barndoors/line-bar/horizontal split-wipe (expanding or converging); F. vertical split wipe/field bar (wipes in or out); G. diagonal (top right); H. fan wipe (in or out); I. diamond wipe-in; J. box wipe-out; K. rotary/clock wipe.

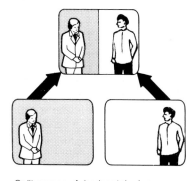

Split screen. A horizontal wipe, stopped mid-way, to show halves of two separate pictures.

Figure 12.4 Water ripple

A spotlight's beam is reflected from pieces of mirror in a dish of water to produce convincing water ripples.

be moved around the background. Flexing the board will alter the reflected shape.

Light reflected from slightly crumpled kitchen foil will throw interesting nebulous shapes and patterns onto a plain background. This is particularly effective behind translucent screens.

Mirror. If you shoot a scene via a mirror, you can apparently:

● position the camera at angles that could otherwise be impracticable (e.g. floor, overhead or outside limited openings),
● take the camera farther away from the subject, in confined surroundings,
● tilt or cant the camera,
● create a wipe from one situation to another on a single camera. The camera shoots the first subject via an angled mirror, which slides aside to reveal the second subject.

A mirror image will always be laterally reversed. If this matters, you can correct it either by using a second mirror (i.e. shoot into a mirror via a mirror), or by electrically switching the camera's line scan circuits (line reversal).

12.8 Pepper's ghost

The old theatrical illusion known as 'Pepper's ghost' was originally used to create transparent ghost effects on the open stage. But it has its application in video too, for although it involves only *one camera*, it can achieve some striking effects:

● to provide backgrounds, that can be faded in/out, and changed in vision,
● to produce transparent superimpositions,
● to light a subject directly along the lens axis, with shadowless illumination.

The principle is extremely simple. The camera shoots through a sheet of clear glass or a semi-transparent mirror (pellicle) held at 45° in front of the lens, and sees both the subject straight ahead, and a reflected image of the background picture (e.g. a large photograph) which is located over to one side.

If you want the background picture to look normal (a 'solid superimposition'), you will need a black surface behind the subject. Otherwise the reflected background will appear as a ghostly superimposition. If your main subject corresponds with a dark area of the background picture,

Figure 12.5 Using mirrors

Part 1 *Confined spaces.* In a confined space, a mirror may make shots possible (although reversed) that would otherwise be impracticable. (Here, shooting into a mirror from a window.)

Part 2 *Inaccessible viewpoints.* When you cannot get a camera and operator into position, a mirror may make a viewpoint possible.

Part 3 *Overhead shot.* A top shot via an overhead mirror may be essential for some table-top demonstrations.

Part 4 *Canted shots.* When you want a canted viewpoint, to suggest instability, horror or madness, a mirror shot may be more convenient than a ground camera.

and the relative scale and brightness of subject and background are reasonably similar, it should not be possible to detect the faking.

The stronger the lighting on the background picture, the bolder it will appear. If you fade out then lighting on the background area, it will vanish and leave you with your subject against a plain black backing.

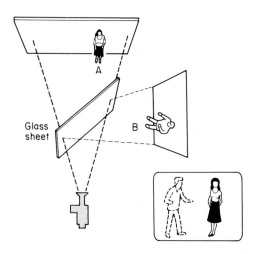

Figure 12.6 Pepper's ghost
A glass sheet reflects a subject, mixing it with the scene in front of the camera. The prominence of the mirrored image of the out-of-shot person (B), depends on the main scene's tones and brightness, and those of the second subject.

The background picture can come from a drawing or photograph, or you could use a translucent screen of frosted plastic sheeting with a rear-projected slide.

Because the lens-to-performer distance needs to be similar to the lens-to-background distance, the overall layout for this effect can take up a fair amount of room, even using a wide angle lens, unless you are working in miniature and using, e.g. model soldiers, or small puppets for the subject.

Superimposition normally requires two cameras with a picture from each. But if you use a Pepper's ghost set-up, you can carry out superimpositions on *one camera*, and that can be an extremely useful facility for a single-camera unit. You could for example, have two photographs: one of a ruined building, and another taken when it was newly built. Place one in front of the camera, and another (printed in mirror image) to be reflected in the plain glass sheet or pellicle, and you can be changing their lighting, fade from one to the other, holding a superimposition if you wish, part way.

12.9 Projected backgrounds

Although you can use commercial pattern projectors (*profile spots*) to project light patterns of all kinds onto backgrounds, a regular slide projector has some very useful applications.

Rear projection. While action is shot in front of a translucent (frosted) screen, you project a slide onto its rear.

You can use this idea to provide a backing outside a window in a studio set, as a display screen during a talk, and even as a complete background for limited shots (close-ups, table-top displays).

Because you do not want light to spill over the screen, washing out its image, the trick is to light *across* the scene as far as possible, and mask off any stray light.

Front projection. Here you use a hidden or suspended unit to project a slide directly onto a light-toned surface. it is essential to avoid action lighting spilling onto the background.

The brightness of the background image will depend on the projector's lamp-power and lens efficiency, its distance, the slide's density, and the background tones.

Reflex projection. This set-up uses a sort of 'reverse Pepper's ghost' arrangement. A slide of the background scene is projected directly along the lens axis via a half-silvered mirror onto a special screen. The surface of this screen is made up of millions of tiny glass beads, which reflect the background image extremely efficiently, and the camera shooting through the mirror sees both the subject and the screen with its background picture.

Figure 12.7 Projected backgrounds

Rear projection. A slide projected onto a translucent screen (frosted plastic sheet) provides a background.

Slide projector

Translucent screen

Figure 12.8 Reflex projection

Part 1 The background scene is projected along the lens axis, via an angled glass sheet, onto a highly directional glass-bead screen. The performer's lighting swamps the image falling on him.

Part 2 The camera sees the person in front of the projected background scene.

Although the projector's image falls on the subject as well as the screen, it is swamped by the subject's lighting, so is not visible on camera. The subject's shadow on the screen is not seen in the picture, provided the projector and camera lens angles are comparable and the system is lined up accurately.

If you cut out a piece of the reflex screen material, to match something in the background picture (e.g. a tree), and stick it on a piece of board, the performer can actually appear to walk *behind* that tree on the slide!

There are disadvantages as always, such as the fact that the camera cannot move during the shot, the light losses through the mirror, and the way light tones in the subject (e.g. a white shirt) may reflect in the screen and cause haloes. But these are unimportant, compared with the visual miracles this *single-camera* arrangement can achieve.

12.10 Color medium ('gels')

Colored images. Shooting through carefully selected color media can produce strange color transformations, without totally destroying color values, e.g. 'surprise pink'.

Multi-colored light. Take two sheets of color media (e.g. light blue and yellow), cut a series of holes in both at random, and staple them together. When light shines through them, it will produce color patches of *three* colors (e.g. blue, yellow, green), for a stained glass effect that can be projected onto a plain background.

Angle two differently colored spotlights onto a slightly crumpled kitchen foil sheet. Multi-colored patterns will be reflected.

12.11 Light effects

Beam of light. To produce a beam of light (e.g. shining into a room, from a window), a smoke-filled atmosphere would normally be necessary. To create the effect, either superimpose a graphic of a white on black beam, or shoot through a gauze painted/sprayed with the beam shape.

Distant lights. To suggest distant lights (e.g. of a town, roadway, esplanade or stars), string out white Christmas-tree lights on a black cloth background.

If you pin the center of a string of these lights to a black background, and bring its separate ends towards the camera, this V-shaped string of lights resembles an airfield landing strip at night. The camera takes an over-shoulder shot of a seated person, facing the black background. Raising and lowering the strings of lamps makes the 'aircraft' appear to dive and climb. As the aircraft gets closer, the strings are parted. Add aircraft noises to complete the illusion for brief shots.

High lamps. A PAR lamp fixed to the top of a vertical hand-held pole can be useful:

● when you are shooting in awkward places, and need a high lamp for a short time,

● as a 'swinging keylight', gently swaying from side to side, to suggest a ceiling lantern on a board a ship at sea, or a hung light set swinging in a bar brawl.

12.12 Scenic effects

Scrims/gauzes. If you paint on scrim/gauze material, the surface will appear solid when lit from the front, provided you leave areas behind the scrim unlit. If you light the areas behind the scrim instead, surface details almost disappear on camera.

So you can create various mystical, magical effects, simply by light switching (e.g. solid room walls disappear, to reveal whatever is beyond). Both white and black scrim can be used. White can create 'misty' effects and soften off the image. Black can provide 'solid' painted features or decoration, apparently suspended in mid air.

Tree branches. Tree branches a few feet long, with or without leaves, can be pressed into service for a number of purposes.

● Near the camera, they appear as undergrowth or small growing trees (nailed vertically to wooden floor supports or pushed into the ground).

● Waved gently in front of a yellow–orange lamp on the floor, a small branch can simulate firelight-flicker. (Alternatively, use a stick with close strips of hanging rag.)

● Supported in front of a lamp, a branch can produce dappled light, to suggest sunlight through leaves, or mysterious shadows in a night scene.

● Do the same thing with *colored light*, and an attractive decorative effect results. Try several lamps, using different colors. (Alternatively,

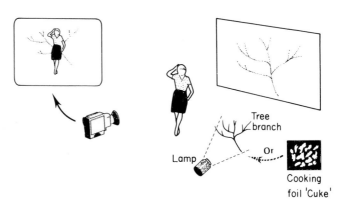

Figure 12.9 Projected shadows
You can cast shadows from a lamp on the ground, using branches, wire, grilles, metal-foil stencils, etc.

use sheets of kitchen foil with a pattern of holes cut in them, to dapple the light.)

● Placed in front of a lamp lighting a translucent screen from the rear (hung, or on the floor), a tree branch will cast decorative shadows.

12.13 Chroma key

This automatic switching device is widely used in most studios. It relies on a blue background behind the subject (it can be other colors), to automatically insert the action into a background scene. Wherever the blue 'keying color' appears in the master shot, the *chroma key* system replaces it with a corresponding area of the background shot instead – rather like inserting a piece of a jigsaw puzzle.

Blue is usually chosen for this keying color as the hue least likely to be found in typical scenes – although you can adjust the system to use any hue to activate the switch, as long as it does not appear in your subject. So if there is an artist with a blue canvas in the master shot, and a real dog on the second camera, you could have a 'living dog painting' on his easel. If the artist then painted the canvas with another color (i.e. *not* the keying color), that part of the dog and its background scene would disappear.

Figure 12.10 Chroma key
The subject is set up in front of a blue background. Wherever this 'keying hue' appears in the master camera's shot, the system switches to a separate background picture instead. So in the combined result, the subject appears in front of the background scene. Any colors can be used in the background picture.

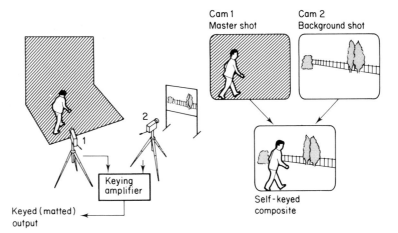

A long shot can take in a width of 12–15 ft (4–5 m) or more, and it may not be convenient to provide an area of blue this large in a studio. So you introduce a blue camera matte in the foreground of the master scene. This is simply a blue card with a hole in the center, as large as you need to accommodate the action in the shot. The lens sees both the blue of this card (separately) and the blue behind the subject, and accepts it all as the keying hue.

Wherever you want the background scene to appear in the composite picture, you must have a blue area in the main scene; whether it is blue backing, a blue flat, blue drapes or whatever. You can have someone in the studio, standing in front of a blue background, with a blue floor, and the chroma key switch will insert them into a background photograph totally convincingly – provided you adjust the proportions, perspective, tones and color to match.

There are snags to this magical process. As we said earlier, you must not have *anything* in the main subject scene (clothing, furniture, scenery, etc.) that is blue, or the system will accidentally insert the background scene there as well! If a performer wears blue jeans, we will see the houses in the background picture, where his legs should be! Anything shiny that reflects the keying color will similarly cause breakthrough.

The blue keying area must be evenly illuminated, because shadows in the master shot can cause poor switching (edge ragging).

In the composite picture, there are normally no natural shadows from the subject, and this can appear strange or unnatural.

The camera cannot move, tilt, pan or zoom while on shot, without causing some pretty strange effects, such as 'growing and shrinking' as you zoom! Useful phenomena when you need them, but otherwise to be avoided. People in the studio, normally appear *in front of* anything in the background picture. This is no problem, unless the effect is unnatural for any reason.

There are methods of minimizing these problems by equipment design, and ingenious staging, but they are usually only available in more extensive facilities.

You can use any video source to provide a 'background' picture, including:

● A second camera looking at a photograph or a projected slide. Try to avoid subjects that would normally be moving; e.g. people, sea waves, traffic. If you want to augment or cover up parts of the inserted background, put something in the foreground master shot at that point.
● A second camera looking at a model. Effective designs are easy to make using card and balsa wood, cut-out photo-prints (e.g. buildings, trees, etc.). Plastic moldings, packaging inserts, etc., enhanced by colored lighting, can create decorative 'settings'.
● A VCR replay or a film channel will provide a moving background.
● A computer can supply graphics, patterns, etc.

As well as providing *complete backgrounds*, you can use a small panel of chroma key blue in a setting to provide a range of effects, from a 'display screen', to a busy street scene outside a window.

12.14 Video effects

There seems to be no end to the methods you can use to control and manipulate the picture image! Some are little more than a passing fashion or an eye-catching gimmick, others provide a useful productional device.

Many video cameras and VCRs now incorporate gizmos that produce changes in the image. As well as more 'ordinary' changes that alter picture tones and color, soften details, etc., there are the various *image enhancers, video effects units, digitizers, computer programs* and whatever, which offer all kinds of 'video magic'. Here is a brief list of typical opportunities:

● *Freeze frame.* Stopping movement in the picture, and holding a still frame. (Held for too long, you can wear and stretch the tape.)
● *Frame grabbing.* A sequence in which a series of single frames are frozen at regular intervals during the action. (From every 2 secs. to almost instantaneous).
● *Strobe.* A similar effect, displaying action as a series of still images flashed onto the screen at a variable rate.

- *Reverse action*. Running the action in reverse.
- *Fast or slow motion*. Running the action at a faster or slower speed than normal.
- *Picture in picture*. A miniature picture inserted into the main shot. By copying and re-inserting, a pattern of up to 81 frames can be created on the screen!
- *Mosaic*. The picture is reduced to a pattern of small single-colored squares of adjustable size.
- *Posterizing*. Reduces tonal gradation to a few coarse steps.
- *Mirror*. Flipping the picture from left to right, or providing a symmetrical split screen.
- *Time lapse*. Still frames shot at regular intervals. When played back at normal speed, the effect is of greatly speeded-up motion.
- *Digitizer*. A frame is grabbed, then treated in various ways (redrawn, colors/texture changed, etc.).

12.15 Desktop video

In *desktop video* the world of the personal computer (PC) combines with that of home video, to provide exciting new productional opportunities. Using ingenious PC programs, Apple Macintosh MAC, Commodore Amiga, and IBM computers for example offer audio/video facilities that not so long ago required specialist broadcast equipment.

However, it is not simply a matter of plugging your PC into your video system and loading appropriate software. Units need to be made compatible. Few PCs produce an NTSC (PAL) broadcast signal, so cannot be used directly with video systems.

Video/television units such as camcorders, VCRs, and TV receivers, are designed to use standard NTSC (PAL, SECAM) type television signals. Personal computers, on the other hand, are essentially *digital* systems. In fact, PC standards can vary fundamentally between brands or even between models. Some have sequential scanning instead of broadcast-type interlacing.

To enable a PC to be used with a video system, some form of scan conversion device is necessary. An *encoder* converts the digital data into an NTSC signal, so allows computer generated graphics and animations to be interswitched with video. *Genlock* units allow you to *intermix* your computer-generated images or titling with live or taped video pictures (as supers, split screen, inlays, inserts).

All genlock units produce a single NTSC (PAL) signal, that is suitable for VHS, 3/4 in. industrial VTRs, Betacam, or 1 in. tape systems. But some also have separate Y (luminance) and C (chroma/chrominance) outputs, which provide higher picture quality with Super VHS recorders.

So what facilities do desktop video software provide? The list of available programs grows ever longer!

The versatile PC

- *Titling*. As a character generator, providing titling/subtitling of all kinds in various fonts. Lettering can form on screen, scroll, collapse, rotate, etc.

You can key titling into live or recorded video, or combine it with computer-generated graphics, plain color backgrounds. etc.

- *Graphics*. You can devise illustrations ranging from charts, graphs, tables, diagrams, to 'watercolor' effects, posters, textured drawings, cartoon, logos, etc.

- *Three-dimensional images*. You can create photo-realistic images of three-dimensional subjects.

- *Paintbox*. A video still or a photo shot can be treated in many ways: e.g. color, texture, etc., can be added, removed, altered. details can be strengthened or redrawn. New features can be inserted, and defects such as color bleeding removed.

- *Animations*. A series of still images can be shown in succession, to create animated effects; e.g. cartoons, moving logos.

- *Picture transition effects*. Pictures can be shifted around, obliterated by straight geometrical wipes, decorative curtain wipes, etc. Areas can be 'flown in/out'.

- *Inserts*. You can take a complete picture (or part of it) and insert it within a shot; e.g. as a 'wall display screen'. You can present a series of different shots (stills or moving) side-by-side.

- *Chroma-keying*. A subject in front of a blue background, can be overlaid into another shot.

- *Music*. Musical soundtracks of all kinds can be generated, using synthesized or digital audio sampled sounds.

- *Sound effects*. You can use effects to simulate or replace natural sounds; to create background noises (e.g. for outer space shots). Even artificial speech is available!

- *Synchronized sound*. Digital sound can be synchronized with animated action.

- *Prompter*. You can provide a moving script for performers/newcasters to read while looking at the camera.

- *Edit decision lists*. Here you check through shots, select which you want to keep, and note their in and out times. This log can be used either as a *guide* to later editing ('off-line editing'), or to actually *drive* the equipment in an editing suite; picking out the chosen shots and joining them in order. Advance preparation considerably reduces costly editing suite time.

- *Storyboarding*. A production planning aid, in which you arrange how you are going to break down action into a series of separate shots.

- *Scriptwriting aids*. Software aided script layout (e.g. two-column display).

- *General organization*. Software programs for creating forms, labels, order sheets, logs, etc.

Desktop video limitations

As you would expect, personal computers do have their limitations:

- *Memory capacity* will restrict the amount of detail, elaboration, or speed of effects.

- *Flicker* can be noticeable in fine detail. where a horizontal line is so thin that it appears in only one TV line, flicker occurs as scanning switches between the odd and even fields.

- Color from computers may be too *highly saturated* (*pure*), and appear dazzling and artificial in a video picture. Desaturated (paled) colors are preferable. Avoid strong red, for it bleeds badly, spreading over nearby areas. Always check out effects before finalizing; especially when inserting titling into a background picture. Look out for woolly edges, chroma noise, poor color harmony.

- *Aliasing* in computer images gives circles or diagonal lines a jagged, 'staircase' appearance. *Anti-aliasing* circuits overcome this effect by reducing the apparent contrast at hard edges; inserting an intermediate color or tone, so that the overall effect appears smooth.

- *Picture shapes* (*aspect ratios*) of computer displays vary. Few accurately match the 4 by 3 NTSC/PAL screen shape so there may be spurious borders or loss of edge information.

- *Detail* in computer graphics may be clearly visible in a computer monitor display, but lost on a TV receiver screen.

Chapter 13

Video basics

How it works.

Figure 13.1 How video works

A. Just behind the camera lens a *prism block* with color filters (dichroics), is used to produce three images, corresponding to the red, green and blue in the scene. Attached to these prisms are three *CCD light sensors*. A pattern of charges builds up on their tiny elements, corresponding to the light and shade in their color images.

B. The pattern of charges on each CCD is read out in a regular series of lines, to produce a *video signal*. Thanks to *synchronizing pulses* the three CCDs are scanned exactly in step (synchronous).

13.1 Technical details

By now, it is obvious that you don't need to understand technical design features, to produce good pictures and audio. But you will meet situations where a general idea of what is going on, will smooth away problems; e.g. when interconnecting equipment. So let's take a look at the underlying principles.

13.2 Producing video

It all begins with the *lens system* which focuses an image of the scene onto a light-sensitive surface within the camera head. In most video cameras, this light-sensor is a solid-state CCD – *charge coupled device* (rather than the 'target' of a *camera tube* previously used).

This CCD is typically ½ in. (12.5 mm) or ⅔ in. (18 mm) across, and consists of hundreds of thousands of tiny independent cells (*pixels; elements*). Each develops an electrical charge – according to the strength of the light falling upon it. The result is an overall pattern of electrical charges on the CCD, that corresponds to the light and shade in the lens image.

To produce the *video signal*, scanning circuits continually read across this charge pattern in a series of parallel paths or 'lines' (525 or 625). The fluctuating voltage produced, corresponds to the strength of each cell in turn.

This basically, is how the monochrome ('black and white') video camera generates its pictures.

13.3 Recreating the picture

To convert this video signal back into a picture, we can use either a picture tube, or an LCD (liquid crystal diode) screen. Most TV receivers, picture monitors, camera viewfinders, use *picture tubes* of various sizes.

In the picture tube, a beam of electrons scans across the screen, causing its phosphor-coated surface to glow. If we use the video signal to contin-

C

C. If we look at a single line as the system reads across the picture...

D

D. ... we see how the strength of the video signal fluctuates with the tones at each moment of the scan.

E

E. The TV receiver is fed simultaneously with the three different video signals – red, green, blue.

The screen of the *picture tube* in the TV receiver or monitor, has a pattern of three different phosphors on its inner surface. Streams of electrons are controlled by the RGB video signals. As they scan across their respective sets of phosphors, these glow red, green, or blue, and build up a color picture.

ually adjust the strength of this scanning beam as it sweeps across the screen, it will 'draw' a light pattern on the phosphor. When the video is strongest (corresponding to a white surface in the original scene), the screen will glow brightly at that point. Where there is little light reflected from the scene, the screen will appear much darker.

In the LCD screen, the density of each element of the screen varies with the strength of the video as the picture is scanned.

13.4 How we see color

Our eyes contain selective 'cones', which detect color by analysing the visible spectrum into three primary color regions – red to orange, green to yellow, and blue to violet.

Most colored surfaces reflect a color mixture of red, green, and blue light in varying proportions. So for instance, the various shades of 'green' we see in foliage, are actually color mixtures reflecting quite a wide spread of the visible spectrum. Even yellow, can be reproduced by adding suitable proportions of red and green light!

13.5 How the camera sees color

The color video camera too, relies on this *additive color mixing* process.

Any light-sensor (CCD or camera tube) can only respond to the *intensity* of light. It cannot directly distinguish *color*. So we imitate the eye. By placing red, green, and blue color filters over three light-sensors, we can analyse the scene into its separate color components. If a subject appears to have similar proportions of all three primaries, we see this mixture as *white*.

In the color video camera, the lens' image of the scene passes through a special prism, which splits it into three identical versions. Three CCD sensors with their red, green, and blue color filters, provide three *video signals* corresponding to the light and shade of these colors in the scene.

13.6 The color picture

Look through a magnifier at the scene of your TV set or picture monitor, and you will see that it has a tiny pattern of three separate sets of phosphors. These glow red, green, or blue as the scanning beam passes over them. The brightness of each point corresponds with the video strength at that moment. Our eyes cannot distinguish these individual phosphor points, but instead, blend their images to form a natural-colored picture.

Figure 13.2 The video signal
The video signal is a varying voltage, corresponding to light and shade in the image. While the scanning system *retraces* at the end of each *line* and *field*, *sync pulses* are inserted to ensure that the entire system scans in step.
A brief *color burst* reference signal (subcarrier frequency) ensures color accuracy.

13.7 Practical cameras

While larger professional video cameras use a 3-CCD format, other camera designs are often simplified in order to provide a more compact unit, and reduce cost.

For example, instead of three separate chips, a segmented multi-color filter may be placed over a single sensor. Although picture detail is reduced, results are very satisfactory for many purposes.

There are a number of variations too, in the types of CCD used, and their resolution.

So how do such technical details concern the video maker? Well they will affect picture clarity (particularly under low intensity lighting). While for example, top-quality cameras can resolve as many as 700 vertical black and white stripes across the picture width, simpler cameras may only manage to reproduce half that number. (Then finer detail will be blurred however carefully you focus.) Color fidelity is less accurate or consistent in simpler designs, and there is a greater possibility of disturbing picture defects (e.g. vertical smear, background patterning). In the best video cameras these are negligible.

As you will see, these issues can become important where pictures are copied several times over during editing or creating special effects.

13.8 Scanning

Let's look more closely at the scanning process we met earlier. The scanning circuits read off the CCD charge pattern 60 times a second.

To reduce picture flicker, the odd lines are actually read first, then the even lines. These odd and even *fields* are *interlaced* to form a complete TV picture or *frame*. So the entire picture scanning process using 525 lines, takes place in 1/30 of a second. (In a 625-line system, there are 50 frames or pictures a second; 312½ lines in each field.)

13.9 Sync pulses

To reproduce the TV picture accurately, in full color, without tearing, breakup, or picture roll, it is essential for the scanning process in the TV receiver or picture monitor to be exactly in step with scanning in the camera. So regular synchronizing pulses ('sync pulses') are combined with the video. These pulses need to pass through the system accurately, to provide stable pictures.

There are two forms of sync pulses:

● those that keep the horizontal or line scanning in synchronism (line syncs),

and

● those that time the vertical scanning rate (frame syncs).

The video information together with its sync pulses (including an additional 'color burst' signal which stabilizes color accuracy), is called the *composite video*.

13.10 Color video

Although it is possible to transmit color from camera to screen in the form of three separate color components – red, green and blue video signals – there are technical disadvantages.

When the American NTSC color TV system was developed, its designers had to ensure that color transmissions could also be received on black and white receivers. This required some ingenious engineering tricks – which are also used in derived PAL and SECAM color systems.

Picture information was coded into:

luminance (Y): which conveys the brightness and light and dark in the scene,

and

chrominance (C): which conveys the color in the scene.

The chrominance component is quite complex, for it has two features: the 'I' signal (red minus luminance) and the 'Q' signal (blue minus luminance) – in PAL systems, called U and V.

Decoding circuits in the color picture-monitor or receiver recover the original RGB components from these signals.

13.11 Transmitting the signal

A regular method of sending a color video signal along a single cable is used in most domestic video recorders. Here the composite video signal, together with its accompanying audio signal, are fed to a small device called a 'modulator'. This produces a modulated radio frequency (RF) which is fed to the antenna (aerial) socket of a TV receiver.

13.12 Forms of video signal

Summarizing then, the video signal can be distributed in several different forms. Each has its advantages. The particular kind used. will affect interconnections between equipment.

- As separate red, green, blue video signals (RGB); perhaps with separate sync pulses.
- As a combined composite video signal (total video plus syncs).
- Video can also be distributed as two separate signals: *luminance (Y)* and coded color or *chrominance (C)*. A 'signal converter' can be used to convert a Y/C signal into separate R G B signals.
- As a modulated radio frequency signal. (A convenient one-wire method of distributing picture and sound, but with a slight deterioration in picture quality.)

13.13 Program sound

The audio accompanying the picture is handled as a single separate circuit (two in the case of stereo sound), routed quite independently of the video circuits. Where an RF modulator unit is used however, the audio channel can be fed into this in addition to the composite video, to provide a signal suitable for the antenna (aerial) socket of a TV receiver.

13.14 Reproduced quality

How much detail can the system reproduce? That will depend on the type of equipment used, and its design refinements. For example, a conventional TV receiver may typically be able to reproduce up to 320 vertical black and white stripes; while a more advanced design can resolve over 560 lines.

A typical VHS recorder can resolve around 250 lines (3.2 MHz), while a Super VHS video recorder can resolve over 400 lines (5.13 MHz).

Audio too, will depend on system parameters. The highest and lowest ends of the audio scale ('top', 'bass') are limited on many receivers and VCR systems, distortion reducing clarity and overall fidelity. For others, audio quality is comparable with that from compact disc systems.

13.15 Units

You will find two approaches to equipment design:

- That in which all circuit functions are incorporated within the same unit.
- Systems in which a series of separate sub-units are interconnected.

While for instance, a broadcast studio, will have separate precision units generating the synchronizing (sync) signals, which are fed to all cameras, switchers, video recorders, etc., a portable video camera has to be entirely self-contained.

In the box on page 227 you will see an outline of typical video and audio units used in a video/television system.

13.16 Monitors and receivers

Although both *TV receivers* and *picture monitors* are widely used in video production, they have important differences.

TV receivers. These are designed to display off-air pictures of broadcast programs, with their accompanying sound. For technical and economic reasons, picture and sound quality are a compromise; although the performance of top-grade receivers can be extremely good.

If a camera system or videotape recorder includes a *modulator* unit, (which converts its video into a modulated RF carrier), its output can be plugged into the regular *antenna (aerial)* socket, of the TV receiver. But there is inevitably a certain amount of picture deterioration.

Many modern receivers have a choice of inputs. A *video input* socket allows the direct video signal from a camera or VCR to be fed to the receiver for improved performance (better detail, less noise). For higher picture quality there are separate *RGB* inputs, and/or *Y/C (luminance/chrominance)* video inputs.

Picture monitors. Specially designed to provide accurate, stable picture quality, their circuit sophistication is reflected in their higher cost. Picture monitors do not include circuitry to receive off-air pictures. Instead, they are fed directly by cable, with a video signal – in encoded form, with picture plus sync pulses, as separate red–green–blue picture components, and/or in Y/C form.

Program sound is reproduced through a separate audio system.

Video equipment

A wide range of equipment is used in the video chain. You can clarify its purpose broadly as:

> *Supplementary* (e.g. switcher),
> *Compensatory* (e.g. TBC),
> *Effects* (e.g. SEG).

Some units combine more than one function (e.g. a switcher that incorporates effects).

Supplementary equipment

Switcher (vision mixer). Equipment allowing the outputs from various video sources (cameras, video recorders, telecine, character generator, etc.) to be inter-switched, faded, mixed.

Sync pulse generator (SPG). This provides

- the *horizontal and vertical drive pulses* that initiate the scanning process,
- the *blanking pulses* that suppress the scanning read-off as it moves on to the next line or frame,
- the *sync pulses* at the end of each line and each field,
- the *color burst* which provides a reference signal to stabilize color fidelity when encoding color information with the luminance information (color sync; color subcarrier).

Sometimes a single 'black burst' signal is generated. This incorporates blanking, syncs, and black level video. This 'black-burst' signal is used as a synchronizing source, and equipment is genlocked onto it.

Distribution amplifier (DA). An amplifier used to isolate and distribute video signals.

Camera control unit (CCU). In multi-camera setups, each camera head is cable-linked to a *camera control unit (CCU)*, where most of the circuitry providing power, scanning, sync signals, etc., is centralized. The CCU has all the camera's main electronic adjustments, affecting picture quality (exposure, black level, gain, etc.). All cameras' CCUs are grouped together, and controlled by a video operator or 'shader', or extended to a central video control panel. Similarly, a BSU (base-station units) or CPU (camera processing unit) controls digital cameras.

Multiplexer. Device with a movable mirror, enabling one camera to see several different picture sources (slide projector, film projector (telecine), filmstrip, captions).

Patch panel/jackfield/jack strip. Rows of sockets to which the inputs and outputs of various video units are permanently wired. Units may be inter-connected with a series of plugged cables (patch cords).

Routing switcher. A unit enabling various video (and audio) sources to be interconnected by pressing appropriate buttons.

Compensatory/corrective equipment

Genlock. All equipment in a video system needs to work from exactly the same synchronizing pulses. Otherwise, when shots are inter-switched (cut) or combined (i.e. mix, wipe, insets and other effects) there will be picture disturbances such as frame roll, displacement, etc. To avoid this, the sync pulses from one of the video sources (e.g. a remote camera) are used to synchronize *all* units via a genlock unit, so that they scan in unison. Similarly, a computer, character generator, slide scanner must be fed with communal syncs.

Genlock systems may generate either a standard NTSC (PAL, SECAM) signal over a single conductor (combined Y and C), or separate Y and C signals (e.g. for S-VHS, Hi8, ED-BETA sources).

Processing amplifier (Proc-amp)/stabilizing amplifier. Corrects errors that develop in the video signal from any source. Because the procamp can correct signals from unstable VCRs, it is invaluable when copying tapes. It can reshape, reinsert, or separate sync pulses from the composite signal (i.e. video plus syncs), and may also correct color errors.

Image enhancer. The enhancer can improve apparent picture detail, crispening edge sharpness of vertical (perhaps horizontal) edges.

However, it cannot compensate for poor resolution or soft focus, or show detail that does not already exist. Over-correction leads to an artificial 'cartoon' effect, with emphasized outlines and increased graininess. The enhancer can subjectively improve picture quality when copying tapes, reducing detail loss effects.

Advanced image enhancers can also remove color fringing around outlines, correct any color displacement, reduce video noise ('snow'), suppress 'ringing' at edges, regenerate syncs, etc.

A *pre-enhancer* between the camera and the VCR can boost detail (higher frequencies) before recording, so improving apparent definition.

Image processors can improve or modify picture quality, by adjusting color saturation, hue, tonal contrast, white/black, picture strength (brightness), detail enhancement. And improve matching in color quality between shots, correct color balance, etc.

Time base corrector (TBC). Circuitry used to insert accurate sync pulses when the incoming sync pulses are lost or distorted. The TBC removes jitter on VCR playback, correcting color and sync errors.

A TBC that includes a *frame store synchronizer* can lock up an unsynchronized video source to your system's sync pulses. If the picture is momentarily interrupted (e.g. shooting on location) it will insert an image of the previous frame during the break. Many TBC units today include *proc amps* (above). Again, over-correction can lead to greater picture noise, degraded grays/blacks, color deterioration.

Color corrector. Circuitry that allows you to correct a chosen color, with minimum effect on others. It adjusts the gain (amplification), black level, gamma (tonal contrast) of the separate red, green, blue channels.

Effects equipment

Special effects generator (SEG). A unit for creating various wipe patterns, keying effects, mattes, etc.

Character generator (CG). A system for providing electronically generated titling of various sizes and forms. As well as letters, numbers, and symbols, the CG may include facilities for creating graphics (logos, maps, charts).

Image enhancer (see above). May also be used for video effects: e.g. reduce color to black and white; create negative images; change selected colors (e.g. red car to green!); tint the picture overall (sepia for old photos, blue for 'moonlight'); dilute (wash out) color; emphasize color; adjust brightness and/or contrast.

Digitizer. An encoder unit used to translate a regular analogue video signal into digital form e.g. for treatment in a *computer* system. You can hold (grab) individual video frames, and modify/adjust/redraw them; e.g. to create graphics, cartoons, animations.

Conversely, a digital/analogue encoder is needed to convert digital signal (from a computer) into NTSC (PAL, or SECAM) form.

Video effects unit. Various designs allow you to *freeze frame*; strobe (grab stills at 0.2–2 s intervals); *mosaic* (break pictures into small squares); *posterize* (reduce tonal gradation to a few steps); *superimpose* (intermixing effects); add *shadowing* and *edging* to titling; *alter colors* of titling/background; *fade* video, titles, or background.

Superimposer. A unit enabling the output of a computer (e.g. providing titling, statistics) to be mixed with the composite video signal (NTSC, PAL) from a camera.

Video test equipment

Picture monitors

There are disadvantages in setting up a monitor so that edges of the picture are lost beyond the screen mask ('over-scanning'). A mike or lights on the edge of the shot may go uncorrected. Synchronizing faults may not be visible.

Underscanning (reducing picture size) so that the entire picture area is visible (no edge cut-off) immediately reveals a bad signal (instability, jitters).

A *pulse-cross monitor* can be switched to displace the picture, and display the edge and bottom of the TV picture in the middle of the screen. With increased brightness, you can detect any synchronizing faults, and check VCR replay (tape tension, tracking). Using a special converter box, a regular monitor can be used in this way.

Waveform monitor

This is an oscilloscope displaying a fluctuating line, which traces the variations of the video signal, the sync pulses, etc. You can select and examine individual picture lines. It has several uses, including: checking for exposure errors, ensuring that the video does not exceed the system's limits (i.e. so that light tones do not crush out or clip off to white; shadows do not merge to black); checking accuracy of sync pulses.

Color bar generator

A test signal comprising a series of vertical bars of standard colors (white, yellow, cyan (blue–green), green, magenta (red–purple), red, blue, black). It is usually generated electronically, although a color chart can be used.

Vectorscope

An oscilloscope used for checking the color accuracy of all parts of the system (cameras, switcher, VCR, etc.). Wrong adjustments can totally wreck color quality! White and black should be neutral, producing a central blob on the screen. When a *color bars* test signal is displayed, a series of e.g. six bright dots appear around the screen – ideally within small engraved boxes.

If the 'chroma gain'/'chroma level' (color strength) is too low, a test color will fall outside its box, closer to the screen's center. Nearer the screen's edge, it is too high. If the dots are clockwise or anticlockwise of their boxes, the 'subcarrier phase' or 'burst phase' (hue) may need adjustment. If some dots appear normal but others are displaced, check white balance and/or color temperature, otherwise the 'encoder level' may be wrong. If in doubt, don't! Ideally, the color responses of all cameras should match. Color bars are recorded at the start of each videotape, to check color accuracy.

Test signal generator/pattern generator

Various signals and patterns can be generated electronically, to check and adjust the system's resolution (definition), tonal gradation and contrast (gamma), tonal limits (black level, white level/clipper), color bars, circles, crosshatch, staircase, split field.

Audio equipment

Audio equipment too can be considered as

Supplementary (e.g. mixer),
Compensatory (e.g. EQ),
Effects (e.g. echo).

Again, some units have more than one function.

Supplementary equipment

Pre-amplifier. An amplifier used to adjust the strength of audio from one or more audio sources to a standard level (intensity). It may include source switching, basic filtering.

Power amplifier. A unit used to amplify the output of the pre-amplifier, and deliver power to drive a loudspeaker unit. A *cross-over filter network* is often used to subdivide the amplifier's output to drive speakers covering sections of the audio spectrum (tweeter, mid-range, woofer).

Patch panel/jackfield/jack strip. Rows of sockets to which the inputs and outputs of various audio units are permanently wired. Units may be interconnected with a series of plugged cables (patch cords).

Audio mixer. A unit or sound desk used to select, control and intermix all audio sources. It may include filter circuits, reverberation control, etc.

Sound control

Audio filters. Audio filters may be used to reduce background noises (traffic, air-conditioners, wind), or compensate for boomy surroundings. They can take several forms.

Slope filters (RSA – response selection amplifiers), which accentuate/reduce the strength of either end of the audible scale (adjust top/treble, bass).

High or low pass filters, which cut off lower or higher audio (bass cut; top cut).

Graphic equalizer (shaping filter), which has a series of slider controls, allowing selected parts of the audio spectrum to be boosted or reduced.

Notch filter (parametric amplifier), filter producing a very steep peak or dip in a selected part of the audio spectrum; e.g. to suppress unavoidable hum, whistle, rumble, etc.

Presence circuits, which boost/cut around 2–6 kHz, to improve clarity, audio separation, bring a sound source 'forward' from others, improve sibilants.

Noise reduction. Circuitry for reducing unwanted noise from tape, disc and other background sounds. This can be done by *noise gate circuits* (suppressing quiet sounds), *compressor/expander circuits* (reducing then restoring the dynamic range), pre-emphasis/de-emphasis boosting higher notes during recording, and reducing them during reproduction (Dolby, dBx systems). A *dynamic noise reducer* simply reduces treble during quieter periods.

Limiter. A device for preventing loud audio from exceeding the system's upper limit (so causing overload distortion), by progressively reducing circuit amplification for louder sounds.

Effects equipment

As well as using audio filtering for effects (e.g. imitating telephone conversations), sound can be manipulated in various ways.

Compressor/expander. Deliberately used to reduce or emphasize the audio dynamic range (i.e. the difference between the quietest and loudest sounds).

Reverberation. Device for increasing or adjusting the amount of reverberation accompanying a sound. Systems include spring delay, echo room, digital methods.

Appendix A

Battery care

If your power supplies fail during shooting, you could find yourself with a lot of expensive equipment. . . that does *nothing!*

Types of power

All electrically powered equipment is designed to be used with a particular form of supply. It may be a.c. (alternating current) or d.c. (direct current).

Public utilities' electricity supplies (mains supplies) vary between countries: 100, 110, 120, 127, 200, 210, 220, 230 or 240 volts, 50 or 60 Hz.

Some equipment is adaptable, and can be powered from several different sources, or from various supply voltages.

Portable video equipment generally uses rechargeable batteries, although a special adapter enables it to be powered from a.c. household supplies. (This reduces the voltage, and converts the a.c. to the d.c. that the system requires.)

The camera may be powered from the VCR, which in turn is powered from battery or household supplies.

In use, equipment draws a certain current (measured in *amperes*), according to its total power consumption (measured in *watts*). Fed from an a.c. mains outlet via an a.c.-adaptor, it can draw this current for as long as you wish. But when supplied by a battery, the chemicals within the cells gradually change, the supply voltage falls, and the battery becomes exhausted.

Whereas the *dry cells* used in flashlights, watches, calculators, etc., are expendable after using up their chemicals, you can restore the re-chargeable cells used for video equipment to their original voltage (i.e. their chemicals reconverted), by connecting them to an appropriate *charger unit*.

Battery sources

Batteries for video equipment may be carried around in several forms;

- Internal ('on-board') battery, fitted within the equipment.
- Battery belt; a series of batteries carried in a waist-belt.
- Snap-on battery-pack; clips to rear of camera.

- Shoulder sling bag; used to power a lamp (e.g. 80–100 W) in a mounting-shoe on top of the camera, or hand-held. May power the VCR.
- Trolley-pack; a wheeled cart/trolley carrying a VCR, monitor and high-capacity battery.
- Car battery; supply run from automobile's engine battery (using cigar-lighter outlet).

Typical battery supply voltage is 12 V (10.5–17 V).

Using batteries

When you are moving around, or working away from household supplies, batteries are an essential power source; and provided they are cared for, they can be used and re-charged many times. But mishandle them or use them incorrectly, and their performance deteriorates and their useful life shortens.

Your video system draws power directly it is switched on. Remember, supplies are needed for the camera (its viewfinder, power zoom, video light), for the VCR (when recording, replaying, rewinding), and any separate equipment (monitor, audio recorder, hand-held lamp).

Apart from the actual shooting/recording time, the equipment will be using power while you are adjusting it, checking shots, rehearsing action, testing lights, and so on; and a surprising amount of time can pass doing these things. (A *film camera* on the other hand, only uses power while it is running.) Thus a battery might only last for a single cassette when shooting and rehearsing, whereas it might last for several cassettes when shooting a news event continuously.

You can conserve battery power by switching units off until they are needed (e.g. monitor), and switching the camera and VCR to 'standby' (warm-up) when possible, ready to switch-on and use. On some cameras, 'auto-switch-off' saves the power when the unit has not been used for several minutes.

A battery is always made up from a series of identical *cells*. Several forms of cells are regularly used: sealed lead–acid, nickel–cadmium cell (NiCad) or silver–zinc.

The *voltage* of a group of batteries is increased if they are wired in 'series', i.e. the +ve (red) of one cell to the –ve (black) of the next (see Table A.1).

The *capacity* of a group of batteries is increased (i.e. they last longer) if all their +ve poles are wired together, and, *separately*, all their −ve poles are wired together.

Table A.1 Typical video camera battery capacities (minimum)

Consumption for 12–14 volt portable camera	1–1.5 hr overall capacity	2 hr overall capacity
10–14 watts	1.2 Ah NiCad	2 Ah NiCad
15–25 watts	2 Ah NiCad	4 Ah NiCad
25–35 watts	4 Ah NiCad	4 Ah NiCad
35–50 watts	4 Ah NiCad	8 Ah NiCad
		12 Ah silver–zinc

Cell capacity

How long a fully charged battery will provide current before its voltage falls, and it needs re-charging, is indicated by its rating in *ampere-hours* (Ah). Knowing this figure, you could say theoretically, that a 2 Ah battery will supply a current of 2 Ah for a camera for 1 hour (*viz.* Ah divided by amperes).

In an ideal world, one should be able to deduce that if, instead, you use that same battery for a lamp drawing 8 amps, it should last about 2/8 = ¼ hour or 15 mins. Unfortunately, batteries do not always behave as simply as that, and it may only last 10 or 11 min.

If a fairly high current is drawn from a lead–acid battery its effective capacity falls, i.e. it does not last as long as you might expect from a battery of that Ah rating, before needing re-charging. The *NiCad* cell's output capacity, though, is more constant.

This is a point to bear in mind when you are supplying several pieces of equipment from the same battery, especially when using high consumption battery-operated lamps.

Not only will the battery's capacity be reduced if it is asked to supply a heavy load, but the supply voltage will fall (voltage drop), and may in fact become too low to operate the camera and the VCR.

So you can use a relatively larger high-rated battery, that lasts longer and permits heavier currents to be drawn; or a similar compact lower capacity one, sufficient for short-period working, that is more frequently replaced with fresh standby batteries. So for instance, a 2Ah 'in-board' battery within a camera may last about an hour, while a power belt 4–7 Ah could give 2–3.5 hours use.

Sealed lead–acid cell

This is the cheapest and toughest, but the bulkiest and heaviest cell. It is tolerant of brief short-circuits and extreme working temperatures. However it is liable to top-leaks. The electrolyte is distilled (chemically pure) water, and may need topping up occasionally (depending on construction).

It has a minimum 2 volts per cell (which falls to 1.65 volts minimum). Typical capacities for lead–acid cells are 2–30 Ah. (Car batteries are up to e.g. 100 Ah).

Nickel–cadmium cell

The popular *NiCad* or nickel cadmium cell (1.2 volts per cell), is smaller, rugged, long-lived and easy to charge, but more costly. Its voltage falls at higher temperatures.

It has a maximum of 1.2 volts per cell (which falls to 1.1 volts minimum). It should not be discharged at over 20 times its capacity, nor recharged at over one-tenth of its capacity, i.e. ½ amp for a 5 Ah battery.

Silver–zinc cell

The silver–zinc cell provides a high storage capacity for its size – three times that of a NiCad cell. But it does not have the high cycle-life of the NiCad battery. It is less tolerant of misuse: overcharging, continuous trickler charging, discharge to exhaustion, and to high temperatures.

Battery care

Look after your batteries, and you will find them a reliable effective power-source. Although they are quite robust, it pays to handle them carefully, for mechanical shock, blows, dropping, or excessive flexing of connections (especially inter-wired cells in power-belts) can cause unexpected breakdown.

Many batteries are ruined by the way they are used. Take care when fitting or charging a battery to avoid connecting it the wrong way round (reversed polarity).

Measure a battery's voltage while it is working ('on-load'), not when you have removed it from the equipment, for then it is liable to give you a higher, more optimistic reading, than it should. A fitted indicator on the camera will usually show you the 'state of charge'.

Avoid storing batteries in extreme temperatures, e.g. leaving batteries in a car in the sun, or out in temperatures below freezing. NiCad batteries retain their charge well in cool storage, losing it rapidly in hot surroundings.

If you are storing NiCad batteries, temperatures of around 68° to –22°F (20° to –30°C) are preferred. Much higher temperatures tend to reduce the life of the battery to half or even a quarter of normal.

Their working efficiency varies with temperature. Best at around 65–75°F (18–22°C), the cell's output falls over 120°F (50°C), or under –40°F (–40°C).

In cold weather, some cameramen shoot with their NiCad battery-belt worn underneath a jacket, to keep it warmer.

Lead–acid batteries can work effectively in temperatures as low as –40°F or up to 150°F (66°C).

The battery's voltage remains reasonably constant in use, falling rapidly when nearing the end of its capacity. It is good practice to carry around several fully charged standby batteries, and you should replace the one in use when its volts are down to the official minimum: 1.6 volts per cell for lead–acid, 1.1 volts per cell for NiCad.

Do not discharge a battery below 1 volt per cell. And certainly never *completely exhaust* a battery ('flat', deep discharge), for example, by leaving the equipment switched on and forgetting it. A new battery can be ruined that way.

Do not leave discharged cells around for long periods (i.e. cells below full voltage), but re-charge them as soon as possible. (However, see the comments on 'memory' in the next section.) If a NiCad cell falls too low, it can actually go into reversed polarity, and when the battery is charged next, the faulty cell will appear satisfactory, but lose its charge quickly, and this can result in the entire belt being permanently damaged.

As batteries age, they tend to *discharge themselves* to a noticeable extent when left, and in the worst cases you could find that, after a few days, a fully charged battery has very little charge left in it. If in fact some cells in a battery are faulty, any attempt to charge the battery may destroy the remaining good ones, which become overcharged.

A battery can only be recharged/discharged a limited number of times ('its 'cycle-life') before its rated capacity falls. If you find a battery's voltage falling quite quickly in use, it could indicate that it is coming to the end of its useful life, especially if during charging, it also seems to be taking less time than normal to reach full charge from a completely discharged state.

The cycle-life for a NiCad battery is typically several hundred cycles, much better than that of a lead–acid type.

Battery charging

A battery charger should always be appropriate for this job. For example, don't use a 'lead–acid' charger for NiCad or silver–zinc cells. They require different charging voltages and rates.

A battery should be recharged at the correct rate for its type, using an appropriate type of charger unit. Normally, a lead–acid battery will take about 15 hours at 2.4 volts per cell, to charge fully from a discharged condition. A NiCad cell requires around 12–16 hours, depending on the charge-rate (current); about ⅛ or ⅒ of its Ah capacity rating. In practice it is best not to continue once charging is complete.

The exception to these charging rates is the 20–60 min taken when using special *fast-charger units* with suitable Nicad batteries.

Fast re-charging sounds like a great boon to the busy cameraman. But unless it is carried out correctly, it can put quite a strain on the battery, particularly if it is not in top condition, or the ambient temperature is unusually high or low.

NiCad batteries should really only be fast-charged at normal room temperature (65°–75°F) (18–23°C). At temperatures under about 60°F (15°C), or above 100–110°F (38°C) damage is inevitable. Many feel that it is safer to carry more batteries, and that a slow overnight charge is preferable.

Avoid *cycling*, i.e. taking a battery from a fully charged to a fully discharged state, for this will reduce its storage capacity. There is the danger that individual cells of the battery will not return to the same maximum voltage (imbalance), and the poorest cell will reduce the battery's overall performance. A battery-belt or pack can never be better than its poorest cell. So never mix new and old cells.

Unlike lead–acid batteries, NiCad cells can develop a 'memory' condition (depressed voltage) if you give the battery an over-lengthy 'trickle charge' (low charging current for a long period), or if the battery has been frequently over-charged, and then left around partially discharged.

If you continually use a battery for a short period (say half an hour), then recharge it fully, you may find that this battery regularly starts to drop after half an hour, instead of giving its full capacity.

A battery that has developed a 'memory' appears normal after full charge, but will not deliver the full running time in use. You can cure this condition, by deliberately discharging the battery to one volt per cell (measured *off*-load, i.e. disconnected), and recharging it for 20 hours at about 77°F (25°C), repeating the process several times.

It is generally recommended that freshly charged cells should be allowed to stand for some time to stabilize, before using them. Take care when using a freshly charged battery for a portable lamp, that it does not burn out ('blow') its bulb (typically 30 volts, 150, 250 or 350 watts).

Appendix B

Useful data

Power consumption

This table shows how much current (in amperes) is drawn by equipment, so that you can avoid overloading supplies. Check the supply voltage. Then add up the consumption of individual units in watts, to find the total current being consumed. (All figures are proportional: e.g. 150 W = 100 W + 50 W.)

	12 V	110 V	120 V	220 V	240 V
50 W	4.2	0.46	0.42	0.23	0.21
100 W	8.4	0.91	0.83	0.45	0.42
200 W	17.0	1.82	1.67	0.91	0.83
300 W	25.0	2.7	2.5	1.36	1.25
375 W	31.25	3.4	3.2	1.7	1.6
500 W	41.66	4.6	4.2	2.3	2.1
800 W	–	7.33	6.66	3.64	3.33
1000 W	–	9.1	8.33	4.55	4.2
1250 W	–	11.4	10.4	5.7	5.2
2000 W	–	18.2	16.7	9.1	8.33
3000 W	–	27.3	25.0	13.6	12.5
4000 W	–	36.4	35.4	18.2	17.0
5000 W	–	45.0	42.0	23.0	21.0

Typical light levels

1 foot candle (fc) = 10.764 lux; 1 lux = 0.0929 fc. For most purposes you can approximate 1 fc = 10 lux.

Light source	Foot candles	Lux
Bright sun	5000–10 000	50 000–100 000
Hazy sun	2500–5000	25 000–50 000
Bright, cloudy	1000–25 000	10 000–25 000
Dull cloudy	200–1000	2000–10 000
Very dull	10–200	100–2000
Sunset	0.1–10	1–100
Full moon	0.001–0.01	0.01–0.1
Television studio	100–200	1000–2000
Office	20–30	200–300
Living room	5–20	50–200
Corridors	5–10	50–100
Good street lighting	1–2	10–20
Candlelight (20 cms away)	1.5	15

Lensless spot	Flood	(fc/lux)	Spot	(fc/lux)	ft/m
250 W	90°	32/350	45°	140/1500	10/3
600 W	90°	74/800	45°	223/2400	10/3
800 W	90°	37/400	45°	130/1400	16/5
2000 W	75°	93/1000	35°	370/4000	16/5

Six-light (PAR) floodlight bank

6 × 650 W		140/1500		74/800	33/10

Typical color temperatures (in kelvins)

Standard candle	1930 K
Household tungsten lamps (25–250 W)	2600–2900 K
Studio tungsten lamp (500–1000 W)	3000 K
Studio tungsten lamp (2000 W)	3275 K
Studio tungsten lamp (5 kW, 10 kW)	3380 K
'Quartz' (tungsten-halogen) lamps	3200–3400 K
Photoflood	3400 K
Fluorescent lamps	3000–6500 K
Sunrise, sunset	2000–3000 K
1 hr after sunrise	3500 K
Sunless daylight	4500–4800 K
Midday sun	5000–5400 K
Overcast sky	6800–7500 K
Hazy sky	8000–9000 K
Clear blue north sky	10 000–20 000 K

Lens angle

When we refer to lens angle, we mean the *horizontal* coverage (angle of view). Its *vertical* angle, which determines the height taken in by the shot, is three-quarters of this value. Thus a 40° lens has a vertical coverage of 30°.

The angle covered by a lens depends on its focal length, and the camera's light sensor (CCD) image size.

Here are the approximate focal lengths (in millimeters) needed to provide typical lens angles, with different size light sensors:

Angle (°)	12.5 mm (½ in.)	18 mm (⅔ in.)	25 mm (1 in.)
50	7.5	10	15
35	10	14	20
25	15	20	30
15	25	33	50
10	37	50	75
5	75	100	150

From these figures, you can see how by referring to the lens angle rather than the focal length, we have a stable standard against which to judge shots. Quoting the focal length can be misleading, for the same lens will produce different shots with various camera sensor sizes. Another advantage is that you can draw a lens angle on any scale plan, and see exactly what the shot opportunities and problems will be, when planning.

To see the maximum detail available in a TV picture, we should ideally sit at around four to six times the picture height away from the screen. At this distance, the picture width covers an angle of about 28–20° to the eye. If the camera lens covers a similar angle, the perspective will appear natural in the shot. So a lens shot of about 28–20° is termed *normal*.

A lens covering much less than 20° is called a *narrow* angle (long focus) lens. One covering over about 30° is called a *wide* angle lens.

Available shots on a normal 25° lens

	BCU	*CU*	*Chest*	*Waist*	*Knees*	*Full length*
Meters	1.0	1.25	1.75	2.0	4	+6.0
Feet	3.3	4	5.7	6.5	13	+20

Typical lens coverage

Angle (°)	*Width at 3 m*	*Width at 10 ft*
5	0.26 m	10 in.
10	0.53 m	1 ft 9 in.
15	0.79 m	2 ft 7 in.
20	1.06 m	3 ft 6 in.
25	1.33 m	4 ft 5 in.
30	1.61 m	5 ft 5 in.
35	1.89 m	6 ft 4 in.
40	2.18 m	7 ft 4 in.
45	2.49 m	8 ft 4 in.
50	2.80 m	9 ft 4 in.
55	3.46 m	11 ft 7 in.

Shot heights

Level shot:	Standing person 4–5 ft (1.2–1.8 m)
	Sitting person 3.5 ft (1.1 m)
Low level shot:	Ground level to 3 ft (1 m)
Very low angle shot:	50–60° upwards
Low angle shot:	20–40° upwards
High angle shot:	20–40° downwards
Very high angle shot:	50–60° downwards
Top shot, overhead shot:	Straight downwards ±5°

Hyperfocal distance

When a lens is focused at its *hyperfocal distance* (H), the scene is sharp from about half this distance, to the farthest distance (infinity). Any action within this distance range will appear in focus.

You can calculate the hyperfocal distance in meters from:

$$\frac{(\text{focal length in cm})^2 \times 100}{\text{lens stop No.} \times 0.05}$$

or the hyperfocal distance in feet from:

$$\frac{(\text{focal length in inches})^2}{\text{lens stop No.} \times 0.002}$$

Aspect ratio

Because the screen has a rectangular 4 × 3 shape, graphics need to be roughly of this aspect ratio, if information round the edges is not to be lost.

Horizontal size (in. or cm)	10	15	20	25	30	35	40	45	50
Vertical size (in. or cm)	7.5	11.25	15	18.75	22.5	26.25	30	33.75	37.5

Audio tape formats

Reel-to-reel tape
Tape width: ¼ in. (6.35 mm)
Spool diameters:
   3 in. (75 mm) with 175 ft of tape; 4 in. (100 mm) with 300 ft;
   5 in. (125 mm) with 600 ft; 5¾ in. (145 mm) with 900 ft;
   7 in. (175 mm) with 1200 ft; NAB 10½ in. (265 mm) with 2400 ft.
Tape speeds per second:
   $^{15}\!/_{16}$ in. (2.35 cm); 1⅞ in. (4.75 cm);
   3¾ in. (9.5 cm); 7½ in. (19 cm); 15 in. (38 cm).

Running time:
   1200 ft = 32 min at 7½ in. (19 cm) per second.
   1 min = 38 ft (11.6 m);
   30 min = 1125 ft (342 m). Other lengths and speeds in this ratio for standard tape.
For other tape thicknesses, multiply duration by:
   long = ×1.5; double play = ×2; triple play = ×3;
   quad play = ×4.

Cassette
Tape width: 3.5 mm. Speed 4.75 cm/s (1⅞ in.).

Cassette maximum durations:
   30, 60 90, 120 min (turning cassette over at the end of first side)

Appendix C

Camera set-up graph

The graph shows how much any lens sees at various distances. (The *height* of the area seen is ¾ of the width.)

1. *How far away does the camera have to be, to get a certain type of shot?* Select type of shot you want on vertical scale ... then down to the *distance scale*.
2. *What lens angle is needed for a certain type of shot?* Trace a line across graph from the shot you want (vertical scale) ... draw another line, up from camera's distance on the bottom *scale*. Where they cross, shows the best *lens angle*.
3. *What type of shots will I get from here?* Draw a line up from the *distance scale*, to the *lens angle*(s) you have available (max and min zoom angles). Then across left, to the *shot* scale.
4. How much will the camera see from here? As 3, but read the scene *width/height scales*.
5. You can get the *same shot size* at different distances, by altering lens angle. Trace a line right from the shot needed (e.g. CU) and note the distance at which it cuts various lens angles.
6. *To make a subject fill a certain proportion of screen width* (e.g. ⅓: Measure the subject width; multiply this by 3 for ⅓ width (4 for ¼, etc.). Look up this screen width on the left vertical *width scale*. Trace across to the *lens angle used*, then down to the *distance* needed. The subject will now fill ⅓ screen width.

Lens angle	
Horizontal	Vertical
5°	3.75°
10°	7.5°
15°	11.25°
20°	15°
25°	18.75°
30°	22.5°
35°	26.25°
40°	30°
45°	34°
50°	37.5°
55°	40.25°
60°	45°

Index

Numbers in **bold** indicate main entries.